For Richard Vena…
with very best
from
Roy Rawlins
On board a Cambrian plane - I.O.M. -
Manchester 13 June 1971

FOUR HUNDRED YEARS OF BRITISH AUTOGRAPHS

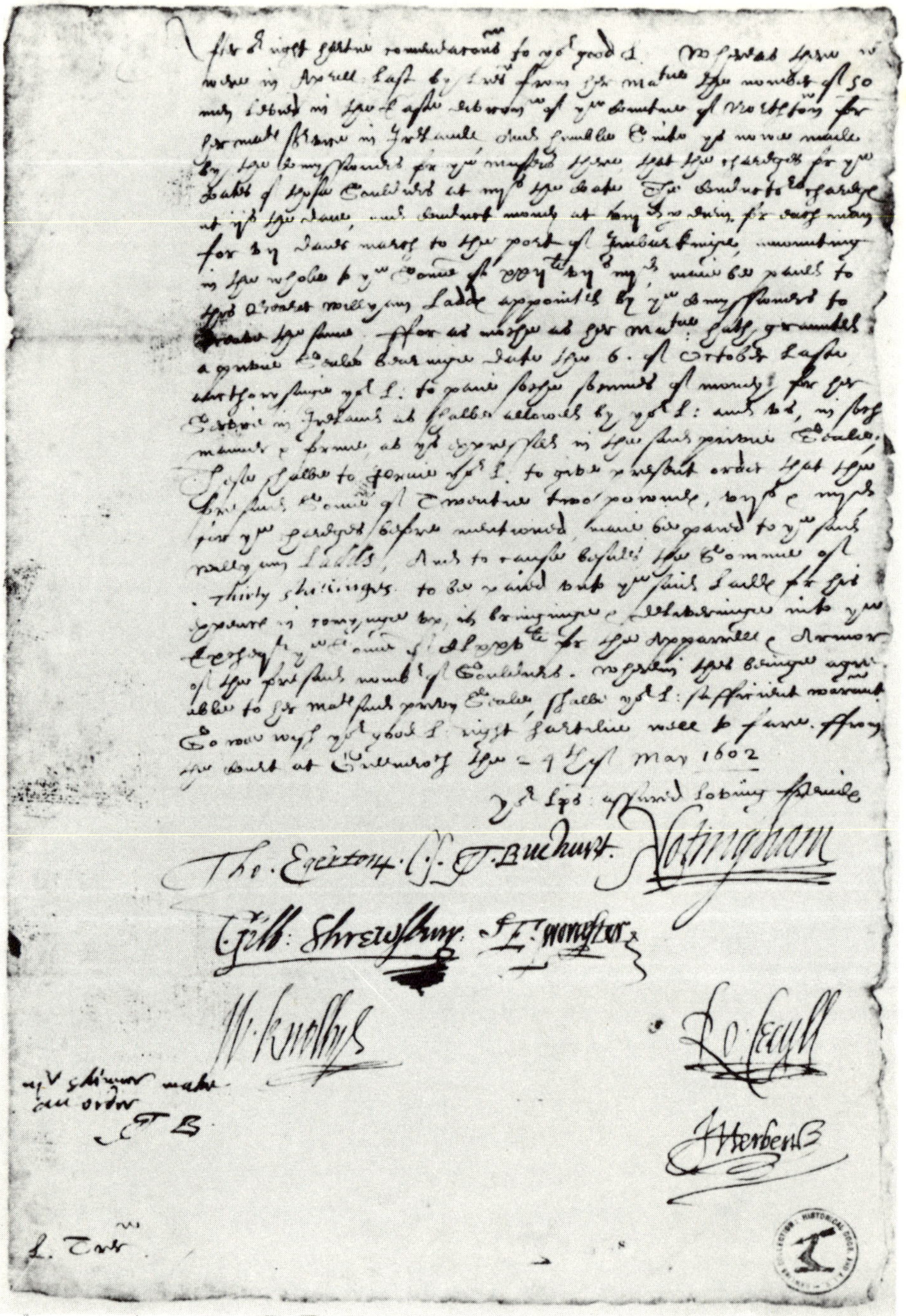

Document signed by eight members of the Privy Council of Elizabeth I. Dated 1602, it concerns provision for clothing for the troops, and its signatories include the Earl of Nottingham (Lord Howard of Effingham, the Commander against the Armada), Robert Cecil (later Earl of Salisbury and Secretary of State) and Thomas, Lord Buckhurst (later Earl of Dorset, the Lord High Treasurer).
Reduced in size

FOUR HUNDRED YEARS OF BRITISH AUTOGRAPHS

A COLLECTOR'S GUIDE

Ray Rawlins

LONDON
J. M. DENT & SONS LTD

First published 1970

Printed in Great Britain by
Lowe & Brydone (Printers) Ltd, for
J. M. Dent & Sons Ltd
Aldine House · Bedford Street · London

To the three Js

ISBN 0 460 03967 9

Contents

List of illustrations

Acknowledgments

One cannot acknowledge individually a thousand people, but my collection has been built up with the help of at least that number, without whom this book could not have been compiled. So I offer them a collective thousand thanks.

The considerable experimental photostatic work necessary in order to decide which originals would best be suited to facsimile reproduction was carried out with patience and skill by Ronnie Shimmin, George Quayle and Geoffrey Cannell of the Isle of Man Government Reprographic Department. I am most grateful to them.

My thanks are also due to my friend and colleague John Wilson for reading through and suggesting many useful amendments to the preliminary sections, to Peter Croft of London, Paul Lutz of Tyler, Texas, and Kenneth W. Rendell of Somerville, Massachusetts, for their advice and encouragement, and to the Vaux family for their invaluable help in proof-reading.

Preface

Autographs have been collected in one form or another for a very long time. Indeed, in Victorian days there was a considerable vogue for them, but it is really only since World War II that they have become things of value and their collection, whilst still a hobby for some, has become a serious study for others.

I myself started collecting forty years ago with the signature of Jack Hobbs. Nowadays I no longer collect plain signatures as such but prefer letters, signed documents and signed portraits. I have over 14,000 of these and though I have become a serious student of the subject it will never cease to remain for me an exciting and fascinating hobby.

This book is therefore intended to serve two purposes: that of being a guide to autograph collecting for beginners and a reference book for all collectors, dealers, librarians and archivists. It is divided into two main parts: an essay on autograph collecting and a large section for facsimiles.

Obviously one cannot claim the collecting of autographs to be an art but there is an art in it, and this is dealt with at some length in the preliminary essay, which provides information on the various forms of autographs, their evaluation, desirability and availability, their generally increasing (but in some cases fluctuating) values and advice on how to build up a collection. Also discussed are the vital questions of correct identification and the many pitfalls for the unwary, such as forgeries and lithographic facsimiles.

Nothing is more important than correct identification and it is for this reason that an extensive facsimile section has been included, to enable readers to check the authenticity of original autograph material. I have kept this book entirely personal. It is, in a sense, a private autographic anthology. The preliminary discourse embodies numerous quotations from letters in my collection and all the facsimiles and illustrations are from originals therein.

Whilst the opening section of the book deals with collecting autographs in general, this work is essentially concerned with British autographs. Although my own collection is an international one, I have restricted this book to British material. A number of publications on international autographs have appeared over the last seventy years, but no book dealing exclusively with the autography of this country has been produced in this century. By confining my subject in this way, I have been able to show a far greater number of facsimile autographs of major British personalities of the last 400 years than has been possible in any single volume in the past. I hope that it will not lose its appeal to collectors in foreign countries because of its restricted field; but there is a considerable interest in British autograph material in all the collecting countries, particularly and understandably in the United States because of our mutual language and historical connections.

Unless one goes entirely on nationality there must be some standards on which to base a selection of national autographs because a considerable number of people very prominent in our islands' history were not actually British. I have therefore chosen to follow two self-imposed rules when selecting names for inclusion in the facsimile section: firstly, all persons concerned must either be or have been at some time in their lives British or Commonwealth nationals; secondly, in addition or alternatively, they must feature in the *Dictionary of National Biography*. Thus included under the first criterion are such distinguished foreigners who later became British nationals as Henry James, T. S. Eliot, Sir Hiram Maxim, Sir Paolo Tosti, Axel Munthe and Benno Moiseivitsch; as are, conversely, British-born Alexander Graham Bell and Australian-born Percy Grainger who both became United States citizens. Under the second rule are included, for example, four great American painters: Benjamin West, John Singleton Copley, John Singer Sargent and James McNeill Whistler. None of these gave up their American nationality but all lived and worked most of their lives in Britain and are included in the *D.N.B.* We cannot but be proud of the part these men played in our history. West, who in any case was of British descent, followed Reynolds as President of the Royal Academy and both Copley (whose son became our Lord Chancellor) and Sargent were also Academicians.

As a result of keeping exclusively to material in my own collection there will be many noticeable gaps. I have no example of Shakespeare (there are none in private hands), nor Milton, nor Bunyan, nor Pope, so that they will not be found in the facsimile section, though certain references are made to them in the preliminary discourse. Collectors need not feel 'let down', however, for I have included a bibliography of earlier facsimile books, in one or other of which they will surely find what they seek. On the other hand I have deliberately concentrated on the inclusion of a considerable number of names which have never before been dealt with in a book on autograph collecting. For example I have put in all forty-eight of our Prime Ministers, from Walpole to Heath. The signatures of many of these have not appeared in earlier facsimile books despite their evident importance in our history. Also I have added many present-day personalities and a fair number of distinguished Commonwealth citizens from all fields of human endeavour.

Although most of the more obvious omissions in the facsimile section are caused by the fact that I have no originals in my collection, some arise only because the originals I have are not good enough for reproduction. Also I possess a considerable number of signed portraits but copyright difficulties prevent these being published.

The facsimile section contains mostly signatures, which are the first essential when checking originals, but in a good number of cases I have included a few words of the handwriting of the subject. This can help a lot in identification, especially where a person's style of handwriting differs from his style of signature or again where someone uses several styles of signature but does not vary his handwriting. Obviously collectors would have been assisted even more had it been possible to represent long holograph extracts as well as the signatures, but had I done this I should have had to reduce drastically the number of subjects to fit into a single volume. We should have been back to the position of including only the very famous names, most of whom are already available in earlier facsimile books.

The selection has been made to link the reigns of the two Elizabeths. Rather more than the four hundred years explicit in the title are covered. A handful of the autographs shown in the facsimile section are of persons who died before the first Elizabeth came to the throne, but all were her contemporaries. Perhaps I needed an excuse for including such pre-Elizabethan autographic rarities as Archbishop Cranmer and the Lord Protector Somerset; I have also included her father, Henry VIII, under the same excuse.

Space has made it virtually impossible to give many biographical details in the notes under the facsimiles but birth and death dates have invariably been given. In addition, where of interest I have added comments on the autographs themselves, concerning their desirability, rarity, variations, and so on.

In several earlier books in which facsimiles have been shown some of these have been reduced in size from the originals. This is not really a serious drawback because everyone's signature varies in size, but too much of it can lead to confusion. I was very anxious to try to keep the facsimiles to the same size as my originals and so no reduction has been made in the whole of that section. The facsimiles of complete documents have, of necessity, had to be reduced from the very large original documents but a note to this effect has been added to each caption.

By the very fact that we have decided to keep to the correct size, design difficulties as to how to space out each page have arisen. I have arranged the facsimiles under headings of the professions of the subjects (e.g. art, politics, literature), duly divided into subdivisions. I have tried also to keep to a more or less historical order of dates within these subsections. But, from a design point of view, it is quite impossible without size reduction to get each person into his proper place. Thus certain writers who were both poets and dramatists, but more famous as the former, may have had to be shown under dramatists. Similarly, a painter-sculptor such as G. F. Watts is shown under sculptors rather than painters because his facsimile autograph fits better on that particular page.

Classification has been treated with great care but certain names just do not fit in very well under any specific heading so that more than one subdivision has had to receive the label of 'miscellany'. I hope that readers will not have too much difficulty in locating their man; the index has been made as complete as possible in order to avoid such an eventuality. Even the index, however, has been limited by practical difficulties. Many persons in our history held several different titles and in other cases authors wrote under several pseudonyms. One cannot index under every name so that I have resorted to doing so under that (or those) by which the person is best known to the average reader.

One final word on selection. It was not easy to decide who to include out of the 10,000 or so British autographs in my collection, even though some had to be rejected automatically for the reasons already given. My primary aim has therefore been to cover as broad a field as possible; so it will be seen that the section for the theatre includes both Garrick and Charlie Chaplin whilst the literature division embraces both Addison and Frank Richards. Though none will deny the greater literary ability and personal fame of Addison I am prepared to wager that the 'Billy Bunter' books are known to a larger section of the community today than are any of the works of Addison. Perhaps this single, albeit absurd example will explain the case for a very wide selection in a book of this nature.

R. R.

Ballakilpheric,
Isle of Man.
1970.

Autograph collecting: a hobby and a serious study

THE MEANING OF AN AUTOGRAPH

What is an autograph? An easy question to answer, surely. It is a signature, many would be tempted to reply. But would they be right?

I learned my lesson early. When I was about fifteen I asked the then Duke of Devonshire to give me his autograph. I had been collecting what I fondly believed to be autographs for some time and had no doubt that His Grace would oblige me with a signature. Instead the Duke took my book, wrote in it 'You are a nuisance', handed it back to me and turned away. I thought him rather unkind and pointed out that he had not signed it. This probably made him consider me even more of a nuisance, but if so he showed remarkable patience. He took the book again and added his signature 'Devonshire', saying that I had not asked for his signature but only for his autograph, which he had in fact given me.

The Duke of Devonshire was quite right. The unsigned statement 'You are a nuisance' did constitute his autograph just as much as if he had signed it. It is not commonly realized that an autograph is not necessarily a signature and a piece of writing does not need to be signed at all to be an autograph. Thus the somewhat pompous old cliché about every lady being a woman but not every woman being a lady can be adapted for this context: every signature is an autograph but not every autograph is a signature.

The word comes from the two Greek words *auto* and *graphos*: self-writing, i.e. anything self-written. Therefore it follows that whilst my signature is certainly a form of my autograph, even if I write down the one word 'no' then that also is my autograph, i.e. in my own handwriting. So the collecting of autographs of famous people means, quite simply, the collecting of their handwriting in such form as appeals to the particular collector. This may take the form of signatures, signed photographs, documents signed by them, complete letters in their own hands, either signed or unsigned, or in somebody else's hand or typewritten and only signed by them, or even only notes or portions of letters, etc., in their own handwriting. As long as there is so much as a single word, or even a single letter, in the handwriting of the person concerned it constitutes his autograph. The two most perfect examples of minimal autographs which come to my mind are both French: the single letter 'N' signed so frequently by Napoleon on documents and the simple unsigned word '*bon*' often written on a petition by Louis XV.

One other word, 'holograph', is almost as frequently used in autograph collecting. This means something entirely in the hand of the writer.

THE CASE FOR COLLECTING AUTOGRAPHS

The reason why people collect autographs must of necessity vary widely because autographs themselves cover so wide a range, from the plain signature of, say, a film star to the complete manuscript of a book or an opera.

Roughly speaking, collectors can be divided into four categories:

1. The signature collector.
2. The general autograph collector.
3. The major collector and depository.
4. The investor-collector.

The present-day signature collector is usually a young person. This was not always so; signatures were avidly collected by all and sundry in Victorian days, when the fearful habit of cutting them from letters and documents and pasting them into albums was in vogue. But more of this abuse anon, when it comes to discussing how and what to collect.

Young people nowadays tend to collect the signatures, and signed photographs, of those they admire in the fields of sport and entertainment: footballers, boxers, film stars, pop singers, etc. This is as good a basis on which to start a collection as any other and should not be decried. My own collecting started with a signed photograph of Jack Hobbs and has gone some distance since. Yet Hobbs, the first professional cricketer ever to receive a knighthood, is still most worthy of my collection.

At precisely the other end of the collecting scale are those who collect only major material. This category consists mainly of the institutional collectors, such as universities, museums and national libraries. Indeed, the collections at such famed depositories as the British Museum, the Bodleian Library and the Public Records Office are to writers and students the primary source of manuscript research information. Private collectors coming into this group will nowadays, of necessity, have to have considerable finance at their disposal to keep up with these standards. All such collectors, private or institutional, will be seeking full letters and documents or manuscripts of important content. Many will be specialists concerned only with the subject of their choice and not with autographs in general.

Between this group and the signature collector comes the general autograph collector with a comprehensive interest in all autography. He too likes material of good content but sets his sights a little lower. Into this category I place myself and in order to try and explain my own reasons for collecting it seems best to give an example.

I have in my collection a document signed by King Charles II. I like to imagine the scene which could have taken place when it was signed. . . . A dignified, bewigged and lace-cuffed nobleman is proceeding gingerly along one of the ill-lit corridors of Whitehall Palace. His aquiline nose is disfigured by a sword scar, gained whilst fighting for the King's father against the Roundheads. He is Henry Bennet, Earl of Arlington, cavalier, courtier and Cabal Minister. He knocks discreetly on the door of the King's antechamber. The King is annoyed. Nell Gwyn is with him and he has no wish to be disturbed. Nonetheless he grudgingly gives the command 'Enter!'. Arlington does so, showing no indication of surprise as he has often seen Nell on the King's knee. He proffers a document for signature. It is a commission of an officer. He probably has several more needing signature or he would not have bothered his Sovereign Lord at so untimely an hour. His Majesty removes the lady gently but firmly and, still slightly irritated, says, 'I suppose these are in order for me to sign?' 'Yes Sire, I have checked them carefully myself.' 'Very well then '; and the monarch signs them hurriedly. Out goes Arlington—backwards, of course, as he must not turn his back on the Royal Presence—and Nell climbs back on the Royal knee.

Three hundred years later one of these documents is in my hands. The Merry Monarch is not my hero. I do not admire him (although I must confess to a sneaking liking for him), but he is a part of history and I love history. He held this document; now I am holding it. It is mine. It is this personal link between Charles and me—in a wider sense the personal link with history—that excites and fascinates me and makes me an autograph collector. If you do not thrill to that feeling of closeness with all historic figures, bad or good (I have Hitler, Mussolini, Crippen and Lord Haw-Haw, just as I have the more worthy), then you will never make a collector, at least not my sort of collector.

It rather adds to my delight when looking at this particular document to see that Arlington slipped up, after all. He had not checked it properly. He had countersigned it himself and let the King sign it but it has not got the officer's name on it nor his regiment. There are blanks where these should be. Once it was out of Arlington's hands anyone could have written his name in and got King Charles's Commission. I have half a mind to fill it in with my own name and if I did who could deny that I had the King's Commission?

Incidentally it is a pity Charles did not let Mistress Eleanor sign it too. She was only capable of writing her initials, 'E.G.', and these are an autographic rarity today.

When I was young and building up my collection (at that time largely signatures), I wrote to the great contemporary composer Ralph Vaughan Williams. He replied to my letter sending me what I had asked for 'with pleasure' but adding that he could not for the life of him understand how I could find any fascination in obtaining the signature of someone I had never met. He was not by any means the only person to express the same sentiments. I wrote back and tried to explain that I was interested in people who made history in all walks of life, politically, by their writings or paintings or, as in his case, by their music. I could not hope to get to know them personally; in the majority of cases they were dead anyway but their works were living and their signatures were a personal reminder of them. He did not reply again—why should he?—but I hope and believe he got my message.

The investor-collector is in a different category. Though all serious collectors would be unwise not to consider the investment angle to some degree, it should not be the major influence in their collecting. I should like to think that no collector thinks first and foremost of the monetary value but such pious hopes have already been shattered for me. I met recently somebody who buys all he can get in the way of fine autograph material and puts it away in a suitcase. He never looks at it and would never dream of documenting, cataloguing or lovingly 'writing-up' these precious acquisitions. He admits, with disarming frankness, that one day he will open the case and sell at a considerable profit. All genuine collectors, who derive pleasure and knowledge from the handling of autographs and the study of autography, will be horrified by this utter disregard of the aesthetics of collecting, but there is no doubt whatsoever that manuscript material is a first-class investment and is likely to remain so as long as the capitalist world itself survives.

The financial value of autographs, speaking in general terms and not of obvious exceptions, was surprisingly low until after World War II. It is really only in about the last fifteen years that it has risen swiftly. Nowadays there are infinitely more dealers in this field (especially in America) than there were only a few years ago, which indicates that there are many more collectors. However, it is not only the private collector who has popularized serious autograph collecting but also such institutions as have already been mentioned. University libraries also show a rapidly increasing interest in first-class autograph material. Britain, France, Germany, Italy and Austria have long been autograph-collecting countries but I think that the swiftest rise in enthusiasm has been in the United States and this has had its effect on prices in a market where, today, demand far outstrips supply. Although Americana is, of course, the most popular subject there, the demand for British autographs is, on the whole, greater than for possibly more illustrious continental examples; the more immediate contact felt with those who think and write in the same language as oneself doubtless explains the added attraction.

By way of an example of a good autographic investment let us take Lord Byron. This poet is not yet strictly rare, autographically, but is much sought after, especially by major libraries. Apart from one or two sold privately, perhaps half a dozen of his letters may appear on the open market this year. They will be snapped up avidly and at least three-quarters of them will go into an institutional depository such as a university or a library. They will not re-appear. It follows that, since the floating stock of Byron holographs obviously cannot go on for ever, the very next year there may well be only four such letters for open sale and these will fetch even higher prices; and so on and so forth. Even the unlikely finding of a cache of Byron letters could not alter this trend for very long. So as an investment autographs are evidently a good thing and a man who buys a Byron letter today may only have to hold on to it for a couple of years to double his money.

I cannot see how the upward trend of autograph values is likely to abate (though obviously it may have its setbacks). The pattern it is following is that of most other collected antiquaria such as pictures, books, objets d'art and even bric-a-brac. All these have appreciated beyond measure.

For anyone who feels the need for a part-time occupation, a hobby of some sort, autograph collecting, started when young, can not only provide great joy and interest during one's working years but can enhance the pleasure and lighten the burden of retirement and old age; and as autographs can combine education, enjoyment and investment value what better reasons need be given for their collection?

WHAT TO COLLECT: THE CHOICE FOR THE BEGINNER

There are two main ways in which to collect autographs: to collect them in general, that is to say to collect the autographs of anybody who interests one in any profession and in any period of history including the present day; or to specialize. There is much to be said for both, and it is almost impossible to advise a beginner on this point, though I do consider that it is something which should be decided by the collector as soon as possible after he has started to collect, if not before. I think one thing is certain, however: that if you specialize you stand a good chance of getting together a more complete collection, whereas the general field is so wide that it is never possible to come anywhere near what might be termed completion.

Perhaps my own collection is a good example. I have letters, signed documents, etc. of well over 12,000 different people and at least 2,000 duplicates, for want of a better word, though of course no autograph item is ever, strictly speaking, a duplicate. Nevertheless I have really only scratched the surface. There are thousands upon thousands of well-known people, past and present, of whom I still have no autographic example. Had I specialized in, say, nineteenth-century English literature, it would have been quite possible to have obtained letters of all but a very few of the literary greats of this era. Certainly I would have had difficulty with Keats, of whom I still have no example, and some trouble over the Brontë family, of whom I have only Charlotte, but with few other exceptions I could have amassed a full collection of at least one autographic example of each name.

This is not the whole case for specialization but it is certainly a point that you can thus reach satisfaction, or at least near satisfaction, before you depart this life; also if you choose wisely you may well be able to build up something quite unique. In British autography, for example, a collection of all the sovereigns of England from Richard III to the present day would be magnificent but not unique. On the other hand a collection of every British explorer might well be so.

It would be impractical to attempt a full list of subjects for specialization but here are some suggestions. They cover British material only; the variations are endless if we go further afield. There are also obviously many possible permutations and subdivisions of each suggestion here listed:

- The famous of any one century or era
- The sovereigns (and their consorts) or all British royalty
- The Prime Ministers (and the earlier Lord High Treasurers)
- Politicians (under centuries or under parties)
- Historical periods (e.g. the Civil War, the Industrial Revolution) or causes (e.g. slavery, history of and abolitionists of, etc.)
- Explorers
- Inventors or pioneers (all, or any particular field)
- Science (all, or subdivisions thereof, e.g. medicine, astronomy, mathematics, physics, chemistry, etc.)
- Religion (all, under centuries, or under denominations or religious appointments, e.g. Archbishops of Canterbury)
- Scholars (all or under subjects)
- Literature (all, under centuries or under media, e.g. poetry, drama, the novel, etc.)
- Art (all, under centuries or schools, or under media, e.g. painting, sculpture, design, etc.)

Music (all or subdivisions thereof, e.g. composers, conductors, instrumentalists)
Entertainment (all or under media, e.g. the stage, cinema, radio, television)
Sport (all or subdivisions thereof, e.g. football, cricket, golf, boxing)
Naval, military or air commanders of any period
Judges and the law
Commerce and industry
Philanthropists
Criminals and rogues
Women in history
Pairs (e.g. Nelson and Lady Hamilton)
Dictionary names (i.e. those whose names are now part of our language, e.g. Spooner(ism), Sandwich, Cardigan)
Philately and postal history
Famous persons of geographic areas (Scotland, Yorkshire, London, etc.)
One particular person (Dickens, Johnson, Churchill, etc.)
Association books only (books containing autograph inscriptions, dedications, annotations and/or signed by their authors or owners)
Signed photographs and portraits only

The ultimate in specialization is the collection of autographic material of a single person. This is not uncommon amongst collectors but he who specializes in, say, only Dickens is really not so much an autograph collector as a collector of Dickensiana. Such collectors will probably be seeking not only the novelist's own letters but those to him, about him and those of his family circle and immediate literary connections—such as Wilkie Collins or Harrison Ainsworth. They may well go outside the purlieus of autographs and collect also first editions of his works, portraits and photographs of him and associates, prints from the illustrations of his books, etc. I suppose this could go on ad absurdum to buying his favourite armchair or obtaining a snip of his hair. (As far as the hair goes one would be safe with Dickens, who had plenty of it, but it would be less easy with Samuel Rogers!)

The case for generalization is an obvious one. A collection of really great men and women of all periods and professions, arranged of course with some degree of consistency, can be immensely impressive and the very fact of its variety can certainly make it more entertaining to others who have no specific collecting interests. For myself I can only give a view that is not in the slightest bit helpful to a beginner: that I often wish I had specialized but that I am very happy with my own general collection!

WHAT TO COLLECT: THE VARIOUS FORMS OF AUTOGRAPHS

Autographs take many forms and their appeal (and value) depends on a number of factors in themselves not autographic. Once you have chosen your subjects you will then need to consider in what form to collect them.

Here is a list of the various types of autographs, arranged in roughly descending order of interest and value:

Signed holograph manuscripts and full musical scores
Original sketches signed by the artist

Signed autograph letters
Unsigned holograph manuscripts and musical scores
Signed non-holograph letters
Signed autograph bars of music (with the composer's signature in particular)
Signed self-sketches
Signed documents
Signed photographs or portraits
Autograph letters in the third person or unsigned
Signed autograph notes or drafts from speeches, letters, etc.
Signed autograph quotations or sentiments
Association books
Signed autograph minutes, etc.
Signed autograph franks (the covers used mostly in the first half of the last century and signed by members of the Houses of Parliament to obtain free postage)
Unsigned autograph notes
Signed end portions of autograph letters
Signed end portions of non-holograph letters
Signatures with autograph date and/or place
Signatures in full
Unsigned autograph covers or envelopes
A few words in autograph unsigned (i.e. part of a letter). If these are authenticated as part of something interesting, they can go higher up the list.
Autograph initials only
A single autograph initial
A single word in autograph, unsigned

The recognized abbreviation for a signed autograph letter is A.L.S. (Autograph Letter Signed). This is a highly desirable form of autograph and one to which most serious collectors aspire. It is therefore a good basis for evaluation purposes and such evaluation may be adapted to suit most other forms of manuscript material.

The value of an A.L.S. depends upon its content, length, condition, date and addressee. The first is by far the most important and indeed the value (and the interest) of all autographic material depends more upon the content than upon anything else. If, therefore, a famous author writes about his work it is evident that this must have far greater value than if he is simply saying that he regrets he cannot come to tea tomorrow. Naturally the more concerned with his writing the letter is, the more valuable is it likely to be but even the briefest mention of his work will make it more desirable.

A short Dickens A.L.S. in my collection may perhaps be a good example. In it he gives permission to a certain clergyman to read *A Christmas Carol* in public but adds that 'my correspondents are too numerous to leave me leisure to explain how I am accustomed to condense it when I read it myself' (see page 20).

In a letter I have of John Masefield he is trying to remember the thought behind certain passages in his poem 'The Seekers'. He regrets that he cannot recollect what was in his mind when he wrote the verses in question and goes on to say: 'Probably the thought referred to users of the imagination, who give up most other things to exercise their imaginations and have rewards not quite of this world.' He adds, a little ruefully, 'the verses were made many years ago and years are bad for the memories'.

I have a long holograph letter of R. D. Blackmore whose permission has evidently been asked for the publishing of extracts from his work and some notes on his career.

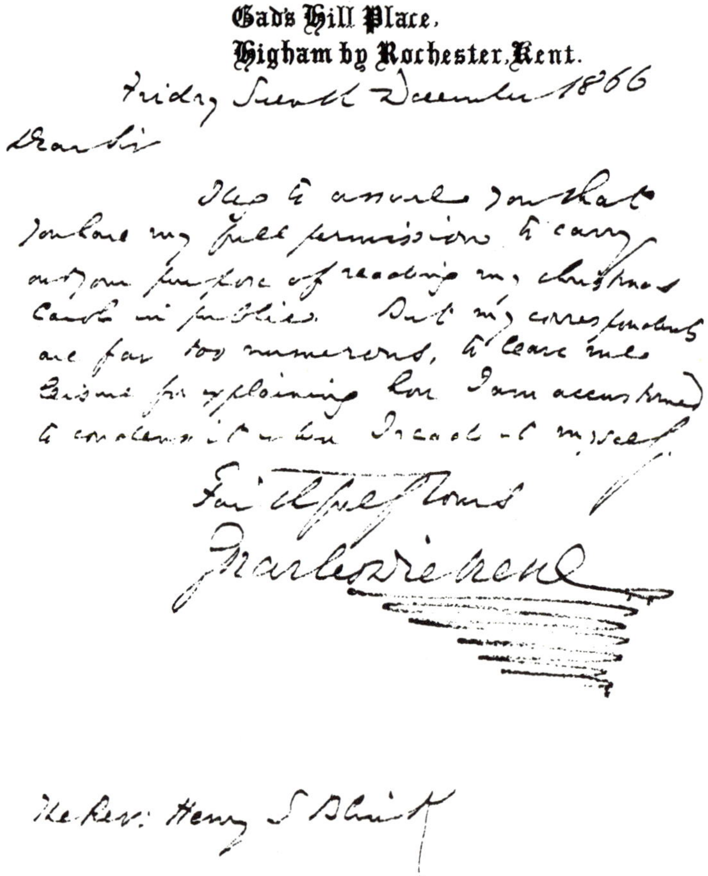
Gad's Hill Place,
Higham by Rochester, Kent.

Friday Seventh December 1866

Dear Sir

I beg to assure you that you have my full permission to carry out your purpose of reading my Christmas Carol in public. But my correspondents are far too numerous, to leave me leisure for explaining how I am accustomed to condense it when I read it myself.

Faithfully Yours

Charles Dickens

The Rev: Henry S Blunt

Autograph letter from Charles Dickens to a clergyman, giving permission for a public reading of *A Christmas Carol.*
Reduced in size

In it he writes: 'I began as most people do, with flying at very high game—a tragedy in sooth, and I sometimes fancy that with much rehandling it would make a good acting play.' He says he has also written a comedy but the interest of this letter is increased greatly with his remark that 'another book, *Lorna Doone*, offers more choice for quotation'. The mention of his most famous novel and his evident pride in it automatically make this letter more valuable.

Nor need a famous author necessarily write about his own work for a letter of his to be of interest. If he touches at all on literary matters it cannot fail to be more pleasing. In one I have of that great Indian poet Sir Rabindranath Tagore he is commenting on his reaction to a book of *Roundels and Rhymes* sent to him by an English lady correspondent. Very gently he gets it across to her that he really has no time to read it. *Inter alia*, he writes: 'I have just had time to take a glance at your poems through uncut pages and they have stimulated my attention. Verses are jealous of neighbouring distractions; they claim around them a whole stretch of perfect leisure—which unfortunately is no longer in my possession since I have been driven out of my obscurity.' Written in 1920, a year after he had tried unsuccessfully to get rid of his knighthood as a gesture of his dissatisfaction with British policy in his country, and seven years after he had been the first Asian to receive a Nobel Prize, these words make this letter all the more poignant.

Just as an author's letter of literary content is to be desired so is the letter of an artist about art or indeed of anyone writing on his own subject. As an example of the former I have a long letter of Sir Stanley Spencer to a fellow artist in which he refers to two of his paintings: 'One is the biggish picture I am doing of disciples and malt houses and God knows what . . . and the other . . . of good and wicked people getting out of graves . . . .' The pictures referred to are evidently those of the *Resurrection*, now in the Tate Gallery.

Many letters in my collection describe or refer to events which were happening at the time of writing and have since become history. A first-hand description of the Chartist Riots is one example and I have a number of letters from ambassadors abroad in the seventeenth and eighteenth centuries reporting on political occurrences in the countries to which they were assigned. These make fascinating reading and are particularly good examples of the value of content. A political A.L.S. of which I am especially proud is a two-page entirely holograph letter of the Baron (John) de Blaquiere, Chief Secretary in Ireland, reporting on the failure of the ill-fated '98 rebellion in that country. The letter is addressed to the first Earl of Liverpool and is dated 8th June 1798, four days after the death of the rebel leader, Lord Edward Fitzgerald.

Another letter of Blaquiere to Liverpool is also in my collection. It reads:

> My dear Lord,
>
> We have this moment issued a proclamation in Council charging Ld Ed Fitzgerald with high treason and offering a reward of £1000 for his apprehension.
>
> I am your most faithful servant
>
> J. Blaquiere.

The letter is dated less than a month before the other one. In little more than a week, poor Fitzgerald was betrayed. Wounded in a fierce struggle to escape arrest, he languished for sixteen days before expiring on 4th June 1798.

Any letter which expresses an interesting opinion will also be of some value, more especially if that opinion concerns an important event or prominent contemporary. In a letter I have of H. G. Wells he considers that the name which appeals to some of the best young men in the Fabian Society is 'not Shaw nor [Sidney] Webb but Professor Karl Pearson'. The letter has a whole lot more to say on Fabian affairs in which Wells had no little interest at that time (1916). Karl Pearson, incidentally, was a mathematician and biologist, said to have been among the most influential university teachers of his time, 'admired and feared rather than loved'.

Even a letter on an entirely personal subject can be worthy of collection. I have a letter of Sir Anthony Hope Hawkins, famed as the author of *The Prisoner of Zenda* under his pseudonym, 'Anthony Hope'. Writing to Lady Balfour he refers to his engagement to 'an American girl . . . an unexpected development in a bachelor of my standing'. He had lasted forty years so I suppose he could qualify for some standing in bachelorhood!

If the content of a letter particularly reflects the character of the writer this would make it a considerable asset to any collector. George Bernard Shaw is a good example of this, for he poured out a plethora of caustic letters and postcards, few of which did not show one or other of his entertainingly conflicting qualities. In one of my letters Shaw writes to a sick woman relative. His kindly side is shown in that he has guaranteed her hospital bill but he cannot refrain from ending with his own brand of astringent advice: 'Fasting will do you good. You were developing an elderly spread. As to your old suitor I daresay you are right. A dead husband is much less trouble than a live one. He costs nothing, and is never unfaithful.'

The gentle complexity of the mind of 'Lewis Carroll' (Charles Dodgson) is highlighted in a letter to a little girl in which he suggests that a life of 'breakfast, lessons, dinner, lessons, tea, lessons, bed, lessons, breakfast, lessons, and so on . . . is a very neat plan of life, and almost as interesting as being a sewing-machine or a coffee-grinder', and goes on to ask her which of these two objects she would prefer to be. The letter wanders on through four pages of typically 'Carroll' flights of whimsy. 'Do you know the way to improve children?' he asks, and replies to his own question: '*Re*-proving them is the best way.' He adds: 'Mr Sampson doesn't send you his love: in fact I haven't asked him; in fact, perhaps he would rather not and it would be *extremely* awkward for him if I asked him to send love, and he had nothing but hatred handy . . . .'

The magnanimity of Winston Churchill is clearly shown in a lengthy and brilliantly phrased letter written at the age of only twenty-five from Bloemfontein, South Africa, in 1900. Addressed to my wife's grandfather, Ramsay Collins, editor of the *Natal Mercury*, he pleads eloquently for the lenient treatment of the defeated Boers by their British fellow colonists. The force of his character comes out in the words: 'Looking on South African matters with an eye which if it be not trained by long experience, is nevertheless undimmed by prejudice, I find much to admire in the Dutch. I regard them as an essential to the development and prosperity of South Africa . . . .' There follows more telling phraseology such as, 'I am not angry when I hear the crime of theft denounced, but I can quite understand thieves being annoyed . . . .' His letter ends with a note of prophetic arrogance: 'It is moreover my instinct to wish to swim upstream.'

A little letter in tiny writing from Robert Louis Stevenson (see page 120) brings out the charm of this brave, sick man. Writing from Vailima in December 1893, he tells his correspondent, Alan Francis of Golden Square, London, how to get hold of some Samoan stamps and administers the very mild reproach: 'I like "living on an island so far away" very much. It is really no further away from me than Golden Square is from you.'

Thus the characters of the writers are continually revealed in their letters, from humorist P. G. Wodehouse telling that old joke about not letting a 'knight out on a dog like this' to that humorist of earlier days, Sir F. C. Burnand, editor of *Punch* seventy years pre-Muggeridge, writing a complete letter in amusing verse.

Length, though important, must take second place. For instance, Henry James, the distinguished American novelist who became a British citizen, was capable of writing a three-page letter when refusing an invitation; half a page with a single literary reference in it would be far more valuable, however. On the other hand, the value of length can be seen from the fact that if the letter were three pages long and at the same time on a literary subject throughout it would be an item of major importance.

It is possible, however, for a letter to be both brief and have some literary content. I am very fond of this little example:

Oct 7, 1882 Harting
Petersfield

Dear Sir,
The Frasers' Magazine is, I believe, dead.
At any rate I am not going to write a story for it.
Yours truly,
Anthony Trollope.
G. N. Richardson, Esq.

The condition of a document obviously influences its value. If a letter is so faded, torn, holed, foxed, creased in the folds, damp-stained, burned or irretrievably dirty as to make any part of it unreadable, this cannot but affect its desirability. Even if it is still readable in its entirety, any of these defects could have such effect, to a lesser degree.

The date can add to the interest if it is one which is outstanding in the life of the writer or connected with the production of any of his work, especially if the latter is specifically mentioned in the letter concerned.

The influence of the addressee on the autographic interest of the letter can be considerable. It is obviously more pleasing, all other conditions being equal, to possess a letter of Shaw to, say, Kipling (though I do not suppose that they ever corresponded) than one of Shaw to a nobody.

Often regarded by dealers and collectors as the two lowest forms of A.L.S. are the letter which replies to a request for an autograph and the 'invitation letter' already

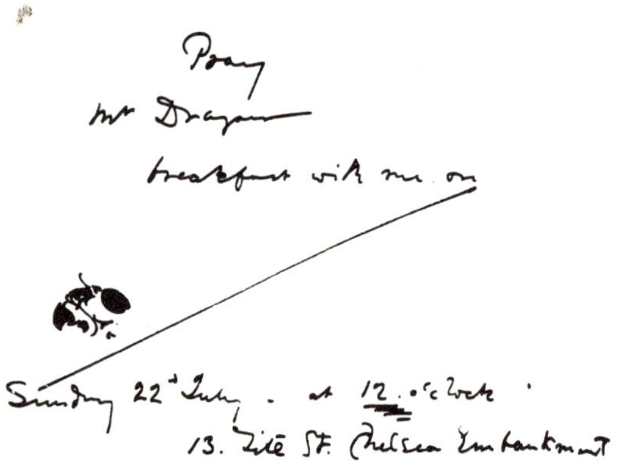
Pray
Mr Draper
breakfast with me on
Sunday 22nd July. at 12. o'clock.
13. Tite St. Chelsea Embankment

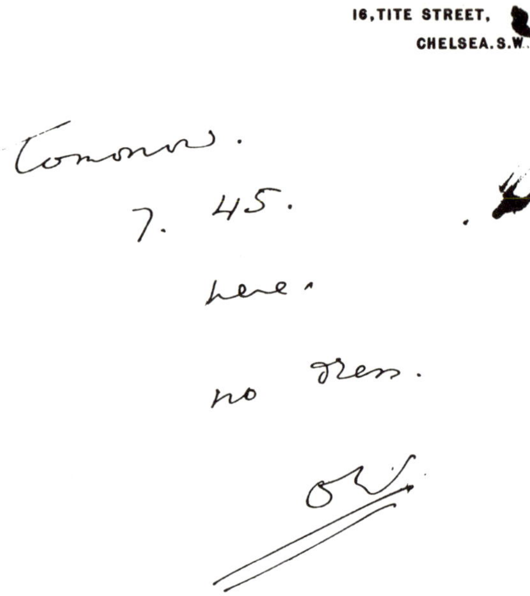
16, TITE STREET,
CHELSEA. S.W.
Tomorrow.
7. 45.
here.
no dress.
O W

Two invitations from Tite Street. *Left:* From James McNeill Whistler, the American painter who lived and worked in London, a brief invitation signed with his 'butterfly' signature. Written from 13 Tite Street. *Right:* From Oscar Wilde, a hastily scrawled, smudged note signed with his initials. Written from 16 Tite Street. *Both reduced in size*

referred to which refuses, accepts or gives an invitation. As a general rule I suppose I must agree that these are least desirable but in the past courtesies were such that even invitation letters can be rather delightful. What about this unusual, entirely holograph, 'summons' from the then Prime Minister:

Downing Street
Sunday, Nov^{b}. 12, 1780.

My dear Lord,
If it will be agreeable to the Cabinet to meet here tomorrow morning at eleven o'clock that hour will be perfectly convenient to
Your Lordship's very humble servant
North.

I somewhat doubt whether Cabinet ministers are called up in so charming a manner nowadays.

And what about this delightfully old-fashioned note from John Abernethy, the great surgeon, in 1820? He writes: 'Dear Sir, if you will dine with me tomorrow at 7 o'clock we may then have the opportunity of colloquising.'

There is another A.L.S. in my collection in which a future Prime Minister, Lloyd George, answers an invitation with the facetious remark that he 'cannot resist the temptation to enjoy an old pro-Boer lunch' (this in 1914). I think these three examples show that the collector must not dismiss invitation letters out of hand.

It will be seen from my list that the plain signature comes fairly far down in value. This is necessarily so if it stands entirely on its own but it will also be noted that the three most important forms of autograph require a signature to help them to the top of the list. There is no doubt whatsoever that to the average autograph collector the addition of a signature to any letter, manuscript or document is important. It is, it must be, the ultimate stamp of its authenticity and of its writer's recognition of his own product.

To collect nothing but signatures alone is a different matter and the more serious collector must strive to do better than this; yet it is a mistake to deprecate this form of autograph. Indeed, with the advent of such increasing interest in autograph material, plain signatures are coming more and more into their own again and I would strongly advise the beginner and even the advanced collector to take a signature if he cannot find (or afford) a letter. Taking the case to the point of absurdity, let us suppose you were to come across an authenticated signature of Shakespeare (only six are known to exist, so the odds are somewhat long). It would be worth several thousand complete letters of lesser mortals!

When including plain signatures in your general collection one example of any particular person is probably enough. But if you are specializing it could be interesting to have several examples showing the differences in your subject's signature at various stages of his life. The signature of Dickens, for instance, changed quite considerably between youth and old age.

In the same way as the humble beginner may have to content himself with a plain signature so it may be possible for a university or a wealthy collector to obtain the ultimate in autography: the complete holograph music score of a famous opera, the entire manuscript of a great play, or that of a classic novel. There is nothing in the collecting of autographs which would be more desirable or more valuable. If you can afford this sort of material then unquestionably it will bring the greatest reward, both as a magnificent possession and as a financial investment. But to form a collection of such items (each running into several thousands of pounds) would be quite beyond the means of most private collectors.

Without doubt one of the most exciting forms of autograph is the complete manuscript of a poem signed by its author. If it is both the original and completely holograph all the better. One of the best examples in my own collection is the full autograph manuscript of Edith Sitwell's powerful poem of outrage against the dropping of the atom bomb on Hiroshima, 'Dirge for the New Sunrise'. I also have holograph signed poems of such diverse poets as Louis MacNeice, A. P. Herbert, Laurence Binyon, Eliza Cook, Hugh Conway and Lascelles Abercrombie.

To collect poems in manuscript can be expensive, but far less so and still very satisfactory is it to obtain a printed poem signed in the original. I have this kind of thing of John Masefield and his successor as Poet Laureate, C. Day-Lewis.

The attraction of collecting signed photographs is an obvious one and such a collection can look extremely pleasant. There are a number of collectors who collect only these and do not touch letters or documents. The collecting of association books can be very satisfactory also, though I do not personally go in for them simply because of

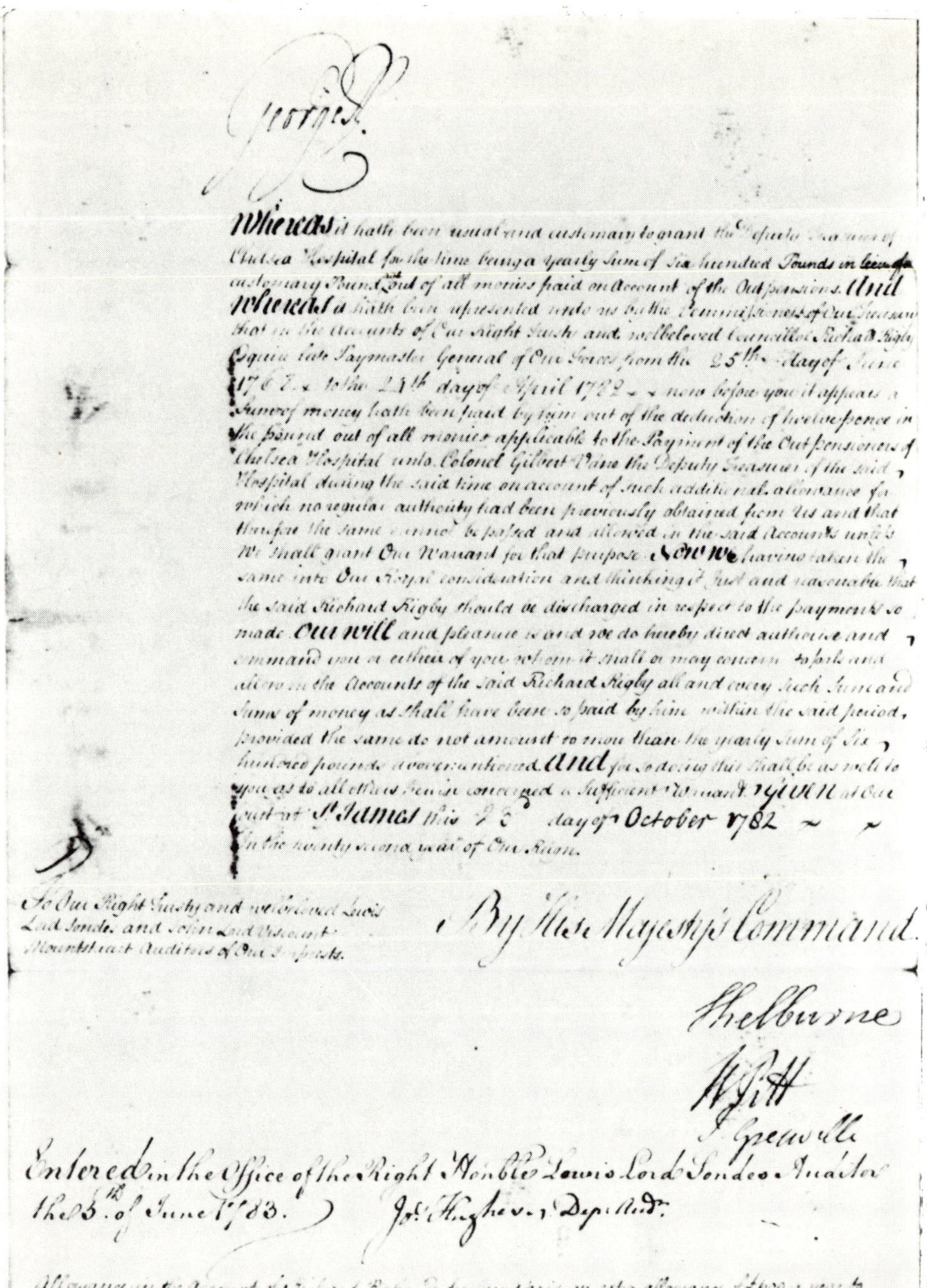

George R.

Whereas it hath been usual and customary to grant the Deputy Treasurer of Chelsea Hospital for the time being a yearly Sum of Six hundred Pounds in lieu of a customary Poundage out of all monies paid on Account of the Out pensioners. And Whereas it hath been represented unto us by the Commissioners of Our Treasury that in the Accounts of Our Right Trusty and wellbeloved Councillor Richard Rigby Esquire late Paymaster General of Our Forces from the 25th day of June 1768 to the 24th day of April 1782 now before you it appears a Sum of money hath been paid by him out of the deduction of twelvepence in the pound out of all monies applicable to the Payment of the Out pensioners of Chelsea Hospital unto Colonel Gilbert Vane the Deputy Treasurer of the said Hospital during the said time on account of such additional allowance for which no regular authority had been previously obtained from Us and that therefore the same cannot be passed and allowed in the said Accounts unless We shall grant Our Warrant for that purpose. Now We having taken the same into Our Royal consideration and thinking it just and reasonable that the said Richard Rigby should be discharged in respect to the payments so made Our Will and pleasure is and we do hereby direct authorise and command you or either of you whom it shall or may concern to pass and allow in the Accounts of the said Richard Rigby all and every such Sum and Sums of money as shall have been so paid by him within the said period, provided the same do not amount to more than the yearly Sum of Six hundred pounds abovementioned. And for so doing this shall be as well to you as to all others herein concerned a Sufficient Warrant. Given at Our Court at St James's this 23 day of October 1782 In the twenty second year of Our Reign.

To Our Right Trusty and wellbeloved Lewis Lord Sondes and John Lord Viscount Mountstuart Auditors of Our Imprests.

By His Majesty's Command.

Shelburne

W Pitt

J Grenville

Entered in the Office of the Right Honble Lewis Lord Sondes Auditor the 23d of June 1783. Jos. Hughes Dep. Aud.

Allowance in the Account of Richard Rigby Esq. for Sums paid on extra allowance of £600 a year to Colonel Gilbert Vane Esq. Deputy Treasurer of Chelsea Hospital.

Document signed by George III and William Pitt, the Younger. Dated 1782, it approves certain accounts submitted by the Deputy Treasurer of Chelsea Hospital. As well as bearing the King's signature at the top, the document is countersigned by the then Prime Minister, Lord Shelburne (later Marquess of Lansdowne), William Pitt, the Younger, and James Grenville.

Reduced in size

their bulk. Knowing my avidity for collecting, I should have to buy a castle to house them and I am not in the castle-buying class!

Signed documents should certainly be collected. It may be difficult to find really historical documents as so many of these are already in museums but an immense variety of documents are still available; some of them, such as old parchments with seals and the elaborate signatures of sovereigns, statesmen and famous commanders on land and sea, are very beautiful. Below is a short list of the kind of documents which may still be found comparatively easily. By way of example I have put in brackets one or two names of persons signing such documents in my own collection:

Commissions of officers (the sovereigns, countersigned by many great statesmen, such as George III with William Pitt, Earl of Chatham)
Naval orders (Admiralty) for movement of ships etc. (Samuel Pepys)
Admiral's orders for restocking of ships at sea (Nelson, Anson)
Lords of the Admiralty: general naval orders (Hood, Howe)
Ordnance office stores orders, etc. (Wade)
Appointments of non-commissioned officers (Marlborough)
Orders for troop movements and routing (Monck)
Permission to exchange or buy commissions (Wellington)
Grants of leave of officers (Frederick, the 'Grand Old Duke of York')
Regimental expenses (Wolfe, a very rare signature)
Treasury documents (Clarendon, Walpole and many Prime Ministers)
Appointments to orders of chivalry (the sovereign, including the present Queen)
Pardons (the sovereign and the Home Secretary)
Privy Council orders (the Council of Edward VI, including Lord Protector Somerset; of Elizabeth I, including Lords Howard of Effingham and Salisbury—see frontispiece)
Judicial documents, including sentences on prisoners (many of the great judges of England, with sentences varying from the public whipping of a woman to the hanging of a highwayman for stealing a threepenny tinder box)
Legal documents, such as wills (Judge Jeffreys, of the 'Bloody Assize')
Old passports, often with decorative coats-of-arms and signatures of Foreign Ministers (Castlereagh)
Land deeds (the great majority are uninteresting but the signatures should always be carefully examined. My own collection contains many of interest, varying from Robert Dudley, Earl of Leicester, to Joseph Addison)
Cheques or payment orders (Sheridan)
Publication and performance contracts (for plays and books signed by the author or for the engagement of actors, concert singers, etc.)
Ecclesiastical courts and appointments (archbishops and bishops, often with fine episcopal paper seals)

Some documents with the Great Seal of the sovereign still intact can be found but these are not often signed. The seals are valuable in themselves but if you are lucky enough to get one with both the seal and the monarch's signature, this will be an exceptionally fine acquisition.

THE VALUE OF AUTOGRAPHS

The financial value of autographs depends on a number of factors, some of which may come as a surprise to the uninitiated. For instance, I am frequently offered documents signed by Queen Victoria commissioning officers in the services. The justly proud owners are nearly always horrified to learn that these are worth only a few pounds. A few shillings may be added to the value if the document is countersigned by a particularly important statesman, say the Prime Minister of the time, whilst a combination of Victoria and Wellington, or Disraeli, might add a pound or so, but the figure will be low in any case. What are the reasons for this?

The position is that Queen Victoria signed every single commission document with her own hand throughout her sixty-four-year reign; also, because she was Queen Victoria, the famous and regal Queen Empress, everyone preserved these documents carefully. Very few will have been lost or destroyed. Hence the number of Victoria commissions still available to this day probably runs into thousands and, despite a growing demand, so thriving a supply cannot do other than keep the price down.

This is a perfect example of one thing the beginner collector (and indeed the would-be dealer) must learn very soon if he is not to get his fingers burned: that the fame of the person does not guarantee the value of his autograph. The recipients usually take so much more care to preserve autographs of the very famous that many are far from rare and thus far from expensive. If a person has lived a long life and written many letters and at the same time been particularly prominent, his autograph will not be scarce. In such a category come several of the greatest names in our history: Wellington, Gladstone and Palmerston were all prolific letter writers who lived into their eighties and are thus very common autographically. Highly acceptable though a letter of the Iron Duke most certainly is, unless its content is important it could well cost less than ten pounds today.

As a general rule then the more rare (and thus valuable) autographs will be those of persons who lived a short life and wrote few letters. Short-lived were the poets Rupert Brooke and James Elroy Flecker and their autographs (especially Flecker's) are uncommon. The artist Aubrey Beardsley and, two centuries before him, the seventeen-year-old imposter-poet Thomas Chatterton, are other examples, as is, of course, Keats.

If fame comes largely after death, this too may play a part in adding value. Shelley is an immediate example. I have a holograph envelope cover of Shelley on the back of which is this note by the recipient, Taafe: 'Percy Shelley, the friend of Lord Byron who was drowned in the Gulph of Genoa.' Not a word about his being a poet, just Byron's friend! Shelley's letters today, because of his early death and posthumous fame, are likely to cost even more than those of Byron.

Another case is that of General James Wolfe. No more than a colonel with a good military record, he was promoted and chosen by Pitt (Chatham) to command against the French in Canada. In his very first action, the taking of Quebec, he was killed, at the age of thirty-two. People do not hoard the writing of unknown colonels, so his autograph, preserved by few, is in demand today by many. It took me over thirty years to get an example of it: a signature on a receipt for expenses of his own regiment.

Like everything in the commercial world, the values of autographs depend on supply and demand. Where demand is very great and supply is very small, as with Keats, then prices will be high. Yet rarity alone is not enough to make for value. If there were no demand for Keats it would not matter how rare his autograph was; it would be worth little.

I am often asked what my oldest document is. When I reply that it is one signed by a judge in the fourteenth century but that it is of little value, this seems to cause surprise. Yet it is a fact that unless the document is in itself interesting or is signed by someone of autographical importance its age will be of no financial consequence unless it is at least fourteenth century. If I particularly wanted to have a document of the thirteenth century, I should have no difficulty whatsoever in getting one. In British autography, it would be less easy to go back further, but in Italy or Germany many documents of greater age can still be found.

My judge's autograph is probably worth about £5 today but my letter of Dylan Thomas (yet another who died fairly young), written six hundred years later, could be worth some twenty times that amount. Could there be better proof of the relative unimportance of the age of a document?

The age factor combined with rarity and desirability is a totally different matter. The documents signed by Shakespeare (the handful that there are) are virtually priceless. No British autograph could be of greater value though there are others which are more rare: Marlowe, for instance. No-one has yet seen a single word in his writing.

A good example of an historical figure who is still not rare but for whom the demand is so great that the price is high is Elizabeth I. This queen has caught imagination throughout the ages and her superb and complicated signature (see page 51) must thrill all collectors. My own document of her is a particularly fine one addressed to the High Sheriff of Kent, ordering him to raise men for a feared invasion of her realm. The magnificent signature of the Queen, as clear as though it were penned yesterday (though it was written in 1597), measures exactly seven inches from the first to the last of its flourishes. Here is a case where rarity takes second place to demand. The autograph of Elizabeth's ill-fated cousin, Mary, Queen of Scots, is much more rare but will cost less.

The rising interest in British autographs in the United States lies mostly in our great literary figures but also in those connected with the American struggle for independence. George III, the sovereign of that time, the elder Pitt, North, the then Prime Minister, Cornwallis, the ill-fated British Commander-in-Chief, etc., are always wanted. George III and North are common, Pitt and Cornwallis less so; the values vary accordingly.

The signatures of the sovereigns of England are not strictly rare until before the Tudors, except for Edward VI, the Boy King, who is excessively so, and Mary I ('Bloody Mary'). Mary II (of William and Mary) is, curiously, also far from common. The monarch's signature is regarded as more valuable if signed as king or queen rather than before accession to the throne. There is little interest, therefore, in George VI signed when Albert, Duke of York and virtually none in William IV signed as Duke of Clarence. George IV signed as Prince would similarly not evoke interest but his signature as Prince Regent, 'George P.R.', is in some demand. The classic example is the still living Edward VIII. As Duke of Windsor his autograph is not uncommon and as Prince of Wales even less so, though both are to be desired. Yet as King, because of his reign having lasted less than one year, this sovereign's autograph is of far greater value than most of his predecessors'. Lesser documents, such as commissions, signed as 'Edward R.I.' can be found but private letters are decidedly rare. In the one I have in my collection, the King refers to an incident during a military parade, when a man threw a gun at him. Writing to Major-General Sergison-Brooke, he congratulates him on the success of the ceremony and ends with the words: 'We have to thank the Almighty for two things; firstly, that it did not rain and secondly that the man in the brown suit's gun did not go off' (see opposite page).

There are trends in interest, and therefore in demand, in autographs both individual and by professions. Taking the latter first, the most sought-after group at present is literature, followed by the sciences, classical music and exploration. Politicians, with notable exceptions, are trailing and, I am sorry to record, 'the Church' is right at the bottom. There is very little interest in ecclesiastical or theological autographs unless the person concerned took some important part in history or in literature. Examples of this would be John and Charles Wesley, Archbishops Cranmer and Laud, and Cardinal Wolsey. There is considerable interest in the autographs of the popes but there has been only one British pope (Nicholas Breakspear—Pope Adrian IV) and one is not likely to find his signature.

Even in literary autographs the whims of collectors are so legion that it is almost impossible for a beginner to know whether he is investing well or not. Milton, Bunyan, Swift, Steele, Cowper, Johnson, Pope and Dryden are all in great demand and letters of any of these will cost well into three figures. So will the later names. Byron, Shelley, Keats, Lamb and Coleridge are high and Wordsworth and Browning are mounting swiftly. Elizabeth Barrett Browning is more expensive than her husband and the Brontës are all highly valued. In this century there is a demand for many British writers from D. H. Lawrence to Dylan Thomas. There is virtually no interest at the moment in Austin Dobson, Henry Newbolt, or even Charles Kingsley, yet Kipling is avidly collected and Conan Doyle is popular, especially if he mentions Sherlock Holmes.

The influence of newly published books, films or plays on autograph values is most noticeable. Because it is fashionable to decry the creation of the Empire, 'Empire builders' and administrators are 'out', autographically. Yet when an excellent film on Gordon, *Khartoum*, was produced not long ago there was a sudden demand for the autograph of that strange mixture of soldier and mystic. Already this has tailed away. *The Right Honourable Gentleman*, a West-End play about the little-known Sir Charles Dilke, suddenly increased the value of his letters from a few shillings to a few pounds, although this interest soon died.

Virginia Woolf's autograph has increased in popularity and thus value, partly because of the recently fashionable interest in the 'Bloomsbury set' and partly, I imagine, because of the purely nominal publicity given to her by the play and film *Who's Afraid of Virginia Woolf? The Quest for Corvo* touched off a quest for the rare autograph of Corvo (Frederick Rolfe) himself, to which a further stimulus has been added by the

St. James's Palace, S.W.

July 16, 1936

Dear Boy -

Please convey through the Lieutenant-Colonels Grenadier Guards, Coldstream Guards and Scots Guards my sincere congratulations to all ranks of the Battalions of their Regiments to whom I have just given new Colours, on the admirable manner in which one and all played their part in the impressive Parade in Hyde Park this morning.

I thought that the drill and manoeuvring was excellent, considering they had only had one rehearsal and that they had to march on grass instead of the hard surface to which they are accustomed.

It was a ceremony I shall never forget.

I would like to add my personal congratulations to yourself and your Staff for the organization and all the arrangements made in connection with the Parade. There was not a hitch, and above all the Parade was not too long.

We have to thank the Almighty for two things: firstly that it did not rain, and secondly that the man in the brown suit's gun did not go off.!!

Yours sincerely,

Edward R.I.

Major-General
B.N.Sergison-Brooke, C.B., C.M.G., D.S.O.

The rare signature of the Duke of Windsor as Edward VIII. On a letter concerning a Guards Regiment Parade in Hyde Park, when a member of the public threw a gun at the King.

Reduced in size

(This letter is reproduced by kind permission of H.R.H. the Duke of Windsor.)

London run of *Hadrian VII*. Even the unassuming author of the former work, A. J. A. Symons, is in demand.

The film *Lawrence of Arabia* added to the already existent interest in his autograph. Whether as 'Lawrence' (the most sought-after form), 'Shaw' or 'Ross', his signature is uncommon. An autograph letter, depending as ever on its contents, could go higher than £100. I have a fully signed autograph note in which he replies to an enquiry from the book department of the Army and Navy Stores concerning private circulation of his most famous book, which is unfortunately referred to as 'The Seven Pillows of Wisdom'! Lawrence has ignored (or missed) the typist's error.

The autographs of artists seem to follow the popularity of their paintings when it comes to values. The Victorian Royal Academicians are almost as dead, autographically, as the dodo, but the moderns are in demand and so are the English Masters. I have a number of the latter, including a fine example of Gainsborough on which he has made a few light pencil sketches of trees. A little item which gives me much pleasure is a holograph receipt signed by George Romney for painting 'two historical pictuers at twenty pounds each'. He would certainly consider he had been underpaid if he could know what his 'pictuers' fetch nowadays. The largest signature in my entire collection is that of an artist: George Cruikshank, the extrovert illustrator of Dickens, whose enormous signature, nearly a foot long and of considerable height, is scrawled all over a fine portrait of himself.

The Pre-Raphaelites were very low in autographic popularity but interest in them has recently revived: a fair demand already exists for William Morris, the Rossettis and John Ruskin. Thomas Carlyle is now voraciously collected also, yet letters of his fellow historian Macaulay are inexplicably worth only a pound or so.

Anything unpublished is of greater financial value than an already published item, especially if it brings out something as yet unknown about the writer's work or his character and, in discussing what to collect, the importance of content with its effect on the financial worth of autograph material has already been emphasized.

The same applies to the relative values of letters which are fully autograph and those which are typed or written in another hand. The rule quite clearly must be 'the more holograph the better the item'. The following is a short list of half-a-dozen values today, based on a one-page autograph letter signed of moderate but not of special interest, as opposed to the same letter in another hand (or typewritten) and only signed by its author (L.S.—Letter Signed).

	A.L.S.	L.S.
Queen Elizabeth I	£2000	£450
Samuel Johnson	800	200
John Wesley	150	50
Winston Churchill	100	40
John Constable	60	15
Robert Southey	30	10

The value of an autograph letter of Sir Winston Churchill brings us full circle back to my remarks regarding the values of letters of people who live long lives and are very famous during their lifetime. It is also an example of a current trend. At present the price of Churchill is high because the days of his greatest fame are still near; but those who are hoarding his letters in the hope of making a greater sum in a few years' time are mistaken in so doing. This great man's vast output must, as the memory of him dims, bring the price down. If this is difficult to believe, I must record that letters of those two great statesmen of earlier eras who also lived long lives, Gladstone and Lloyd George, were once very valuable but are now worth only a few pounds. Churchill letters will never be so inexpensive as these but they will not remain forever at their present price level.

Times and interests change and he who seeks to speculate in autographs should pick his way warily. Whilst, generally speaking, he is on an excellent wicket, if he does not keep a close watch on these trends he may be clean bowled.

HOW TO BUILD UP A COLLECTION

Until the end of the last war it was not difficult to build up a worthwhile collection of autographs without too much financial outlay. In the 'good old days' one's friends and relations would happily give one autograph letters they might have in their possession. Few people thought of asking for payment. Indeed one did not even have to be a friend. I remember shortly after the war picking out the name of a doctor at random from the telephone book as I needed a health certificate. I had never heard of him before, yet somehow we began talking about Washington, from whose family he was descended, and the interview ended with me the richer by a delightful little document signed by his distinguished ancestor which the doctor insisted on my having. This was extremely good of him and I doubt if anyone would give away such an item so lightly today.

I was given literally hundreds of autographs in my early days of collecting and even when it came to having to buy some I was able, in my late teens and early twenties, to purchase for 3/6 many a letter which would cost me £3 nowadays.

So what hope is there for the beginner collector today? How should he set about building a collection?

I started with signatures only and I should say that for an impecunious young collector this is still the best way. Albums crammed with pasted-down signatures assiduously collected by the Victorians can still be found at the smaller auction rooms and second-hand booksellers. They will contain many dull names of nobility, churchmen and politicians but the signatures of the Prime Ministers Palmerston, Peel, Melbourne, Russell, Gladstone and Salisbury will probably be included and these are a good enough nucleus for any collection.

As has already been mentioned, from the latter portion of the eighteenth century until half way through the next, all Members of Parliament and peers were allowed free postage but had to 'frank' their covers with their signatures in order to obtain this privilege. They frequently abused it by franking the covers of letters by other people, presumably relatives or friends. These covers, bearing the signature, the address and often the date all in holograph, as well as the postal date stamp, are attractive little items which the Victorians also collected with avidity. They are a little more pleasing than mere signatures and they too can be had from the same sources as the latter. So also can inexpensive letters of less prominent but nevertheless interesting people of the past. As an example let us take this little autograph note to his tailor by Sir Philip Francis of *Letters of Junius* fame:

> Monday morning 11 January (1813)
>
> Sir P. Francis desires that Mr Cook will *immediately* make and send home a pair of flannel drawers, with a flap before. They are wanted as speedily as possible. After that, another Do [ditto].

I paid next to nothing for this: indeed it is of no political or literary import, but is it not rather fun? Poor old Sir Philip to be feeling so cold in his nether regions in January 1813! The winter of 1812–13 (the winter of the retreat from Moscow) was bitter indeed. At much the same time, though the note is undated, Thomas Hamilton, M.P. (later Earl of Haddington, First Lord of the Admiralty) was yet another who apparently needed warming up: he sends a note to the steward of the Carlton Club from his Whitehall office asking for 'a curry of fowl to be ready for me in one hour'. Obviously he intended to enjoy his lunch break!

I confess to a fondness for utterly unimportant but, to me, fascinating notes such as these two, of which I have innumerable examples, all purchased at fractional expense.

Self-sketches are a pleasant and less usual form of autograph. I have several, including signed self-caricatures of those two knights of music hall, Sir Harry Lauder and Sir George Robey. Indeed any sketch can make an autograph more welcome. In my collection I rather like the pig which Lord Baden Powell, founder of the Boy Scouts, drew blindfold (and signed) in the year of Mafeking, 1900 (see page 94).

The direct approach for the signature of a living person has long been a way of collecting. Like many youngsters today, I used to ask well-known people for their signatures whenever I got the opportunity and later I wrote hundreds of letters applying for them. In very few cases was any request refused or unanswered. I must have been a dreadful nuisance, and Lord Devonshire was right to call me one, but many of the signatures I received in answer were accompanied by very courteous letters which I still have to this day.

Writing for autographs is certainly one way for the young collector to start, for it is the easiest and least expensive. People in the public eye usually understand the price of fame and pay it philosophically; those who do not wish to be forgotten even pay it gladly! Judges and others with legal minds often sign right at the top of the sheet of paper so that nothing can be inserted above their signature: both the Lord Chief Justice of England, Lord Goddard, and the Chief Justice of South Africa, Judge Centlivres, signed for me in this way.

I recall that one of the few people who ever refused my request was George Bernard Shaw who sent a printed reply, the words of which I have forgotten but which contained a reference to autograph collecting being 'unsporting'. As a young fellow I was a bit hurt because I could not think what on earth was unsporting about it and Shaw's card gave no explanation of this. However I was amused not long afterwards when, on looking in a current volume of *Who's Who*, I found that Shaw had listed his recreations as being 'anything except sport'!

Exchange with other collectors will certainly help to build up a collection and if you can afford a little outlay an inexpensive advertisement in a hobbies paper may bring worthwhile results. You may well find a stamp or coin collector with whom you can make an exchange to suit you both.

By these methods you should be able to get together the basis of a collection even though quantity may exceed quality. One must face the fact however that the world-wide increase in interest in autographs has made it impossible to build up a major collection without financial outlay. The serious collector must have a certain amount of money, although his collection will cost him less and give him more satisfaction if he acquires some knowledge of his subject and is prepared to make considerable personal effort.

If you can afford it the easiest way to collect is undoubtedly to buy through the major auctions or from dealers. I myself buy little, except when asked to on behalf of others, at auctions. Bargains can certainly be had but one is frequently disappointed by being out-bid. If one lives close to auction rooms it is certainly a good thing but to travel some distance and come up against the often international opposition of some of the most highly endowed institutions in the world can be heart-breaking. A dealer on the other hand has a fixed price and you know what an item is going to cost you.

You will not get far in serious autograph collecting unless you bring in a dealer to some extent. He has the knowledge, he can advise on price and the investment value, being a business man, and he will go out of his way to get hold of what you require and report on it to you without obligation. He will also guarantee authenticity of anything he sells you and this in itself is of vital concern.

The specialist collector is particularly advised to go to dealers who themselves specialize. A number of British dealers, whilst not trading exclusively in one subject, are particularly known for their interest in, say, literary or in historical autographs. If you intend to collect the autography of classical music you will be particularly fortunate in Britain as there are several dealers who specialize entirely in this subject. There are also dealers whose speciality lies in 'Empire' or in 'Africana' material.

It may not be generally realized that many American dealers are particularly well stocked with excellent British autographs. Their prices must, of necessity, be higher but if you really need a particular British item, you may well find it in the United States.

By buying through the trade you may end up with a fantastic collection but I cannot advise any collector, however rich, to work entirely through a dealer or an agent. This would be terribly unenterprising. No-one will get far without the use of his cheque-book but pure cheque-book collecting is not for me. I cannot see any fun unless you do at least some of the work yourself.

Advertise your interests: ask everyone you know to look out for these things for you—nearly everybody knows someone who knows someone else who has a letter of so-and-so. Get it out of them by any means, short of robbery with violence! If you are young, implore your father to persuade his influential friend to part with that letter of his notorious ancestress, one of George IV's mistresses. If you are older, bribe your son to get his headmaster to sell you that letter of Kipling he showed him the other day.

But seriously, one must make some real endeavour oneself: that is half the joy of collecting.

If you are going to be a really successful collector then no stone must be left unturned, no second-hand bookshop or even market bookstall passed without a good deal more than a second glance. Autographs of interest may well be discovered in books. The one-time owner may have been someone of distinction and may have written his name on the flyleaf. Nor is it uncommon for old bookshops to have the occasional autograph letter for sale.

One must never neglect the antique dealer and the junk shops. In these places I have found letters of Florence Nightingale, Rider Haggard, Wordsworth, Warren Hastings and even Beau Brummell. The famous dandy's letter was a sad epistle in French, from Calais, after he had fled from his creditors in England but was still defiantly insisting on yellow curtains in his bedroom. The Beau must have been a real trial to his creditors. Frequently ordering more expensive clothes, he was less frequently paying for them, witness this little note to his tailor:

> Chapel Street,
> Sept 16
>
> Fogg
>
> I could not call upon you yesterday according to my intention—and leave town this morning. I will return before the end of the present month, and will settle with you about the things I selected.
>
> Yrs
> George Brummell

The letter is undated but the paper bears an 1811 watermark. I hope Fogg got his money and did not have to end his days in the poor-house. Brummell ended his in a French lunatic asylum.

For years I have pursued autograph material not only in England but all over the world. Even if you are on holiday abroad it is worth looking around. You will undoubtedly come across autographs of the country you are visiting but you may also uncover some excellent British items. On recent visits to Italy I have found letters of Wordsworth and Walter Scott; in France, Mary, Queen of Scots and Jeremy Bentham (a friend of mine also found one of the latter in Germany); and in South Africa, many interesting figures of the South African and Zulu Wars. On my travels I also look out for specific material required by fellow collectors and they in their turn look out for any items I may be seeking. This is yet another way in which one can increase one's collection.

These then are the various ways of acquiring autographs. I would say that the mature collector should combine each and all of them to gain his end, though perhaps the actual bothering of a famous man for his signature should be left to the young!

IDENTIFICATION

Signatures are often indecipherable and only long experience will make it possible to identify on sight the writer of an illegible signature or to pick out the writing of a famous man even without looking at the signature at the end of it. The beginner will not be able to do this and even if he can read it he will not know automatically if it is genuine. Right from the start, therefore, it is essential that he should acquaint himself at least with the more rudimentary methods of identification.

Correct identification is of major import because it is no exaggeration to say that hundreds of pounds may be involved if mistakes are made, and such mistakes are only too easy. The signature of Byron's successor, for example, was so similar to that of the great poet that it can very easily be confused, yet it has virtually no value whatsoever. It would be almost equally unfortunate to confuse Charles Dickens, junior, with his eminent father.

The first step in identification is to see if the autograph you are being offered looks like that of its purported author. If you are fortunate enough to live near one of the great depositories such as the British Museum or the Public Records Office, the National Library of Scotland or the Bodleian, Oxford, you will be able to check with originals in their fine collections. County archives and museums all over the country will also provide originals for these purposes. Constant visits to such institutions will take up a lot of time however and it is perhaps best to resort to them for final confirmation if necessary.

For research at home one should surround oneself with as many books on autograph collecting—especially those containing a large number of facsimiles—as possible. These are absolutely essential to all collectors, whether beginners or of long experience, and even if out of date they will always be helpful for the identification of signatures of the past. I shall be including a bibliography of this sort of book but, alas, there are all too few of these, especially when it comes to British autographs. Autograph dealers, second-hand bookshops and book 'scouts' will all be able to help you to build up a useful reference library, which should also contain at least one good biographical dictionary.

When checking an autograph with an original or facsimile it must always be remembered that a person's writing changes considerably throughout his life and may also be affected by mood and circumstance at the time of writing, illness making it wobbly, hurry making it less formed, etc. Thus it does not necessarily follow that a signature is not genuine just because it is not exactly like the facsimile. A perfect example of this is the signature of Sir Winston Churchill (see page 64). Throughout most of his younger life and at the time of his later fame he signed 'Winston S. Churchill' with the bold, firm, flowing hand one knows so well. But during his years 'in the wilderness' he frequently signed just 'W. Churchill' and his signature tended to be more upright and rounded. He often signed in this way in extreme old age, probably because it was less fatiguing than the longer signature.

No British king's signature changed so much as that of George III (see page 53). The variations are considerable, some with a large, carefully written 'G', others (especially his very early ones) with a much smaller one, and indeed with the whole signature being less carefully executed. One is perfectly safe with officers' commissions, for they will almost certainly have been signed by him, whatever the signature looks like. The poor old gentleman was even made to sign commissions with his own hand when he was blind, and his blind signature, splodged, unformed and tottering, is well worthy of a place in any historical collection.

Nelson's writing changed completely from a flowing hand sloping to the right to a shaky upright or even backward-sloping one (see page 90) after the loss of his right arm at Santa Cruz in 1797. Thackeray employed two totally different handwritings, one upright and one sloping (see page 126), and added to the confusion of autograph collectors by now and again signing himself with strange pseudonyms such as 'Titmarsh' and 'Yellowplush'.

Confusion between the signatures of father and son of the same name is exceedingly common especially as the handwriting is often quite similar. Particularly disconcerting examples are those of Sir Robert Peel and his son, the 3rd Baronet. In earlier life the famous Prime Minister's signature had a very different capital 'R' but it changed later to be so like that of his son that they are virtually indistinguishable. The younger Peel made matters worse by hardly ever dating his letters, a habit the father also fell into in later life. Thomas Hood and his son Tom Hood wrote very similarly; so did Charles Reade and Charles Reade, junior. Even the two Pitts' signatures are not all that different and the writing of the younger Pitt can be further confused with that of his contemporary, the minor politician William M. Pitt.

Also contemporaneous to each other were the three Rowland Hills: Sir Rowland Hill, the postal reformer; Rowland Hill, the famed preacher; and the Field-Marshal who later became Lord Hill. Their autographs are, luckily, not alike: 'Postman' Hill's was small, 'Padre' Hill's large and 'Soldier' Hill's medium-size and sloping to the right.

The two politicians John Bright, the famous Free Trader, and the lesser-known Jacob Bright are another couple who can be confused. Both usually signed their full Christian names but occasionally only their mutual initial 'J'; and when it comes to Henry James we have no less than three to contend with. The most sought-after is, of course, Henry James the novelist, who wrote in a large flowing hand, but there were also a military geographer and a Cabinet Minister (later Lord James) of the same name. All three, to the misfortune of the unwary, lived at the same time.

This brings one to the fact that the date of a letter is important in the identification of a signature, whether the latter is legible or not. It is particularly useful in establishing the identity of a peer. No facsimile will be available in the case of lesser known peers. If, for instance, you have a letter signed 'Beaufort' or 'Norfolk' the date will be the one certain way of knowing which Duke of Beaufort or Norfolk has written it. A reference to Burke's or Debrett's peerage will soon establish your man. But what if he has not dated it? Well, if it is written in the early- to mid-nineteenth century there may well be a watermark in the paper showing the year of its manufacture. It may not be the year in which the letter was written but it is not likely to be very much earlier, and obviously not later.

If no watermark date exists, there may be other watermarks and a really perfectionist collector may find it worth his while to make a study of these things. But there are other ways of establishing the approximate date; these include the type and age of the paper and even its size, the kind of ink used, the calligraphy (such as the long first 's' in words with two successive 's's used from the seventeenth to the late nineteenth century) and the content. Some reference to a contemporary event or figure in the letter may also give a clue to its date.

The address from which it is written and the name of the addressee can be most useful. For example, if a letter is written from Gads Hill, Rochester, even if unsigned it may well be written by Dickens (or a member of his family), as this was his home for many years. If the address means nothing to you it is possible, by enlisting the help of a county council library, to find out the former occupants of almost any house in the area for quite a long way back.

As an example of the assistance which the addressee's name can give toward identification, let us take a short scribbled note dated 1820, signed with the initials 'W.S.' and addressed to 'My dear Sharpe'. Get out your *Dictionary of National Biography* and look under Sharpe; it will not be long before you'll find 'Charles Kirkpatrick Sharpe, antiquary . . . lifelong friend of Scott'; the initials 'W.S.' would then seem almost certain to show the writer to be Sir Walter Scott and final identification is then easy since many facsimiles of Scott's writing exist. Scott, incidentally, signed his name equally frequently as 'W. Scott' or 'Walter Scott'. The distinguished lawyer and judge Sir William Scott invariably signed 'W. Scott' and is often confused with the poet-novelist, of whom he was a contemporary. His writing is heavier and a good deal larger however and from 1821 onwards no confusion need arise as he was then created Baron Stowell and signed as such.

Most of these methods can also be used for the identification of the writer of a completely indecipherable signature, but there will always be some which will remain unidentified even after you have asked the help of expert collectors and dealers. The only advice I can give in such a case is that if a letter seems to be of interest, especially in content, do not throw it away. Something may crop up one day which will give you a clue as to its writer and you may find yourself with a greater prize than you could ever have conceived. I held on to a letter for many years until one day I was able to identify it as by Edmund Burke, whose signature when written in haste is illegible; Burke, the great orator and controversialist, was probably our most famous statesman never to have headed a ministry and is one of the comparatively few politicians whose autograph is much in demand.

We now come to the 'hidden' signature. A perfectly readable signature which may on the face of it be difficult to identify will crop up frequently. The most common case of this sort in British autography is that of a change of name. A good number of the great men throughout history were made, or became through inheritance, Peers of the Realm. Signatures always change when this happens, though if the title is the same as the original surname the only difference is the dropping of the Christian names or initials. But in cases where the titles differ from the surname—and these are legion—identification is less easy. If you have a letter signed 'Orford' you may be on to a good thing: several of the Earls of Orford were quite unimportant but if the date is around 1744 it will be the signature of Robert Walpole, the first Prime Minister of England (and the first Earl of Orford). If the date is around 1794 it will be a much more scarce and valuable autograph because the Earl of Orford in that year was none other than the distinguished man-of-letters Horace Walpole, whose holographs are avidly sought by today's collectors.

So much for 'Orford', but when it comes to Horace Walpole before he succeeded to the title we are in for real difficulties. His uncle, who was for forty years his contemporary, bore exactly the same name and both frequently signed as 'H. Walpole'. The uncle was created Lord Walpole of Wolterton, but only a year before his death. Unfortunately, although I have several documents signed by Horace senior, I have no signature of the great author, but a comparison of their signatures is available in Netherclift and Sims (see Bibliography) which, though over a hundred years old, can still be found in antiquarian bookshops. There are several other Horace Walpoles but they are fortunately not contemporaneous.

A signature 'Chatham' may well be that of the elder Pitt and 'Beaconsfield' will be Disraeli. These may be known to many people but, coming to modern times, it is surprising how few are able to identify 'Avon' with Anthony Eden and even fewer 'Passfield' with Sidney Webb. Once again Burke's or Debrett's (or, with contemporary signatures, *Who's Who*) will help towards identification of this nature but collectors should familiarize themselves with the titles of as many famous men as possible so that they can spot these immediately. Burke's is hardly the size of book to carry around in one's pocket for such purposes!

The signatures of kings always change on their accession, either by the addition of 'R' (Rex) or 'R.I.' (Rex Imperator) or their substitution for 'P' (Princeps). The Protectors, Oliver and Richard Cromwell, also signed 'P' after their Christian names during their reigns: in this case the 'P' stood for Protector. Queens sign 'R' for Regina.

Sometimes the sovereign's name changed completely. I believe it was in deference to a wish of Queen Victoria that no prince named Albert has used this name on becoming king. Edward VII always signed 'Albert Edward' before accession and George VI as Duke of York signed 'Albert'.

The signature of Edward VIII has perhaps varied more than that of any other British monarch. As a small boy he signed 'Edward' and often to his family 'David'. On becoming Prince of Wales it was 'Edward P', as King-Emperor 'Edward R.I.' and in retirement it has varied between 'Edward' and 'Edward, Duke of Windsor'.

Many literary people write under pseudonyms and the collector should try to memorize as many of these as possible, but great assistance can be had from such publications as *The Writers' and Artists' Yearbook*, which gives a goodly list of pseudonyms of writers both past and present. The best example I know of a writer whose signature can be found in several forms is that of Marjorie Bowen who wrote under three names and signed (because of two marriages) three other signatures as well. This prolific writer can be found as Marjorie Bowen, Joseph Shearing, George R. Preedy, Gabrielle Long, Gabrielle Costanzo and her maiden name, Gabrielle Campbell! Thus attention should also be paid to female authors' married names.

An elementary error, but one into which the inexperienced may be led, is the confusion between the methods of signing of bishops, peers and peeresses. Such confusion can be added to in the case of a non-titled person whose surname is the same as the title of some peer. Peers sign only their titles but this was not always so. In Tudor and earlier days some of them did add their Christian names or initials. For example, if you find an old document signed 'Fr Verulam Canc' you may have to go in for some research but it will work out like this: 'Canc' is short for the Latin word *Cancellarius* (Chancellor); 'Fr' is short for Franciscus (Francis). So you have Francis Verulam, Chancellor. Verulam (Latin, *Verulamium*) was the name of the Roman town before St Albans and Sir Francis Bacon was both Viscount St Albans and Baron Verulam. As he was also Lord Chancellor you have got your man—and a very valuable document into the bargain.

Reverting to the danger of confusion between peers and bishops, the Prime Minister Lord Liverpool signed 'Liverpool' but the Bishop of Liverpool, John Ryle for example, signed 'John Liverpool'. In addition, if a Lord Liverpool has a wife called Jane, she will sign 'Jane Liverpool' or merely 'J. Liverpool'. There is really no need to mix these identities providing due care is taken.

Several bishops, and both Anglican archbishops, use the Latin name of their episcopal city for their signatures. The Archbishops of Canterbury and York sign '[John] Cantuar' and '[John] Ebor'. A signature 'Canterbury' will be that of Viscount Canterbury, not the Archbishop. The Archbishop's wife will not confuse the issue because she will simply sign her ordinary Christian and surname. British Roman Catholic bishops sign their ordinary names and prefix their signatures with a cross. In addition they may add below the words 'Bishop of Leeds' or whatever see they may occupy.

Only recently I was offered what was claimed to be a signature of Thomas Gainsborough, but it was not his. It read 'Gainsborough' and was, thus, one of the quite obscure Earls of Gainsborough.

In the days of the franked free postage covers already referred to there was some fear of forgers making use of the signatures for nefarious purposes. To avoid this, certain Members of Parliament resorted to the strange remedy of putting the word 'free' between their Christian names (or initials) and their surnames. The great slave trade abolitionist William Wilberforce and the Benthamite politician Sir Francis Burdett were two notable examples.

Then there is the 'proxy' signature where someone else signs on behalf of the writer, using a signature which resembles the original. In the United States many senior executives, including a number of the presidents, have made a practice of allowing specific secretaries to sign in the same way in which they themselves sign. Similarly the French kings from Louis XIII (even occasionally some of the earlier ones) until the Napoleonic era employed *secrétaires de la main* who did precisely the same thing. Indeed it is often very difficult even for experts to know for sure whether a French document of that period is or is not signed by the king.

In British autography proxy signatures are, fortunately, not nearly so common. If anyone else signs on behalf of the writer he usually puts 'p.p.' or 'for' the person concerned. Nevertheless, Tennyson, for example, used to let his wife write and sign many letters for him (see page 42). Confusion is easy because her writing, though larger and often in lighter ink, is not unlike his. Conan Doyle's 'signature' is another which is occasionally signed by someone else. In modern times it is very common for people in the entertainment world to get their secretaries to sign photographs for them, whilst others employ a stamp.

Most British state letters and documents were copied for the record and although

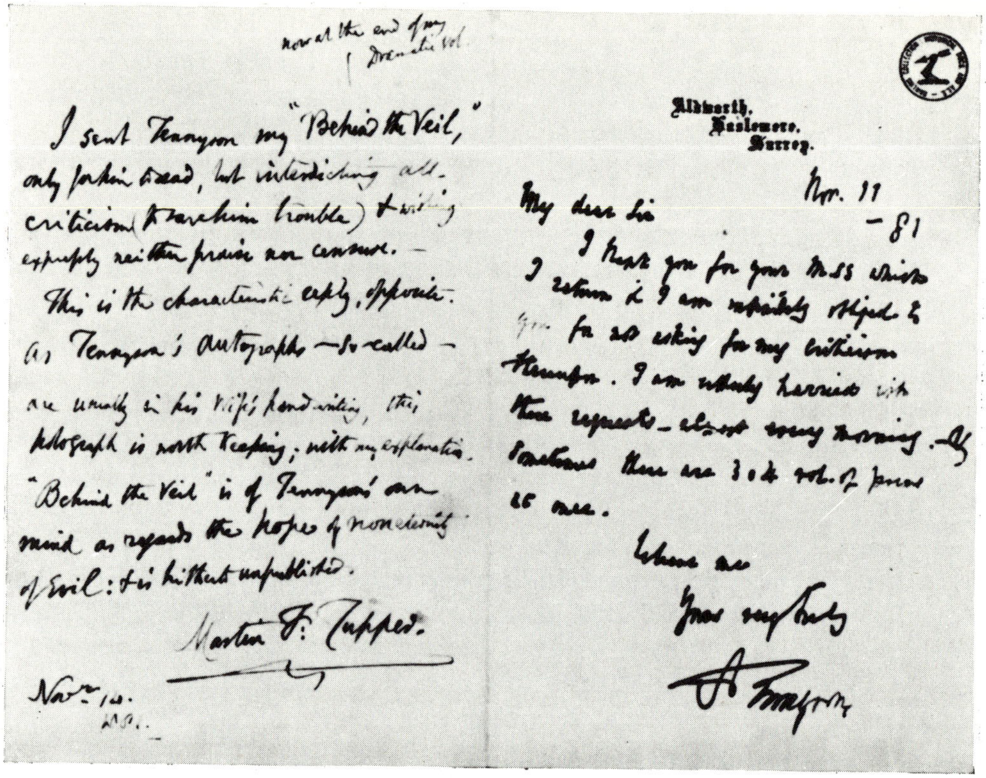

now at the end of my
Dramatic Vol

I sent Tennyson my "Behind the Veil," only for him to read, but interdicting all criticism (to save him trouble) & writing expressly neither praise nor censure. —
This is the characteristic reply, opposite. As Tennyson's autographs — so called — are usually in his wife's handwriting, this autograph is worth keeping; with my explanation. "Behind the Veil" is of Tennyson's own mind as regards the hope of non-eternity of Evil: & is hitherto unpublished.

Martin F. Tupper.

Nov 12.

Aldworth,
Haslemere,
Surrey.

Nov. 11
-81

My dear Sir

I thank you for your MSS which I return & I am infinitely obliged to you for not asking for my criticism thereupon. I am utterly harried with these requests — almost every morning. — Sometimes there are 3 or 4 vols. of poems to one.

Believe me

Yours very truly

A Tennyson

Right: Autograph letter from Alfred, Lord Tennyson, thanking Martin Tupper, the versifier, for sending him a manuscript. *Left:* Tupper's note explaining the circumstances under which the manuscript was sent. He comments that this genuine Tennyson autograph would be worth keeping as Tennyson's letters were often signed by his wife.
Both reduced in size

the clerks were never permitted to reproduce the signatures as such, one must be on the look out here as they may appear to be signed by the monarch or the Lords of the Treasury, Admiralty, etc. Old Treasury documents can be particularly confusing because they may contain a mixture of original signatures and those written in by the clerks.

There are probably more pitfalls in identification than in any other feature of autograph collecting and it is no easy task to steer a safe course through all the rocks on which one can so easily founder. The moral is always to take a second look at anything offered unless it has the guarantee of a dealer or a private expert.

FORGERIES AND FACSIMILES

Forgeries and facsimiles are the plagues of autograph collecting. Though some may not agree with me, I find a really good facsimile can be an even greater menace than a forgery. A forger has to be brilliant to be able to produce writing exactly like that of his subject but a facsimile is that subject's writing, though not original.

There is certainly plenty of forgery in autography in general but it never ceases to surprise me that there is not a good deal more. British autographs have not been forged anything like as much as one might expect and I can only suppose that the reason is that autographs as a whole have only fairly recently become valuable. This may well mean that we should have an increase in forgery in the future but in the past it has seldom been worthwhile.

The three major forgers of British autographs, with their main subjects in brackets, are:

William Ireland (Shakespeare)

Alexander Howland ('Antique') Smith (Burns; also some of Cromwell, Burke, Mary Queen of Scots, English royalty and statesmen)

'Major' George Gordon Byron (Byron, Shelley, Keats)

Ireland—his full name was Samuel William Henry Ireland—is perhaps the most extraordinary of these three, because he was only seventeen when he forged his first deed, apparently signed by Shakespeare. He is said to have started it all in order to delight his father, a Shakespearian enthusiast. The latter was easily deceived, possibly because he so much wanted to be. Young Ireland then continued to produce more deeds and letters by or concerning the Bard of Avon and rose to his highest level of audacity by forging the manuscripts of *Hamlet* and *King Lear*. He finally came unstuck when he wrote and forged as by Shakespeare an unpublished play, *Vortigern and Rowena*, which no less a person than Sheridan produced and no less a person than John Philip Kemble acted in. Its failure led to Ireland's downfall, causing many red faces among the experts whom he had duped.

'Antique' Smith, so called because of his skilfully 'aged' forgeries, flourished at the turn of the century and ended up with a comparatively short sojourn in gaol.

Byron, who claimed to be the poet's son, had a successful career in forgery half a century before Smith but he allowed inaccuracies to creep into the contents of his forged letters, which led to his unveiling.

These three men were masters of their art and bemused such great authorities as (in the case of Ireland) Samuel Parr and Joseph Warton, but common forgery is in a very different class.

Fortunately for the average collector, many of these forgeries are instantly detectable. Often they bear but little resemblance to the handwriting of their subject. I have seen 'letters' of Oliver Cromwell, Monmouth, Sir Walter Scott, Charles Dickens, Edward Lear and several others, falling into this category. So crude were these that one wonders if in fact they were ever intended to be forgeries at all, rather than just elaborate copies.

Cleverer forgeries may be detected by the age and size of the paper on which they are written (the latter varied in different eras), the type of writing used, the ink, the watermarks, the shakiness or uncertainty of the writing and inconsistencies in the contents, or the spelling or style being inconsistent with that expected of the purported writer. Though the writing may look the same, even the method of signing may give away a forger. For instance, Sir Robert Peel nearly always signed either 'Robert' or 'Rob' Peel. A signature 'R. Peel' would be suspect. A knowledge of postal history, too, can help in exposing a forgery if the cover or envelope bears a postal mark or stamp inappropriate to its date.

In my experience there are more forgers of poets (and other writers) than of any other professional group, so that it is as well to be particularly careful when checking authenticity of literary autographs. At the time of writing, a group of fairly well executed portrait sketches with forged signatures affixed of such persons as Shelley and his entourage are being disseminated. A dealer friend of mine, who was most certainly not fooled by them, had an unusual experience with one of these. He put it temporarily in a drawer, intending to experiment on it by exposing it to ultra-violet examination (one of the recognized professional ways of testing doubtful material). When he came to take it out weeks later, he was startled to find the 'signature' had completely faded from view!

Also being similarly circulated are a number of counterfeit autograph letters and I was amused to be shown by the same dealer one which purported to be a forgery by William Ireland of a Shakespeare letter to Anne Hathaway. Genuine—a strange word under the circumstances—Ireland forgeries are themselves valuable nowadays, but this was clearly a case of the forger forged!

A crude little collection, ostensibly once owned by someone called Norris, occasionally crops up here and there. It contains badly done forgeries of Oliver Goldsmith, Nelson, Tennyson (a little A.L.S. about an invitation: 'I had laid a fork for you . . .'), Burns and more modern names such as Dame Millicent Fawcett and Sarah Bernhardt. Any collector encountering a rather messy little bunch of uneven bits of paper roughly bound together in a cover and containing all or most of the above names should be warned that this is almost certainly one of the several 'copies' made by this unknown and unskilled forger.

In the past there have been several forgers who would be more rightly described as 'hoaxers'. The most distinguished of these was that remarkable seventeen-year-old (he killed himself in 1770 at that age) Thomas Chatterton. He invented a fifteenth-century monk, 'Rowley', and produced some exceedingly fine manuscripts supposedly by this non-existent figure. These compositions were in fact his own and were so brilliant that, despite his unmasking, Chatterton has been accepted as a poetic genius ever since. Autographically he is excessively rare. It would certainly be poetic justice if someone were to seek to fill this gap by forging him. Perhaps the forger would be called Rowley?

Facsimiles are rife in the autograph collecting world. I am sent them every week. Lithographic facsimiles of letters of the great were often made by their proud recipients, without the slightest intention to defraud anyone but simply to send to their admiring friends. Equally many were made by publishers for the enhancing of books. Often these look incredibly real, especially to the unpractised eye, and it is not really possible to advise on any certain way of checking them. One can try to erase with an ink rubber (and considerable caution) a tiny unimportant portion of the writing but if any pressure is used this might also rub out a printed facsimile, thus proving nothing. A more successful way is to use a chemical ink eraser, but this will erase only modern ink.

Lithographic reproductions are not confined to the past and there are none so common at present as those made by Sir Winston Churchill. These were sent out in their thousands by his secretaries to acknowledge the enormous number of letters of congratulation which he received during his terms of office. The reproduction, on 10 Downing Street paper, is very clever, though one soon realizes that Churchill would hardly have had time to sit down and acknowledge a hundred or so letters every day whilst conducting a war! (See page 64.)

The modern process of the photostat need cause no confusion, but a good xerox machine can reproduce a letter which has been newly written on clean white paper with startling accuracy. However, a xerox copy of older material will be immediately recognizable, so there really is little danger from this source.

The following is a short list of some of the facsimiles of British autographs which turn up frequently and against which the collector must be on guard. All are realistic.

The Byron Vampire *letter*: from Byron to Galignani refuting authorship of *The Vampire*. Three pages, with cover. Found in a book of his collected verse.

The 'Tilt' facsimile of Sir Walter Scott: a short half-page A.L.S., addressed to Charles Tilt, referring to himself as author of *Waverley*. Sometimes accompanied by the (separate) address cover which is stamped 14 May 1830, but which has been reproduced onto paper watermarked 1832. A first-class give-away!

Nelson's letter in Southey's biography: found inserted in certain editions of Southey's works.

Sir Winston Churchill acknowledgments: already referred to. Found in various forms but always missing any prefix, such as 'Dear Sir', and without any valediction, such as 'yours faithfully'.

Edward VII A.L.S.: to Campbell-Bannerman from Buckingham Palace, 1906, concerning the Education Act.

George V: welcoming letter to the American troops on their arrival into World War I.

George V: welcoming back returning British prisoners-of-war.

George VI and Queen Elizabeth: Dorothy Wilding portrait (in Coronation robes with Princess Elizabeth), signed by both and dated, in the King's writing, 22 May 1937.

Elizabeth II: letters written when Princess, thanking for wedding gifts, etc.

Queen Alexandra: thanks for sympathy on death of Edward VII. Also quite a number of open letters to sections of the public.

Queen Victoria: signature and date of her Diamond Jubilee on fine portrait of herself. Also letter to the women of England concerning a subscription towards a statue of the Prince Consort. Dated 22 June 1887.

Lord John Russell, Lord Palmerston, Lord Salisbury and other Foreign Ministers: on the old (folio) passports; sometimes, however, these are signed in the original.

Many composers: the signature of the composer, cleverly printed, is often found on the cover or first page of old printed music.

Signed portrait prints: thousands of these portraits of the great of all eras and walks of life have well executed facsimiles of their signatures below. Only a handful ever bear an original.

Finally, the stamped signature. This should fool nobody, but it does. For example, as

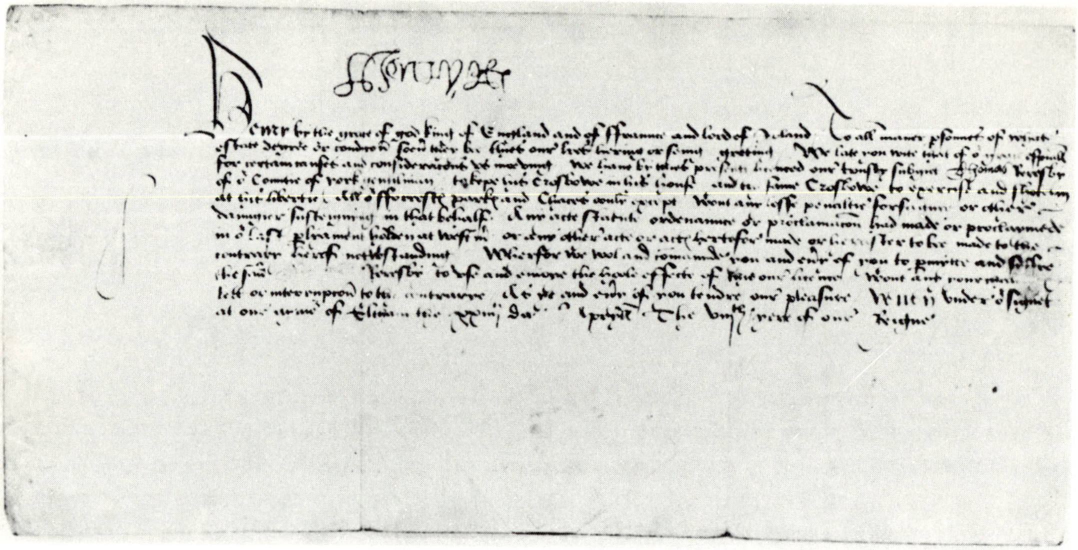

Stamp signature of Henry VIII at the head of a document permitting the possession of a crossbow by one Thomas of York. As the document is of early date (1517), the stamp will have been affixed by Henry himself. *Reduced in size*

an alternative to the printed signature of a composer referred to above, a stamped signature is frequently found on old printed music.

A stamp signature very much in use is that of the sovereign. On ordinary commissions this did not appear until Edward VII and even then his original signature on them is much more common than his stamp. During World War I, however, so many commissions were granted that it was impossible for the King to sign them all, so that George V military commissions (of 1914–18 especially) are mainly stamped. Often even the countersignatures on these are either stamped or printed, so they are of no autographic interest.

From then on it has not been unusual for less important royal documents to bear the stamped signature. Our present Queen's commissions are usually stamped. On the other hand all senior diplomatic appointments and all higher appointments to the Orders of Chivalry are personally signed and always have been.

One form of monarchical stamped signature which can sometimes cause confusion, as it does look rather convincing, is that used by Henry VIII (see page 51). Henry had a stamp of his signature which would appear to have delighted him almost as a toy, for he wielded it zealously himself all the earlier years of his reign. In a sense a document 'signed' in this way is almost autographic because the monarch's own vast hand will have pressed down on it in no uncertain fashion! So jealous was Henry of his stamp that, when he became old and his hand wobbled too much for him to employ the stamp himself, three officers of state were especially appointed to use it for him and no-one else had that right. Documents bearing this stamp are obviously not worth as much as those signed in Henry's own hand but they are less common (because he was obliged by the rules to sign most in the original) and as curios are of historical interest and some financial value.

PRESERVATION AND PRESENTATION

An autograph collection can give a good deal more pleasure to its owner, and to anyone he may show it to, if it is well set out.

Nearly all young people starting to collect make the terrible error of sticking their signatures or letters into books. This practice, referred to as 'laying down', is a fundamental sin but there are few beginners who do not commit it. I was no exception.

Laying down can cause deterioration of the item and will also render it very likely to tear if it ever has to be removed. On no account must any piece of autograph material, however humble, be spoiled in any way. Sticking tape or gum must never be used. Even the stickers sometimes used in stamp collecting should be avoided. There must be no mutilation. Never cut down any item to try to squeeze it into a smaller space. If it is only a signature and the paper is plain it may make little difference but a letter so cut will lose its 'look' and some of its worth.

Under no circumstances cut a signature off a letter. Without its signature a letter, even in autograph, may lose from a fifth to a half of its value. Conversely a signature without its letter could be virtually worthless.

Preservation is most important. Documents must not be kept in damp places nor must they be left where the sun can get at them and fade their ink. Some people like to display them in frames and certainly this can look very pleasing; but a document under glass can sweat and develop the brown spotting known as foxing so that it is as well to remove it from the frame now and again for cleaning. Foxing cannot be eradicated, though fortunately there are chemical treatments which can prevent the spread of it.

Whilst everything must be done to see that you are not responsible yourself for the defacement of any item, the inevitable position will arise where an autograph in an advanced state of deterioration will come into your possession. If a document is in real danger of destruction or serious loss of value and interest because of its condition, it must be repaired. Few collectors will be able to do a really professional job themselves however, so that I would advise at the outset that repair of a valuable document be left to an expert. It is quite astounding what a qualified document-repairer can do. He can virtually build up again a crumbling and torn piece of paper by such processes as silking, re-backing and laminating.

Minor repairs and cleaning are, of course, within the power of any collector providing sufficient care is taken. Never use sticking tape for repair work as this will eat into the material of the item itself. Be extremely careful when cleaning up dust or dirt that you do not tear the document or rub away any of the writing. The strengthening of folds about to tear is best done with paper.

I do not propose to enlarge on the subject of repair because, in the first place, I am not an expert on it and I never attempt major repairs myself; and secondly because I hold the firm view that the less a document is 'disturbed' the better. Repairs, I feel, should only be carried out when absolutely essential. But what the collector can and must do is to make sure that he himself keeps his documents carefully.

There are several ways of ensuring this and, since the manner in which material is kept will also affect the way it is displayed, it must be a matter of personal choice. Framing has already been mentioned but a large collection in frames, however attractive, would take up too much room. Many collectors keep their material in the transparent, acetone-treated cellulose folders which one can buy at any stationer's. These can then be housed in concertina or box files or between the pages of albums. Whenever I have to remove a document temporarily out of my books, for the purpose of taking it some distance to a lecture, exhibition or whatever it may be, I always use a folder of this nature. Semi-stiff, it holds securely the item which can be thus seen clearly without being handled.

My own method of keeping my collection is fairly simple. I have special large guard books made for me, a good deal bigger than normal folio. These books are of about 120 pages and have been specially treated to be proof against the ravages of insects. I put the document into an envelope, which is transparent in front and has ordinary white paper at the back, and hinge it into the album. The item can then be clearly seen and, should it be of more than one page, it is easy enough to slip it out to read the rest. I then try to make it more pleasurable and more useful to those who may come after me by various embellishments which other collectors are at liberty to follow or ignore.

I believe in illustrating my collection with portraits. These can be obtained from print dealers and from art galleries. In London, for example, the National Portrait Gallery will provide photograph copies of its paintings at very reasonable prices and close by are the print dealers of Charing Cross Road and its side streets. Even photographs cut from magazines will be better than nothing.

Illustrations definitely add to the appearance of the collection and help to hold its interest for a non-collector who might otherwise become bored by unrelieved handwriting. All the same I hope you never have the experience I once suffered. I was reluctantly showing my collection—at her request I hasten to say—to a particularly dumb blonde. After about half an hour of apparent interest and appreciation, she said: 'Now do tell me what the letters and bits of writing are under all these nice pictures.' That should have put me off illustrations for good!

It is vital to enter the name of the writer under each autograph. Very many Victorian collectors failed to do this, with the result that their albums are crowded with unreadable signatures, some of which may never be deciphered. This can be frustrating beyond words, and all because the former collector never bothered to make such a record, knowing himself who the writer was and never thinking about future generations.

I like to include a short biography of each subject but this is going further than is necessary and I often wish I had not started it. If the effort is made, however, it does add to the reference interest of the collection.

The actual lay-out of a collection is important. Some form of grouping must be applied both for easier reference and to provide some sort of consecutive order. It would seem better, surely, to show Nelson with Wellington rather than with Charlie Chaplin, and I can see no point in putting Oliver Cromwell next to Thackeray, nor in having Gladstone ogling Sarah Siddons. Group, therefore, under professions or periods of history.

Good documentation is strongly advisable. It will help you to control your collection and make it very much easier for those who follow you. A catalogue should be kept in which every item (with its page or folio number) is recorded under its sectional heading; also, an alphabetical index is essential with a large collection. All this may seem rather a bore but a future generation will bless you and you will bless yourself when you find how easily you can trace any item you want to look up. I remember the very distinguished German collector Dr Herbert Adam once commenting that, with minimal delay, he could put his finger, 'metaphorically speaking', on Mary, Queen of Scots. In a collection as vast as his that could only be achieved by good documentation; I am glad to say that I, too, can put my finger on that same sad sovereign and, equally metaphorically, on Brigitte Bardot.

SOVEREIGNS: ELIZABETH I, HER FATHER AND MARY, QUEEN OF SCOTS

1.

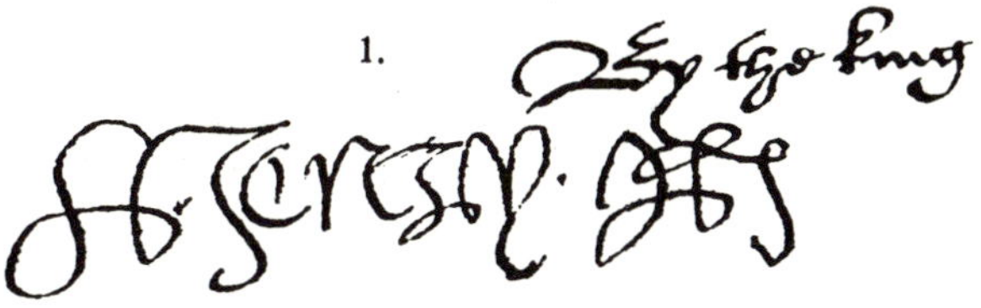

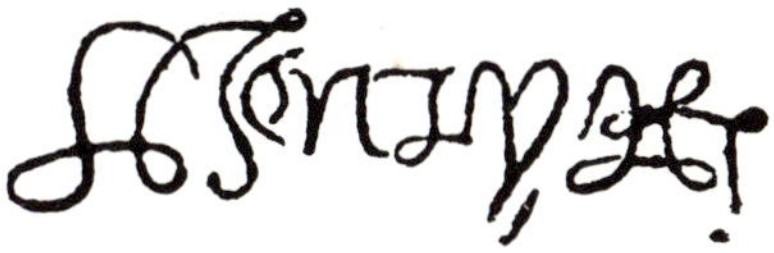

2.

3.

4.

1 and 2. **Henry VIII.** 1491–1547. Reigned 1509–47. Example 1 above is from an autograph signature on a document of 1514 relating to the royal estates in France (Tournai). Example 2 above is of his stamp signature (see page 46), affixed by the King personally on a document granting the use of a crossbow to Thomas of York, 1517.

3. **Elizabeth I.** 1533–1603. Daughter of Henry VIII and Anne Boleyn. Reigned 1558–1603. A particularly large example (7 inches) of her magnificent signature, from a document concerning the defence of her realm, 1597.

4. **Mary, Queen of Scots.** 1542–87. Signed in 1567. Her signature 'Marie R' is easily confused with that of her mother, Mary of Guise, who, whilst Regent of Scotland during her daughter's minority (1554–60), signed in exactly the same style and with a nearly identical signature.

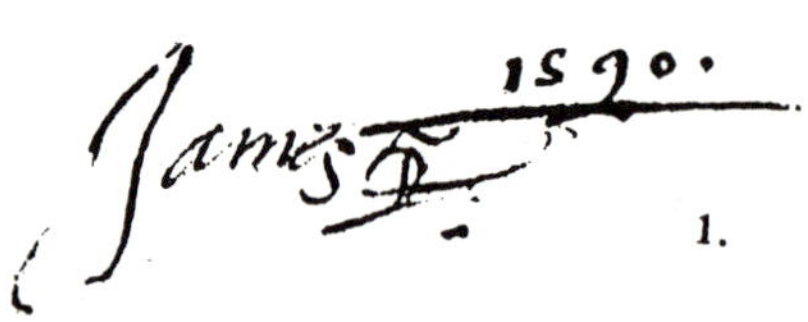
1.

2.

3.

4.

5.

6.

7.

8.

9.

1. **James I.** 1566–1625. Reigned as James VI of Scotland 1567–1603 and as James I of Britain 1603–25. Signed in 1590 as King of Scotland.
2. **Charles I.** 1600–49. Reigned 1625–49. Executed by Parliament.
3. **Oliver Cromwell.** 1599–1658. Lord Protector, 1653–8. Signed during his rule: 'Oliver P'. His signature as 'O. Cromwell' is regarded by some as more desirable.
4. **Richard Cromwell.** 1626–1712. Lord Protector. Richard's signature, as shown above, during his short rule (Sept. 1658–May 1659) is exceedingly rare. In later life he called himself 'Clarke' and his handwriting became more flowing and less formal.
5. **Charles II.** 1630–85. Acceded 1649, restored after protectorate rule and reigned 1660–85. His signature closely resembles that of Charles I.
6. **James II.** 1633–1701. Reigned 1685–8.

7 and 8. **William III (William of Orange).** 1650–1702. His wife **Mary II.** 1662–94. Reigned jointly 1689–94, then William continued alone until 1702.

9. **Anne.** 1665–1714. Reigned 1702–14.

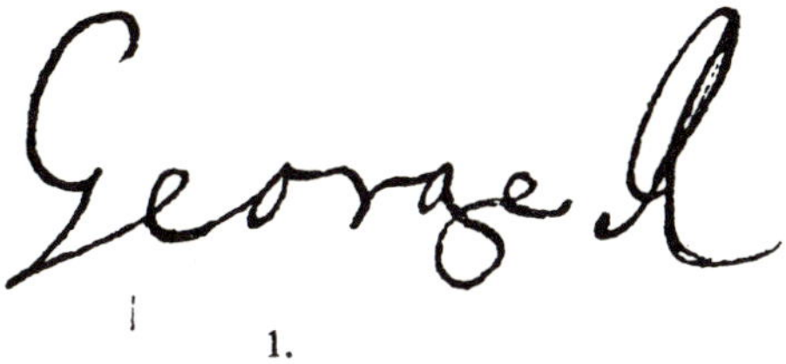

1.

2.

3.

4.

5.

6.

7.

8.

1. **George I.** 1660–1727. Reigned 1714–27.
2. **George II.** 1683–1760. Reigned 1727–60.

3, 4 and 5. **George III.** 1738–1820. Reigned 1760–1820. The signature of this monarch changed more than that of any other. Example 3, from a document countersigned by Pitt and dated 1782, is fairly typical of his signature for most of his reign. Example 4 is an early signature, from the second year of his reign: an uncommon form. When he was nominal King only (1811–20), both blind and insane, his signature became eccentric and ill-formed, as in example 5.

6. **Charlotte Sophia.** 1744–1818. Of Mecklenburg-Strelitz. Queen of George III.
7. **George IV.** 1762–1830. Reigned 1820–30. During his regency (1811–20), he signed as 'George P.R.'
8. **Caroline.** 1768–1821. Of Brunswick. Queen of George IV. Signed as 'Prs' (Princess).

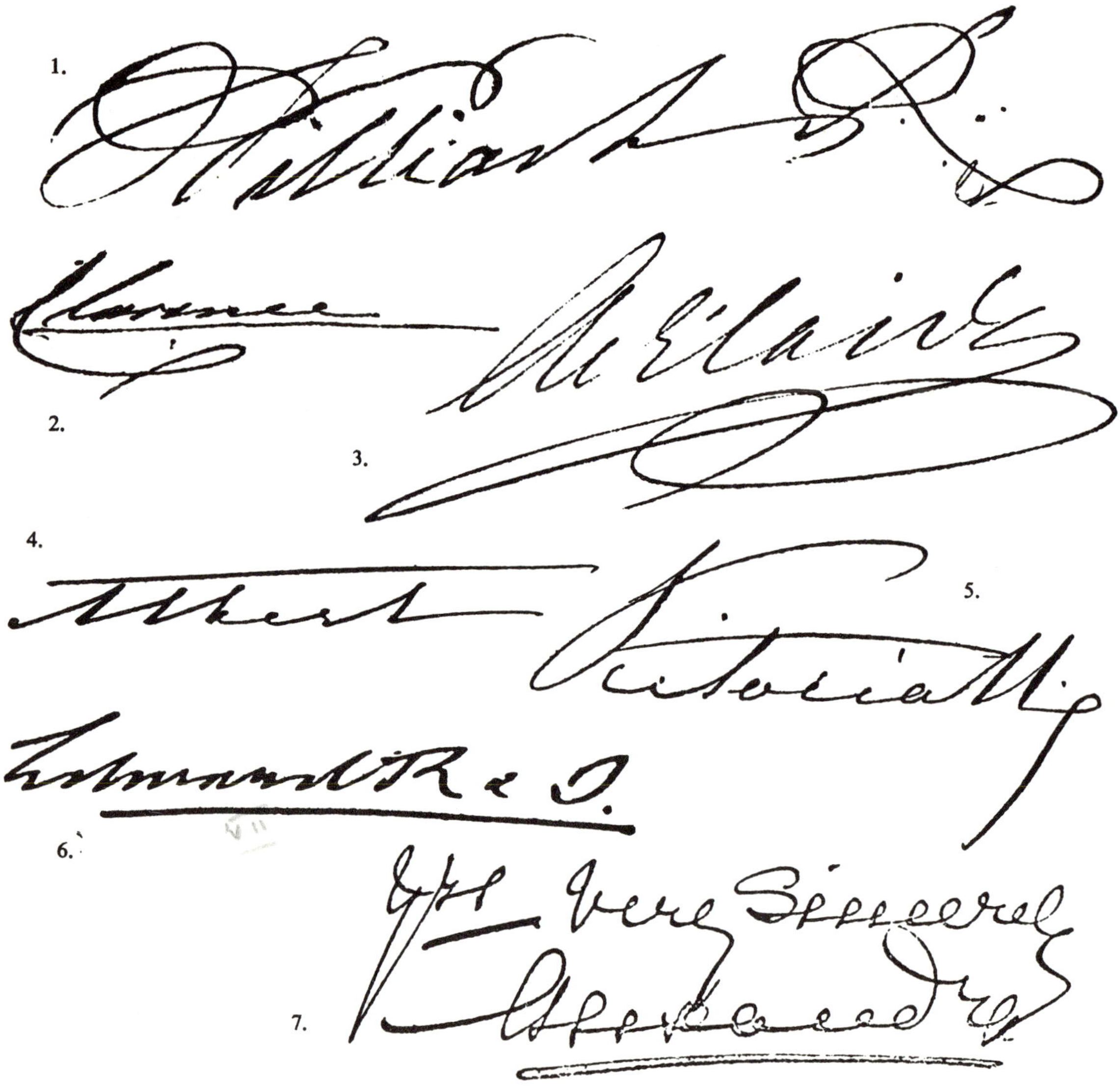

1 and 2. **William IV.** 1765–1837. Reigned 1830–7. Example 1 is of his signature as King, 2 as Duke of Clarence.

3. **Adelaide.** 1792–1849. Of Saxe-Meiningen. Queen of William IV. Adelaide, Australia, named after her.

4. **Albert, The Prince Consort.** 1819–61. Consort of Queen Victoria. Son of the Duke of Saxe-Coburg-Gotha.

5. **Victoria.** 1819–1901. Reigned 1837–1901.

6. **Edward VII.** 1841–1910. Reigned 1901–10. First and only monarch of the House of Saxe-Coburg. For many years before accession he signed as 'Albert Edward', frequently shortening this to 'A.E.'.

7. **Alexandra.** 1844–1925. Of Denmark. Queen of Edward VII.

1.

2.

3.

4.

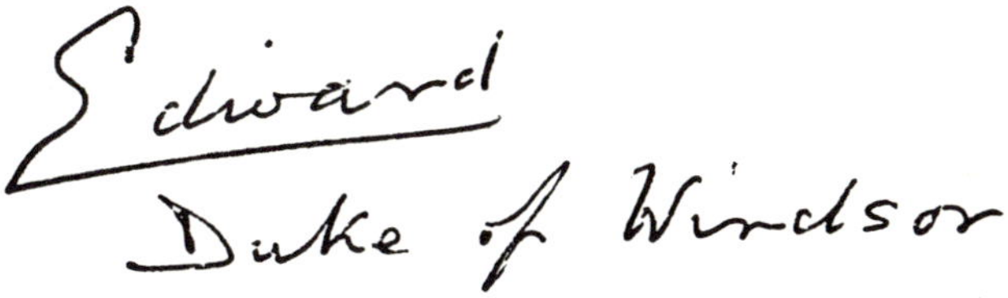

5.

6.

7.

1. **George V.** 1865–1936. Reigned 1910–36. Between 1901 and 1910 he signed 'George P', earlier only 'George'.
2. **Mary.** 1867–1953. Of Teck. Queen of George V. Before becoming Queen she signed 'Victoria Mary'.

3, 4 and 5. **Edward VIII.** 1894– . Reigned 20th Jan.–11th Dec. 1936. Signed as Prince of Wales (3), King (4) and Duke of Windsor (5). As he reigned for only 325 days, his signature as King is rare and will eventually become excessively so. Since his abdication he has signed either as 5 above or as 'Edward'.

6 and 7. **George VI.** 1895–1952. Reigned 1936–52. Signature 6 as King, 7 as 'Albert' whilst Duke of York, before accession.

1.

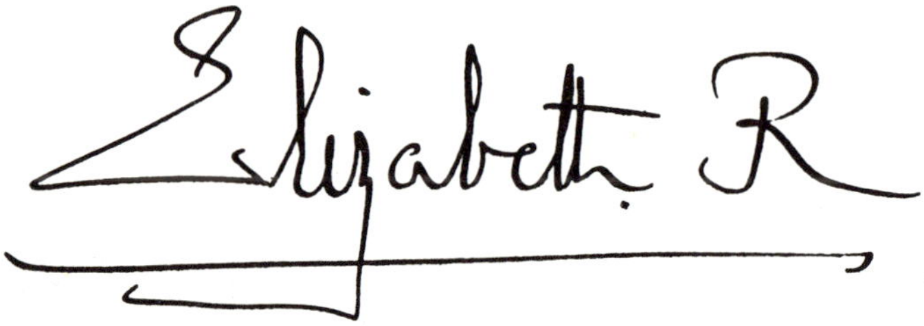

2.

3.

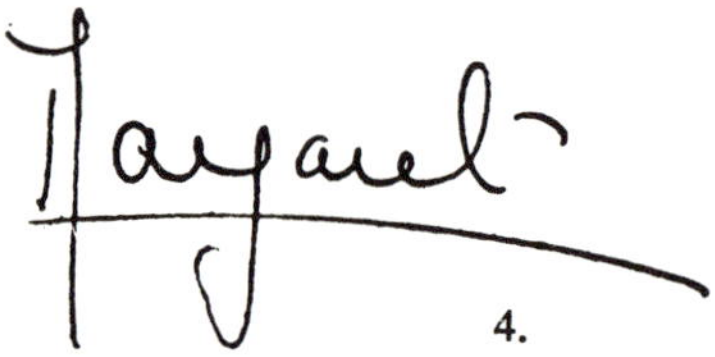

4.

5.

6.

7.

8.

1. **Elizabeth II.** 1926– . Acceded 1952.
2. **Elizabeth, The Queen Mother.** 1900– . Queen of George VI. Formerly Lady Elizabeth Bowes-Lyon, daughter of the Earl of Strathmore.
3. **Philip, Duke of Edinburgh.** 1921– . Consort of Elizabeth II. Son of Prince Andrew of Greece.
4. **Margaret, Countess of Snowdon.** 1930– . Sister of Elizabeth II.
5. **Mary, Countess of Harewood.** 1897–1965. Princess Royal. Daughter of George V, and aunt of Elizabeth II.
6. **Henry, Duke of Gloucester.** 1900– . Uncle of Elizabeth II.
7. **George, Duke of Kent.** 1902–42. Uncle of Elizabeth II and father of the present Duke of Kent.
8. **Marina, Duchess of Kent.** 1906–69. Princess of Greece and wife of 7 above.

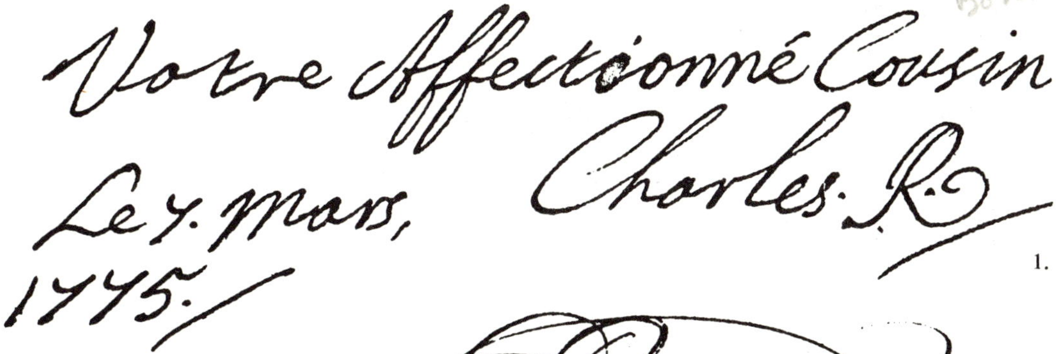

1.

2.

3.

4.

5.

6.

7.

1. **Charles Edward Stewart (Stuart).** 1720–88. Known as 'Bonnie Prince Charlie' and 'The Young Pretender'. Grandson of James II. Signed above as King – 'Charles R' – from exile in France, 1775.
2. **Augusta (Sophia).** 1768–1840. Daughter of George III.
3. **Augustus Frederick, Duke of Sussex.** 1773–1843. Sixth son of George III.
4. **Ernest (Augustus), Duke of Cumberland and King of Hanover.** 1771–1851. Fifth son of George III, he succeeded in 1837 as King of Hanover on the death of his elder brother, William IV.
5. **Frederick, Duke of York and Albany.** 1763–1827. Second son of George III, he was Commander-in-Chief of the Army and the subject of the rhyme 'The Grand Old Duke of York'.
6. **Victoria (Mary), Duchess of Kent.** 1786–1861. Mother of Queen Victoria, whose signature when young, before accession, is very similar.
7. **Edward, Duke of Kent.** 1767–1820. Fourth son of George III. Father of Queen Victoria.

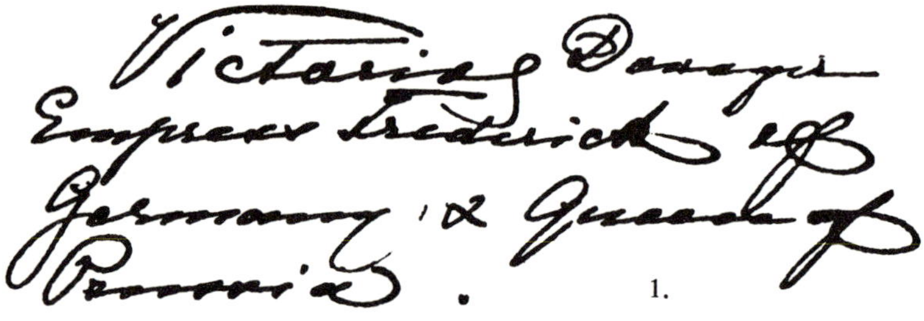

1.

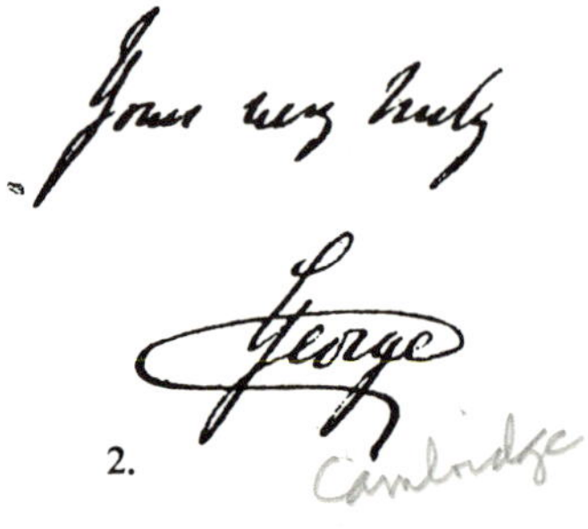

2.

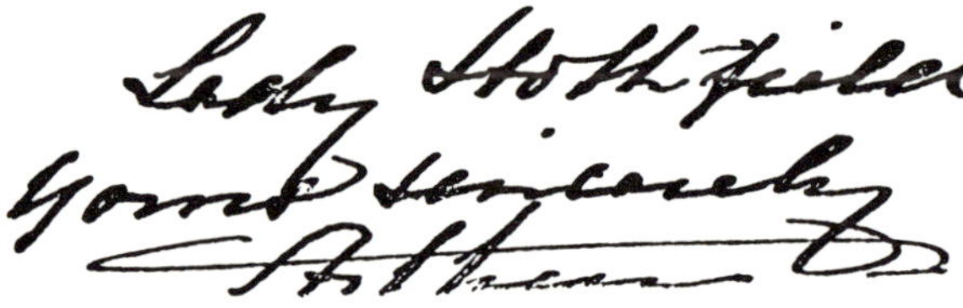

3.

4.

5.

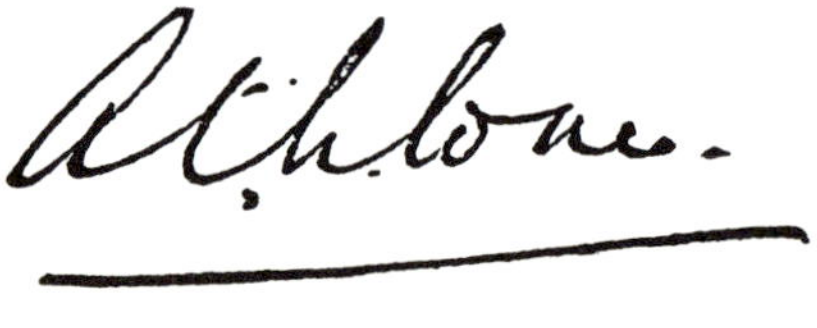

6.

7.

1. **Victoria, Empress of Germany.** 1840–1901. Princess Royal of Great Britain. Eldest child of Queen Victoria. Mother of Kaiser Wilhelm II.
2. **George, Duke of Cambridge.** 1819–1904. Grandson of George III. Commander-in-Chief of the Army. Care should be taken not to confuse his signature with that of George V as Duke of York.
3. **Arthur, Duke of Connaught.** 1850–1942. Son of Queen Victoria. Governor-General of Canada.
4. **Alfred, Duke of Edinburgh and Saxe-Coburg-Gotha.** 1844–1900. Second son of Queen Victoria.
5. **Victoria Eugenia Ena, Queen of Spain.** 1887–1969. Daughter of Princess Beatrice and grand-daughter of Queen Victoria. Queen of Alfonso XIII.
6. **The Earl of Athlone.** 1874–1957. Formerly Prince Alexander of Teck; brother of Queen Mary. Governor-General of Canada.
7. **Princess Alice, Countess of Athlone.** 1883– . Daughter of Leopold, Duke of Albany. The only surviving (1970) grandchild of Queen Victoria.

1.

2.

3.

4.

5.

6.

7.

8.

9.

10.

N.B. Although the title of Prime Minister was not officially recognized until 1905, it is generally accepted that the office dates from 1721, when Walpole was the first to hold the appointment.

1. **Sir Robert Walpole, Earl of Orford.** 1676–1745. Premier, 1721–42. He signed 'Orford' from 1742.

2 and 3. **Spencer Compton, Earl of Wilmington.** 1673(?)–1743. Premier, 1742–3. Signatures before and after being made a peer in 1728.

4. **Henry Pelham.** 1695(?)–1754. Premier, 1743–54.

5. **Thomas Pelham-Holles, Duke of Newcastle.** 1693–1768. Premier, 1754–6, 1757–62.

6. **William Cavendish, 4th Duke of Devonshire.** 1720–64. Premier, 1756–7. One of our youngest Premiers, his comparatively early death makes his autograph uncommon.

7. **James, 2nd Earl Waldegrave.** 1715–63. Waldegrave is not accepted as a Prime Minister by most authorities, but he was in fact Premier for four days, 8th–12th June 1757.

8. **John Stuart, Earl of Bute.** 1713–92. Premier, 1762–3. Bute's autograph is not easily found.

9. **George Grenville.** 1712–70. Premier, 1763–5.

10. **Charles Watson-Wentworth, Marquis of Rockingham.** 1730–82. Premier, 1765–6, 1782.

1.

2.

3.

4.

5.

6.

7.

8.

1. **William Pitt, Earl of Chatham.** 1708–78. Premier, 1766–7. Possibly the most sought-after autograph of any Prime Minister. He signed as 'Chatham' after 1766.
2. **Augustus Fitzroy, Duke of Grafton.** 1735–1811. Premier, 1767–70. At thirty-two he became one of the youngest Prime Ministers.
3. **Frederick, Lord North, 2nd Earl Guilford.** 1732–92. Premier, 1770–82.
4. **William Petty, Earl of Shelburne, Marquis Lansdowne.** 1737–1805. Premier, 1782–3. The American colonies received their independence during his government.
5. **William H. Cavendish-Bentinck, Duke of Portland.** 1738–1809. Premier, 1783, 1807–9.
6. **William Pitt ('The Younger').** 1759–1806. Premier, 1783–1801, 1804–6. Britain's youngest Prime Minister.
7. **Henry Addington, Viscount Sidmouth.** 1757–1844. Premier, 1801–4. Received his peerage after resigning as Prime Minister and signed 'Sidmouth' from 1805 onwards.
8. **William, Lord Grenville.** 1759–1834. Premier, 1806–7. Not to be confused with George Grenville (see page 59).

1. 

2.

3.

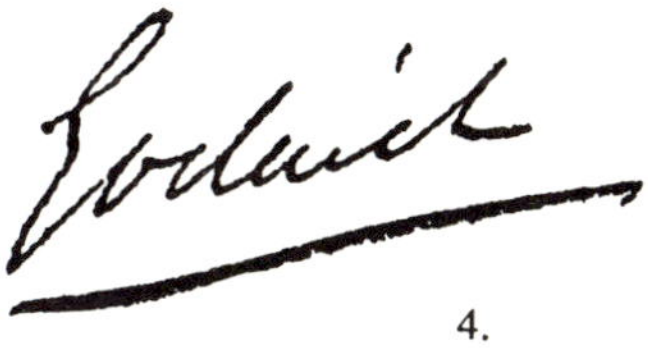
4.

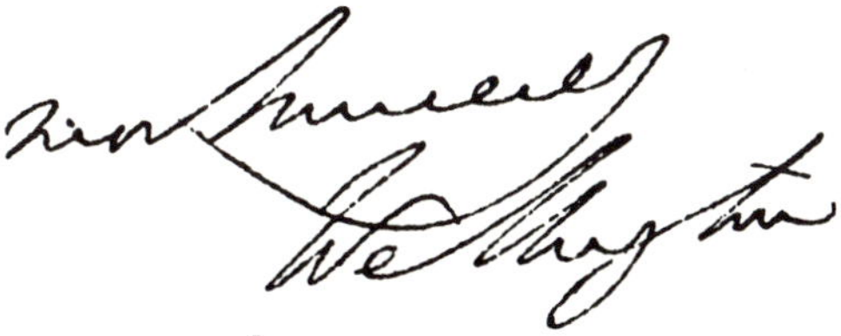
5.

6. 

7.

8. 

1. **Spencer Perceval.** 1762–1812. Premier, 1809–12. The only Prime Minister to have been assassinated.
2. **Robert B. Jenkinson, 2nd Earl of Liverpool.** 1770–1828. Premier, 1812–27. Signed 'Hawkesbury', his earlier title, until 1808.
3. **George Canning.** 1770–1827. Premier, April–Sept. 1827.
4. **Frederick J. Robinson, Viscount Goderich, Earl of Ripon.** 1782–1859. Premier, 1827–8. Signed 'Goderich' 1827–33 and 'Ripon' thereafter.
5. **Arthur Wellesley, Duke of Wellington.** 1769–1852. Premier, 1828–30. More famous as a soldier than as a politician: see also page 92.
6. **Charles, 2nd Earl Grey.** 1764–1845. Premier, 1830–4. Passed the Reform Bill, 1834.
7. **William Lamb, Viscount Melbourne.** 1779–1848. Premier, 1834, 1835–41. Melbourne, Australia, named after him.
8. **Sir Robert Peel.** 1788–1850. Premier, 1834–5, 1841–6. Reorganized the police force, hence 'peelers' and 'bobbies'. Confusion often arises between his signature and that of his son (see page 174).

1.

2.

3.

4.

5.

6.

7.

8.

9.

1. **Lord John, 1st Earl Russell.** 1792–1878. Premier, 1846–52, 1865–6.
2. **Edward Stanley, 14th Earl of Derby.** 1799–1869. Premier, 1852, 1858–9, 1866–8. Created Lord Stanley in 1844, he signed as such until 1851.
3. **George Gordon, 4th Earl of Aberdeen.** 1784–1860. Premier, 1852–5.
4. **Henry John Temple, 2nd Viscount Palmerston.** 1784–1865. Premier 1855–8, 1859–65. His autograph is possibly the most common of the Prime Ministers'.

5 and 6. **Benjamin Disraeli, Earl of Beaconsfield.** 1804–81. Premier, 1868, 1874–80. His writing varied from comparatively small to large. Example 5 is larger than average. He frequently signed just 'D'.

7. **William Ewart Gladstone.** 1809–98. Premier, 1868–74, 1880–5, 1886, 1892–4.
8. **Robert Cecil, 3rd Marquis of Salisbury.** 1830–1903. Premier, 1885–6, 1886–92, 1895–1902.
9. **Archibald Primrose, 5th Earl of Rosebery.** 1847–1929. Premier, 1894–5.

1.

2.

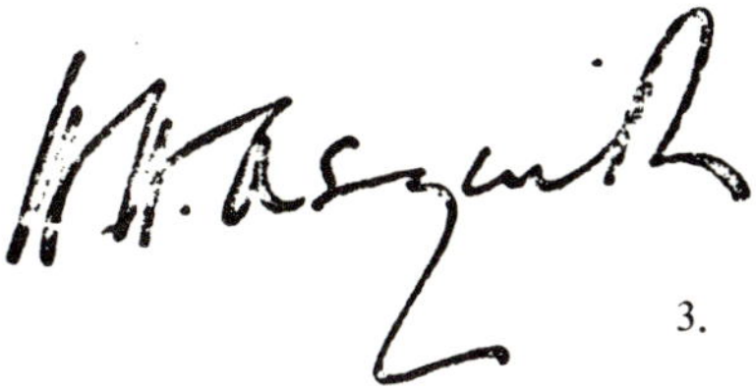
3.

4.

5.

6.

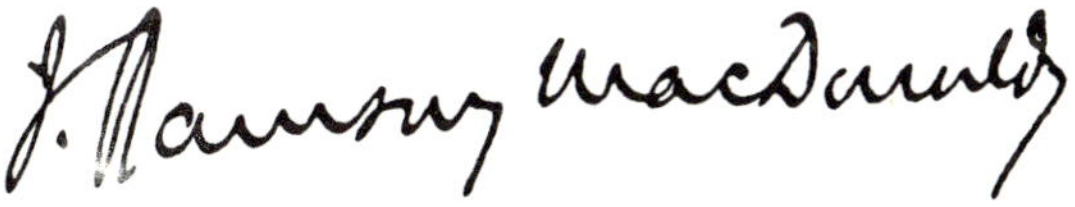
7.

8.
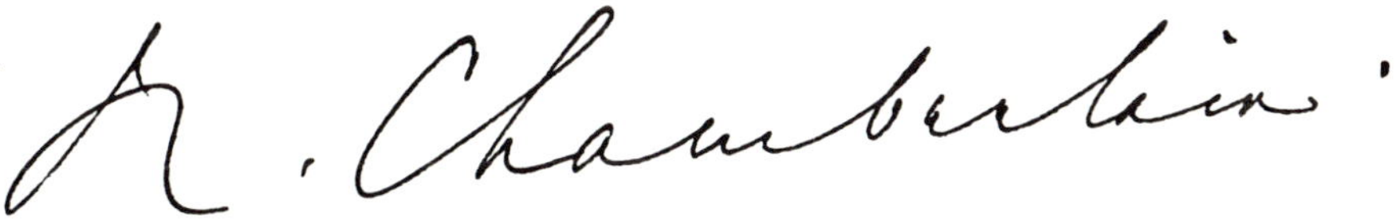

1. **Arthur James, Earl Balfour.** 1848–1930. Premier, 1902–5.
2. **Sir Henry Campbell-Bannerman.** 1836–1908. Premier, 1905–8.
3. **Herbert H. Asquith, Earl of Oxford and Asquith.** 1858–1928. Premier, 1908–15, 1915–16.
4. **David, Earl Lloyd-George.** 1863–1945. Premier, 1916–22.
5. **Andrew Bonar Law.** 1858–1923. Premier, 1922–3.
6. **Stanley, Earl Baldwin (of Bewdley).** 1867–1947. Premier, 1923–4, 1924–9, 1935–7. Lord Baldwin's signature before his peerage (1937), as 'Stanley Baldwin', is far better known. It is normally much larger and more rounded than the facsimile above which, as most collectors are familiar with his normal signature, has been chosen as a less common example.
7. **J. Ramsay MacDonald.** 1866–1937. Premier, 1924, 1929–31, 1931–5. The first Socialist Prime Minister.
8. **A. Neville Chamberlain.** 1869–1940. Premier, 1937–40. A rather larger signature than normal.

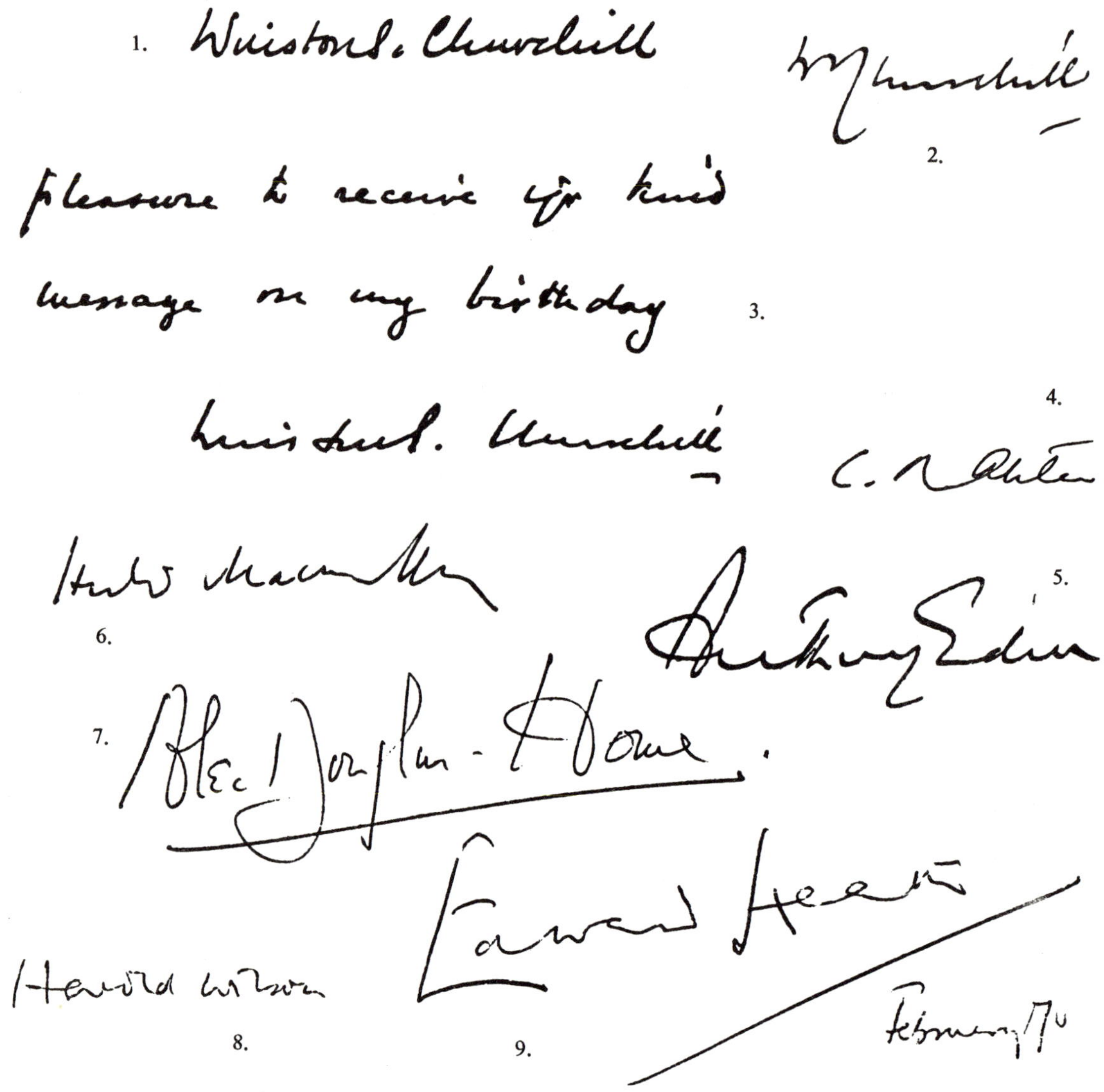

1, 2 and 3. **Sir Winston L. Spencer Churchill.** 1874–1965. Premier, 1940–5, 1945, 1951–5. 1 is an example of his signature in his earlier years and 2 of the shortened signature he employed frequently in his years out of office and again in his old age. 3 is taken from one of his facsimile 'thank-you' letters discussed on page 45.

4. **Clement Richard, Earl Attlee.** 1883–1967. Premier, 1945–51.

5. **Sir R. Anthony Eden, Earl of Avon.** 1897– . Premier, 1955–7. Has signed 'Avon' since 1957.

6. **Harold Macmillan.** 1894– . Premier, 1957–63.

7. **Sir Alec Douglas-Home.** 1903– . Premier, 1963–4. Formerly Earl of Home, he signed 'Home' until disclaiming his peerage for life in 1963.

8. **J. Harold Wilson.** 1916– . Premier, 1964–70.

9. **Edward R. G. Heath.** 1916– . Premier, 1970–

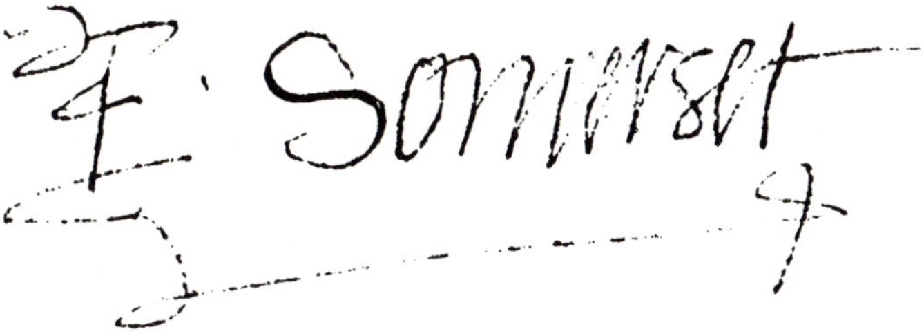

1.

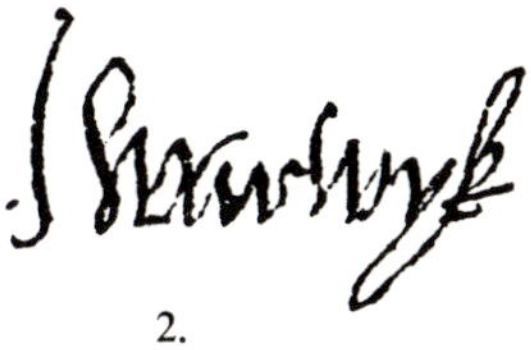

2.

3.

4.

5.

6.

7.

8.

1. **Edward Seymour, Duke of Somerset.** 1506(?)–52. Protector of the Realm during minority of Edward VI. A rare signature.
2. **John Dudley, Duke of Northumberland (Earl Warwick).** 1502(?)–53. Father-in-law of Lady Jane Grey, he was executed for supporting her succession against Mary I. Signature as 'J. Warwick'.
3. **John Russell, Earl of Bedford.** 1486(?)–1555.
4. **William Paulet, Marquis of Winchester.** 1485–1572. Lord President of the Council. His signature is often found as (Baron) 'St. John'.
5. **William Cecil, Lord Burghley.** 1520–98. Queen Elizabeth's chief adviser (as Lord High Treasurer) for twenty-five years.
6. **Sir Francis Walsingham.** 1530–90. Secretary of State. A small faction considers him to be the author of Shakespeare's plays.
7. **Sir Richard Sackville.** (?)–1566. First cousin of Anne Boleyn.
8. **Sir Walter Mildmay.** 1520(?)–89. Chancellor of the Exchequer.

POLITICIANS: ELIZABETHAN AND JACOBEAN STATESMEN AND COURTIERS

1.

2.

3.

4.

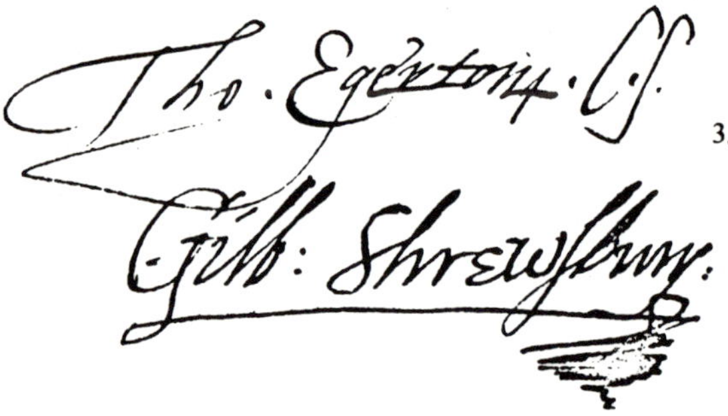

5.

6.

7.

8.

9.

10.

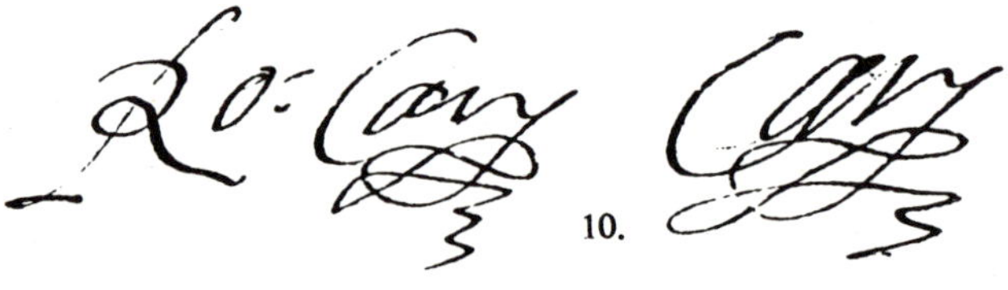

11.

1. **Robert Dudley, Earl of Leicester.** 1532(?)–88. Queen Elizabeth's favourite.
2. **Robert Devereux, Earl of Essex.** 1566–1601. Succeeded Leicester as Elizabeth's favourite but was executed for treason.

3 and 4. **Sir Thomas Egerton, Lord Ellesmere.** 1540(?)–1617. Lord Chancellor, later Viscount Brackley.
Gilbert Talbot, 7th Earl of Shrewsbury. 1553–1616. Both signatures are from the same document (Privy Council, 1601), hence their proximity to each other.

5 and 6. **Thomas Sackville, Lord Buckhurst, Earl of Dorset.** 1536–1608. Lord High Treasurer and man-of-letters. Variant signatures, 1601 and 1607.

7 and 8. **Robert Cecil, 1st Earl of Salisbury.** 1563(?)–1612. Secretary of State to both Elizabeth and James I. Variant signatures, 1601 and 1607.

9. **William Knollys, Earl of Banbury.** 1547–1632.
10. **Robert Cary, Earl of Monmouth.** 1560–1639. Variant signatures: after 1626 he signed as 'Monmouth'.
11. **Edward Somerset, 4th Earl of Worcester.** 1553–1628. Lord Privy Seal.

1.

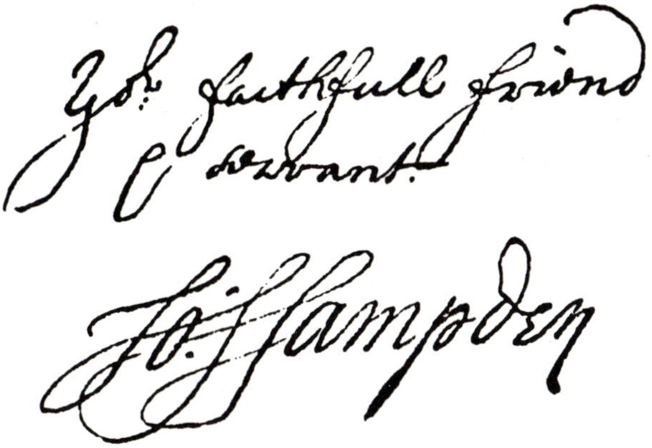

2.

3.

4.

5.

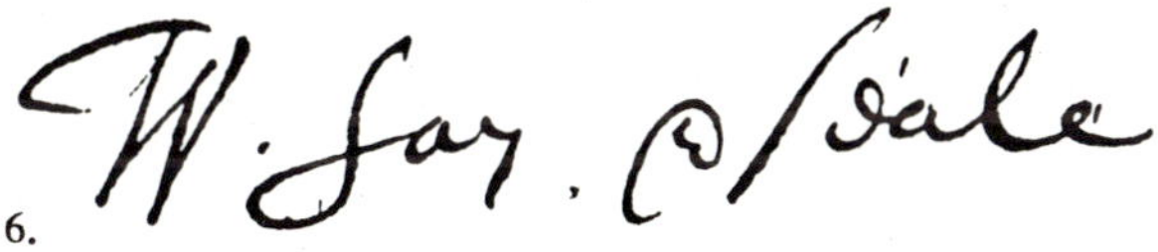

6.

7.

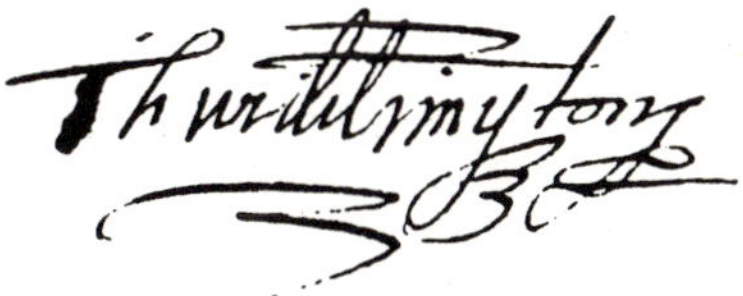

8.

1. **John Hampden.** 1594–1643. A distinguished and patriotic Parliamentarian. His autograph is scarce.
2. **Sir Henry Vane ('The Younger').** 1613–62. Member of Cromwell's Council of State. Executed after the Restoration.
3. **Algernon Percy, 10th Earl of Northumberland.** 1602–68. Member of the Parliamentary Committee of Safety, but opposed the trial of Charles I.
4. **Cornelius Holland.** fl. 1649. Regicide. Member of Cromwell's Council of State.
5. **William Cecil, 2nd Earl of Salisbury.** 1590–1668. Member of the Joint Parliamentary Committee. His signature closely resembles that of the first Earl: see page 66.
6. **William Fiennes, Viscount Say and Sele.** 1582–1662. 'Old Subtlety'. A somewhat half-hearted Parliamentarian.
7. **Bulstrode Whitelocke.** 1605–75. President of the Council of State on the fall of Richard Cromwell, this nowadays unknown man was, temporarily, virtual ruler of England.
8. **Sir Thomas Widdrington.** (?)–1664. Speaker of the House under Cromwell.

1.

2.

3.

4.
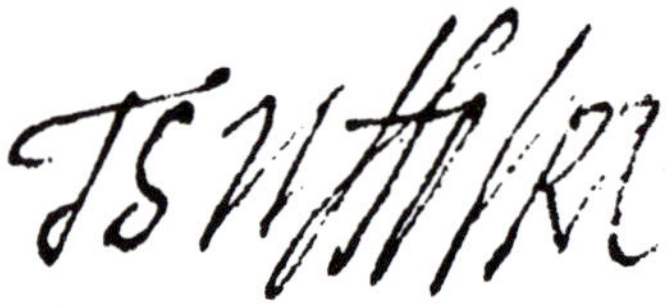

5.

7.

6.

8.

9.

1. **Sir Robert Naunton.** 1563–1635. Secretary of State under James I.
2. **Sir Julius Caesar.** 1558–1636. Chancellor of the Exchequer under James I.
3. **Thomas Wriothesley, 4th Earl of Southampton.** 1607–67. Lord High Treasurer under Charles II.
4. **Thomas Howard, Earl of Suffolk.** 1561–1626. Lord High Treasurer under James I.
5. **Archibald Campbell, Marquis of Argyll.** 1598–1661. Scottish soldier and politician. Executed by Charles II.
6. **Thomas, Lord Clifford.** 1630–73. Lord High Treasurer under Charles II. His name supplies the 'C' of the famous CABAL ministry.

7 and 8. **Henry Bennet, Earl of Arlington.** 1618–85. Secretary of State under Charles II. The first 'A' of the CABAL ministry. Variant signatures, both in the same year, 1665.

9. **Anthony Ashley Cooper, 1st Earl Shaftesbury.** 1621–83. Lord Chancellor and President of the Council. The second 'A' of the CABAL ministry. Signed as Lord Ashley.

1.

2.

3.

4.

5.

6.

7.

8.

9.

10.

1. **Edward Hyde, Earl of Clarendon.** 1609–74. As Charles II's Secretary of State, he wielded great influence.
2. **Arthur Capel, Earl of Essex.** 1631–83. First Lord of the Treasury, 1679.
3. **Robert Bruce, Earl of Ailesbury.** (?)–1685. Lord Chamberlain under Charles II.
4. **George, Earl of Berkeley.** 1628–98. Councillor to William III.
5. **William, Earl of Craven.** 1606–97. Supporter of Charles I and statesman under Charles II.
6. **Robert Spencer, 2nd Earl of Sunderland.** 1640–1702. Lord Chamberlain under William III.
7. **Thomas Osborne, Earl of Danby, Duke of Leeds.** 1631–1712. Lord High Treasurer in 1674. Signed 'Leeds' from 1694.
8. **Laurence Hyde, Earl of Rochester.** 1641–1711. Lord High Treasurer. Son of Clarendon and brother-in-law of James II, he signed 'Rochester' from 1681.

9 and 10. **Sidney, Earl of Godolphin.** 1645–1712. Queen Anne's Lord High Treasurer. 9 is an early signature. As he climbed to power his signature became larger and more confident, as example 10.

1.

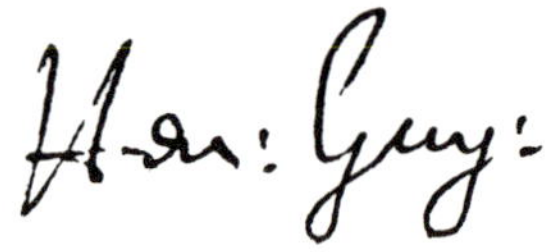

2.

3.

4.

5.

6.

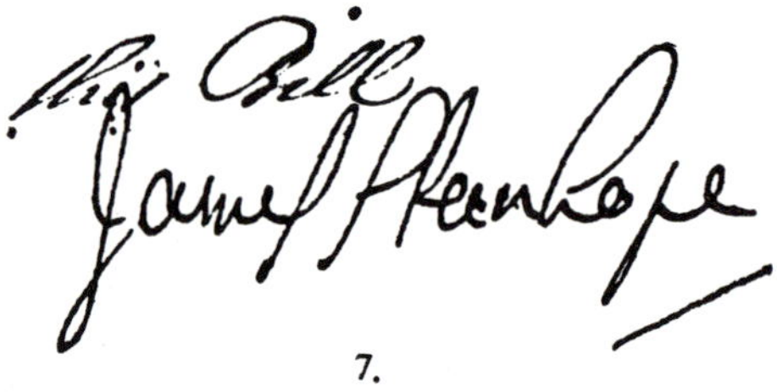

7.

8.

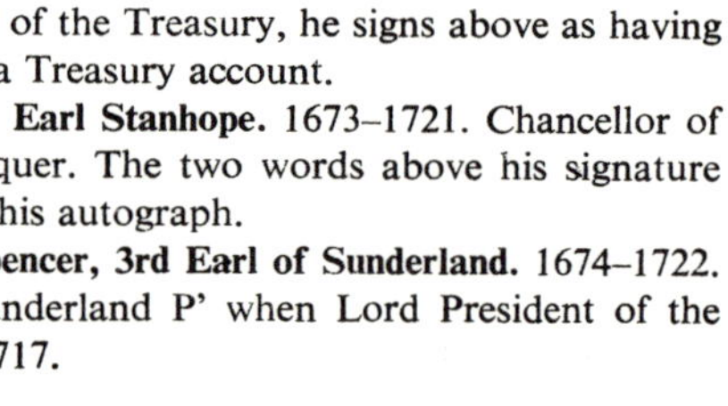

1. **William Bentinck, 1st Earl of Portland.** 1649–1709. Trusted friend and foreign agent of William III.
2. **Henry Guy.** 1631–1710. Companion of Charles II.
3. **Charles Talbot, Duke of Shrewsbury.** 1660–1718. Secretary of State. Swift's 'favourite of the nation'.
4. **Richard Lumley, Earl of Scarborough.** (?)–1721. Soldier and politician.
5. **John Sheffield, Duke of Buckingham.** 1648–1721. The suffix after his signature stands for (Lord) President (of the Council), which post he held under Queen Anne.
6. **Charles Montague, 1st Earl Halifax.** 1661–1715. First Lord of the Treasury, he signs above as having examined a Treasury account.
7. **James, 1st Earl Stanhope.** 1673–1721. Chancellor of the Exchequer. The two words above his signature are not in his autograph.
8. **Charles Spencer, 3rd Earl of Sunderland.** 1674–1722. Signed 'Sunderland P' when Lord President of the Council, 1717.

1.

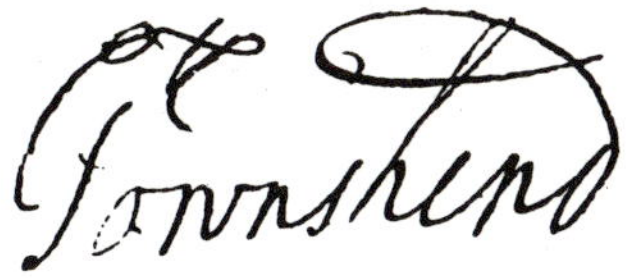

2.

3.

4.

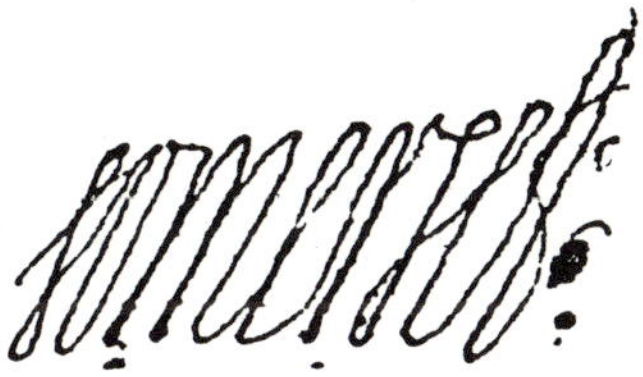

5.

7.

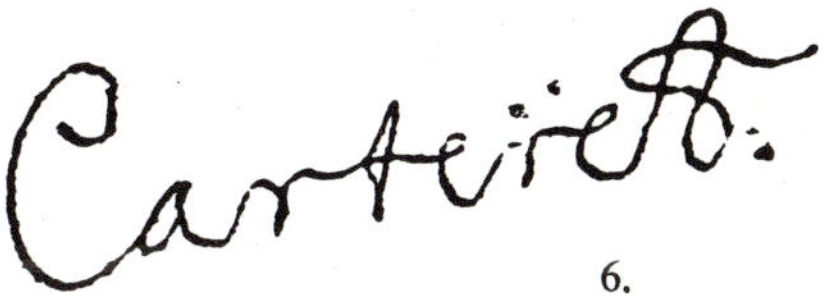

6.

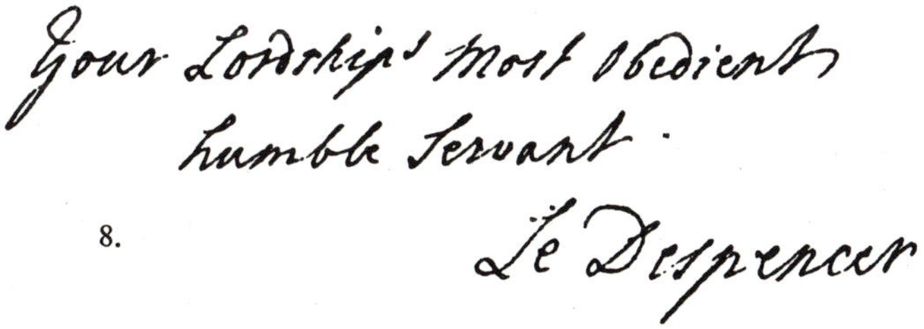

8.

1. **Henry Boyle, Lord Carleton.** (?)–1725. Lord President of the Council. Patron of Addison.
2. **Charles, 2nd Viscount Townshend.** 1674–1738. Lord President of the Council.
3. **Robert Harley, 1st Earl of Oxford.** 1661–1724. Lord Treasurer under Queen Anne. Manuscript collector.
4. **Edward Harley, 2nd Earl of Oxford.** 1689–1741. Added to his father's great manuscript collection which thereafter became the property of the British Museum: the famous Harlean Collection. Signed before succeeding to the earldom in 1724.
5. **Charles Seymour, 6th Duke of Somerset.** 1662–1748.
6. **John, Lord Carteret, Earl Granville.** 1690–1763. Secretary of State under George I and George II.
7. **George Montagu Dunk, 2nd Earl Halifax.** 1716–71. Secretary of State, 1771. Halifax, Nova Scotia, named after him.
8. **Sir Francis Dashwood, Lord Le Despencer.** 1708–81. Founder of the notorious Hell Fire Club. Chancellor of the Exchequer.

1.

2.

3.

4.

5.

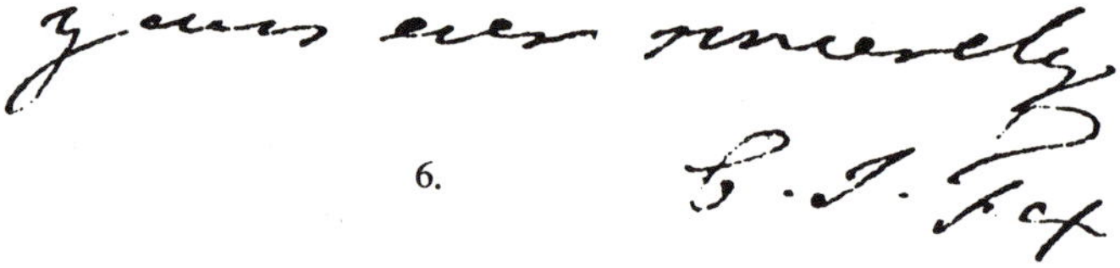

6.

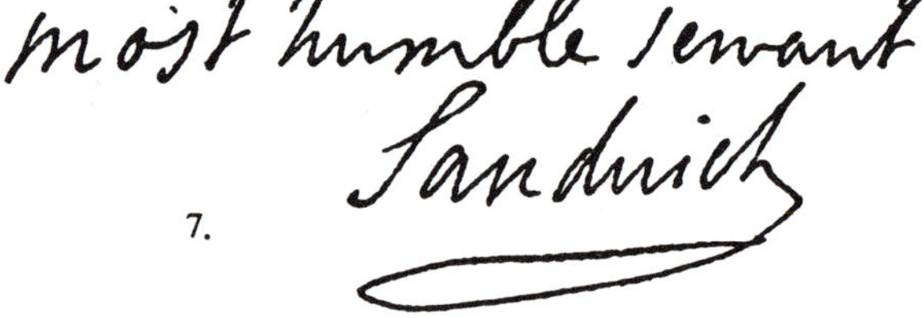

7.

8.

9.

1. **Philip D. Stanhope, Earl of Chesterfield.** 1694–1773. Statesman, orator, wit and man-of-letters.
2. **Henry Fox, 1st Lord Holland.** 1705–74. Secretary of State. Not to be confused with Henry R. V. Fox, the third Baron.
3. **John Wilkes.** 1727–97. The most controversial politician of his time.
4. **Charles Pratt, Earl Camden.** 1714–94. Lord Chancellor and Lord President. Signed as the latter.
5. **Edmund Burke.** 1729–97. Statesman, orator and man-of-letters.
6. **Charles James Fox.** 1749–1806. Liberal statesman.
7. **John Montagu, 4th Earl Sandwich.** 1718–92. Originated the sandwich to eat whilst at the gaming table. Sandwich Isles (Hawaii) named after him.
8. **George, 2nd Earl Spencer.** 1758–1834. First Lord of the Admiralty under Pitt.
9. **Henry Dundas, Viscount Melville.** 1742–1811. Secretary of War.

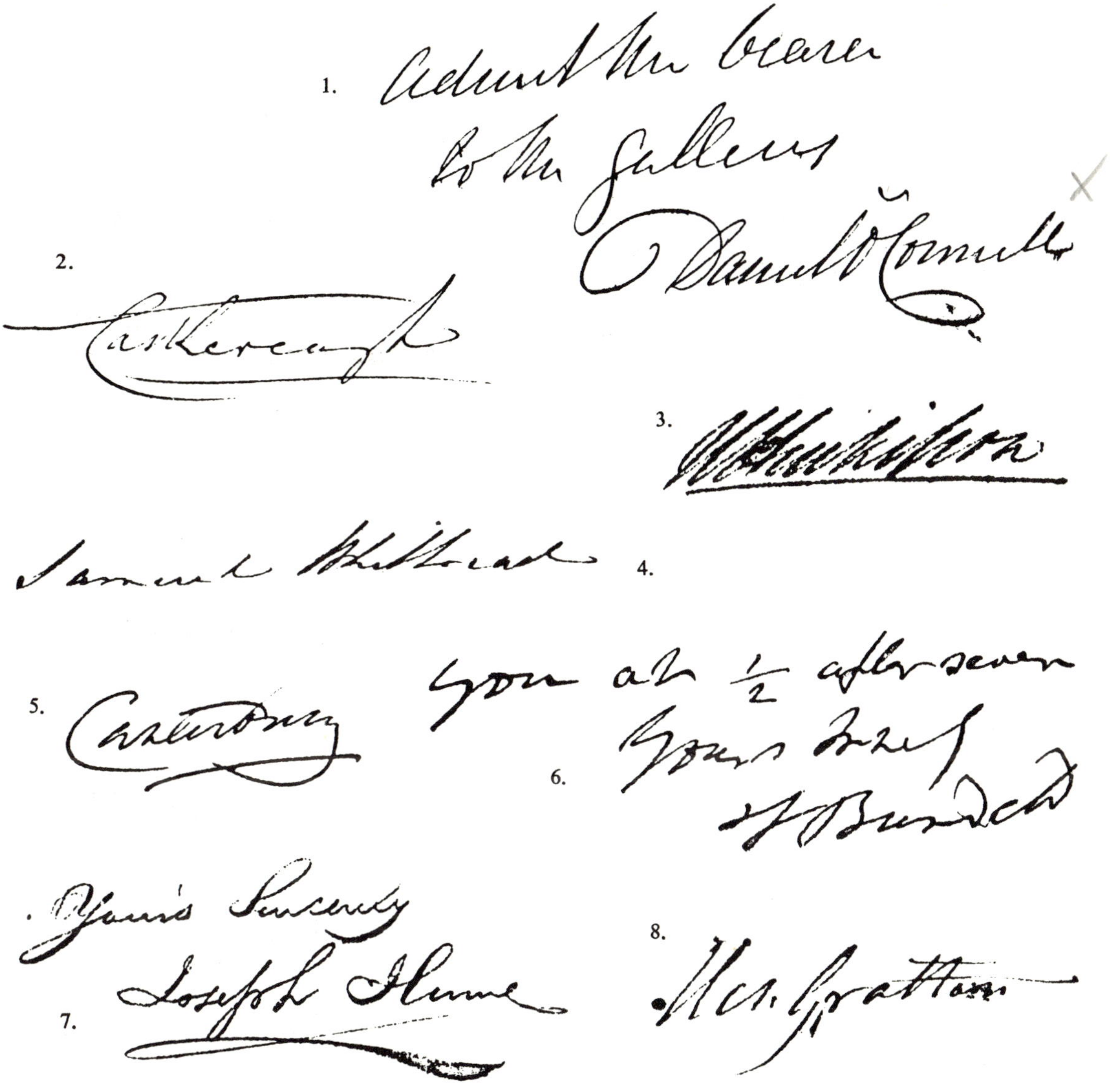

1. **Daniel O'Connell.** 1775–1847. 'The [Irish] Liberator'.
2. **Robert Stewart, Viscount Castlereagh (2nd Marquis of Londonderry).** 1769–1822. Foreign Minister. He signed as 'Londonderry' for only one year (1821–2).
3. **William Huskisson.** 1770–1830. Pioneer of Free Trade. Killed by a locomotive at the opening of the Liverpool and Manchester Railway.
4. **Samuel Whitbread.** 1758–1815. Political reformer.
5. **Charles Manners-Sutton, Viscount Canterbury.** 1780–1845. Speaker of the House of Commons, 1817–35. Note signature as 'Canterbury', not to be confused with that of his Archbishop father of the same name: see page 80.
6. **Sir Francis Burdett.** 1770–1844. Political reformer and Benthamite.
7. **Joseph Hume.** 1777–1855. Radical statesman.
8. **Henry Grattan.** 1746–1820. Irish political reformer and orator.

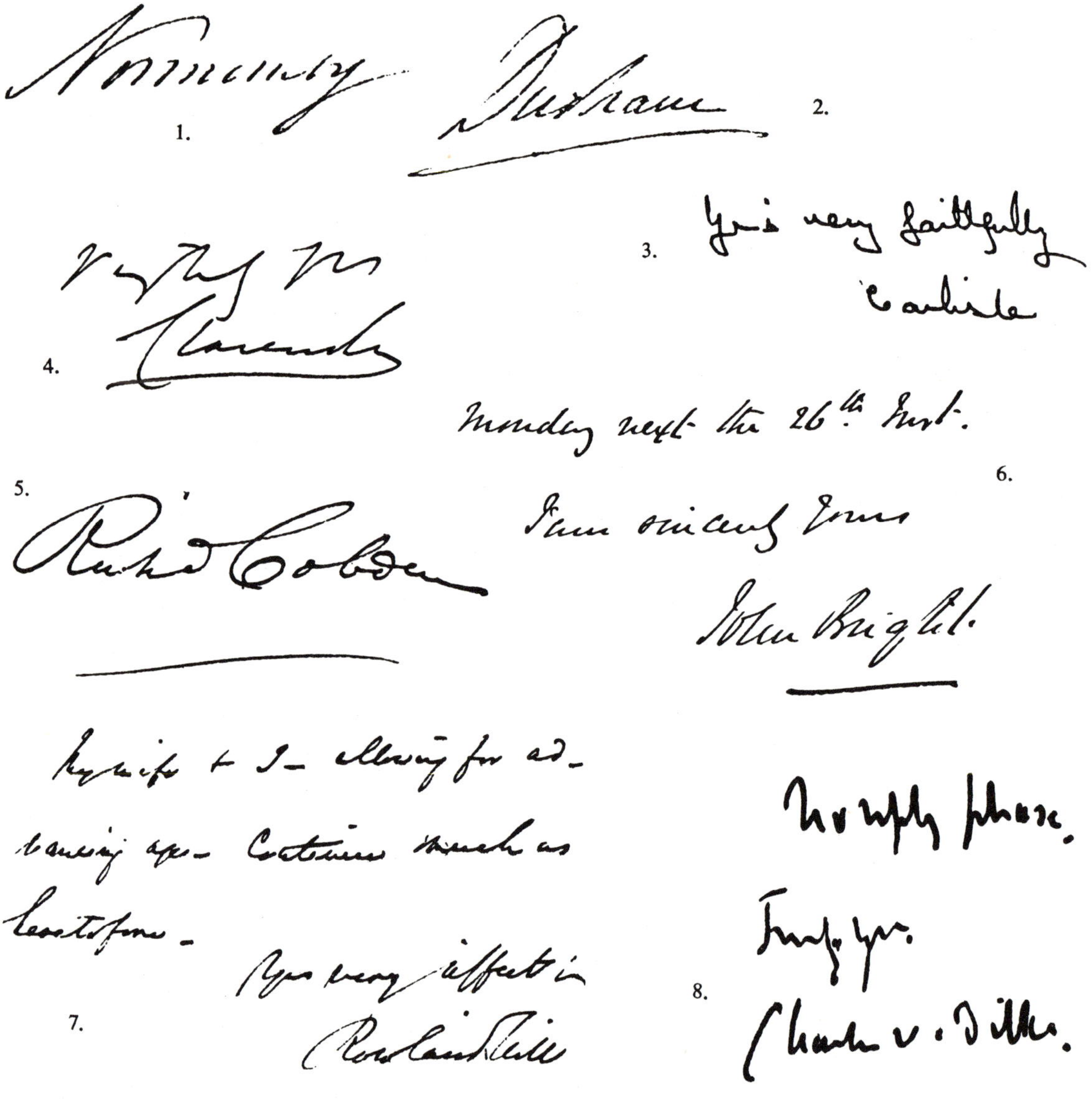

1. **Constantine Phipps, Marquis of Normanby, 2nd Earl Mulgrave.** 1797–1863. His father also signed 'Mulgrave' or 'Normanby', but his writing was smaller and less regular.
2. **John Lambton, Earl of Durham.** 1792–1840. Governor-General of British North America.
3. **George W. F. Howard, 7th Earl of Carlisle.** 1802–64. Orator, poet and Viceroy of Ireland.
4. **George Villiers, 4th Earl of Clarendon.** 1800–70. Foreign Minister.
5. **Richard Cobden.** 1804–65. Free Trader, reformer and economist.
6. **John Bright.** 1811–89. Radical statesman and orator. His signature can be confused with that of Jacob Bright but both usually signed their Christian names in full.
7. **Sir Rowland Hill.** 1795–1879. As the originator of penny postage, his autograph is in demand by philatelists and postal history collectors.
8. **Sir Charles W. Dilke.** 1843–1911. Radical politician whose private life inspired the play *The Right Honourable Gentleman.*

1.

2.

3.

4.

5.

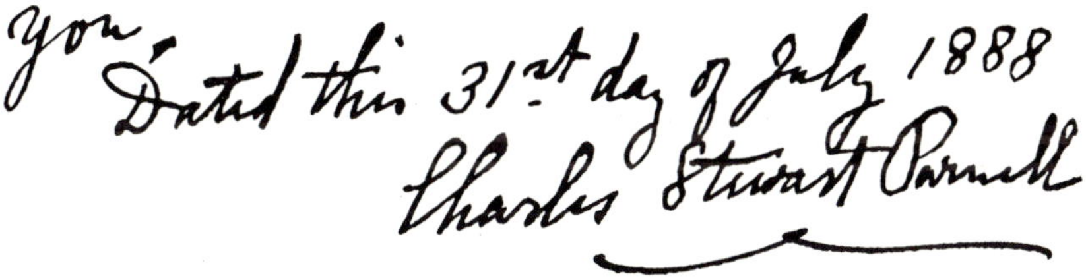

6.

7.

1. **William E. Forster.** 1818–86. Liberal statesman. Remembered for having carried the Elementary Education Act (1870).
2. **Sir Benjamin Hall, Lord Llanover.** 1802–67. 'Big Ben' named after him.
3. **John Poyntz, 5th Earl Spencer.** 1835–1910. Liberal statesman.
4. **Lord Randolph Churchill.** 1849–94. Chancellor of the Exchequer. Father of Sir Winston Churchill.
5. **Charles Stewart Parnell.** 1846–91. Irish Nationalist leader.
6. **Edward, Viscount Cardwell.** 1813–86. As Secretary of War he reorganized the Army.
7. **Joseph Chamberlain.** 1836–1914. Colonial Secretary. Father of Austen and Neville Chamberlain.

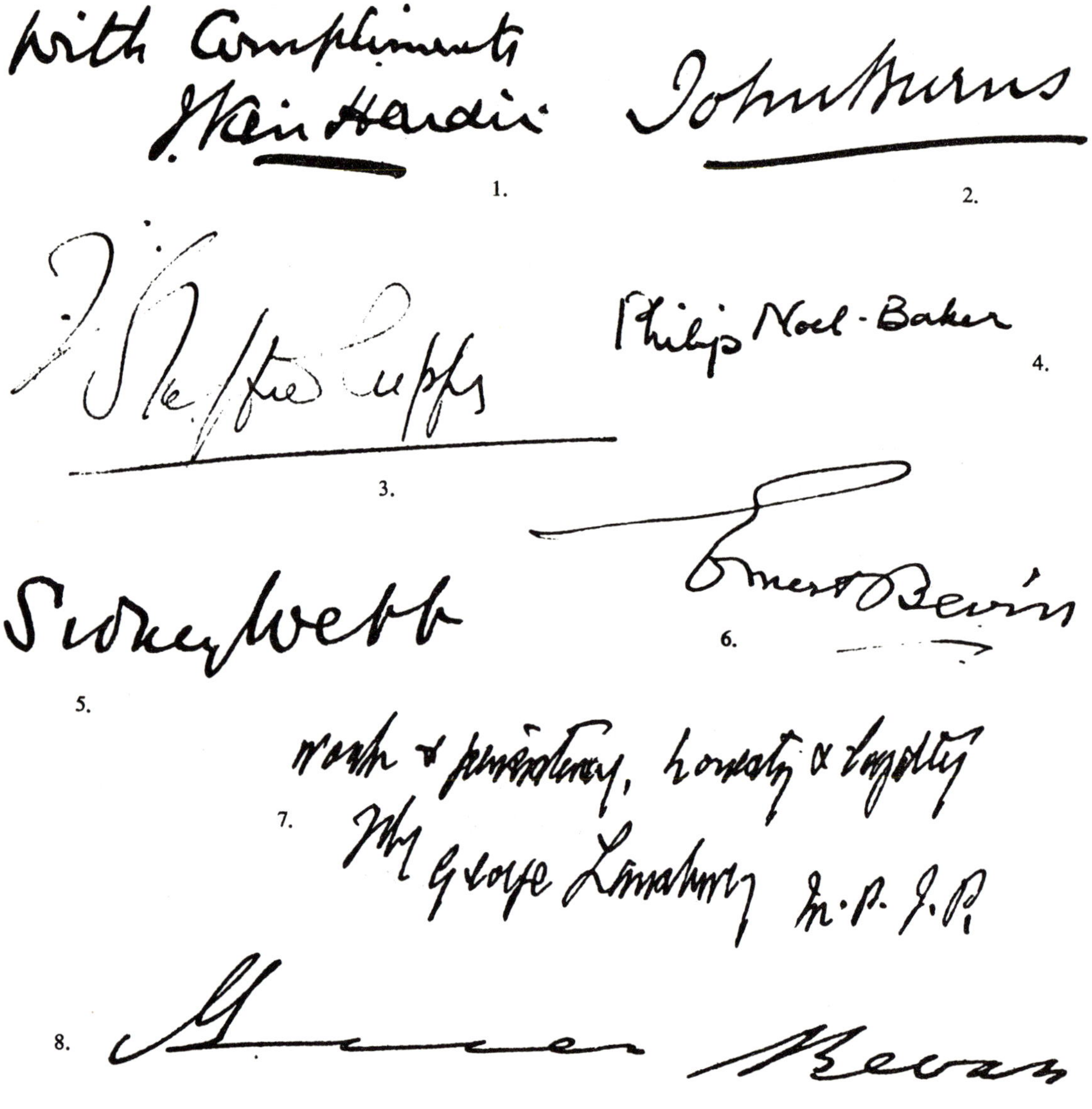

1. **James Keir Hardie.** 1856–1915. One of the founders of the Independent Labour Party.
2. **John Burns.** 1858–1943. Britain's first working-class Cabinet Minister.
3. **Sir Stafford Cripps.** 1889–1952. Chancellor of the Exchequer.
4. **Philip Noel-Baker.** 1889– . Winner of the Nobel Prize, 1959.
5. **Sidney Webb, Lord Passfield.** 1859–1947. Social reformer, Fabian and a founder of the *New Statesman* and the London School of Economics.
6. **Ernest Bevin.** 1881–1951. 'The docker's K.C.'. Minister of Labour throughout World War II.
7. **George Lansbury.** 1859–1940. Leader of the Labour Party (1931–5) and founder of the *Daily Herald*.
8. **Aneurin Bevan.** 1897–1960. Left-wing Labour leader and orator. During his term of office as Minister of Health (1945–51) the National Health Service was established.

1.

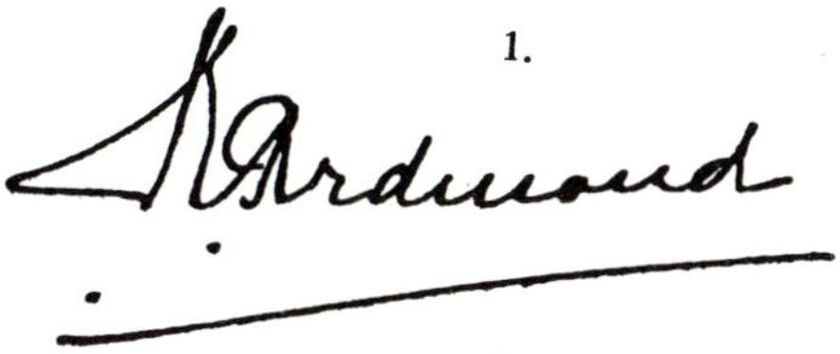

2.

3.

4.

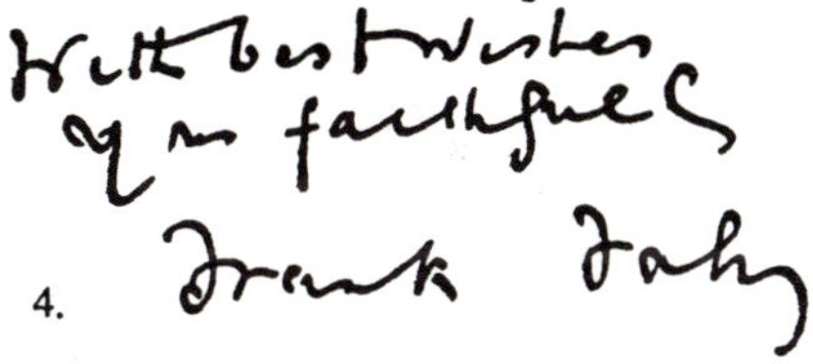

5.

6.

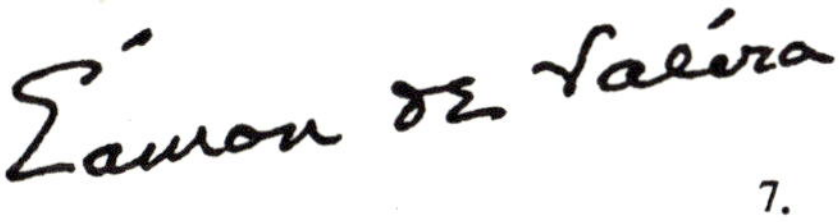

7.

8.

1. **John E. Redmond.** 1856–1918. Irish Nationalist.
2. **Roger Casement.** 1864–1916. A former British consular official, he became an Irish Nationalist and was hanged for high treason during World War I.
3. **Edward, Lord Carson.** 1854–1935. Ulster leader and Lord of Appeal.
4. **Francis (Frank) Fahy.** 1880–1953. Irish Nationalist. Speaker of the Irish Parliament.
5. **James Craig, Viscount Craigavon.** 1871–1940. First Prime Minister of Northern Ireland.
6. **Sir Basil Brooke, Viscount Brookeborough.** 1888– Prime Minister of Northern Ireland, 1943–63.
7. **Eamon de Valera.** 1882– . Irish Nationalist leader and President of Eire.
8. **William Thomas Cosgrave.** 1880–1965. The first President of the Executive Council of the Irish Free State.

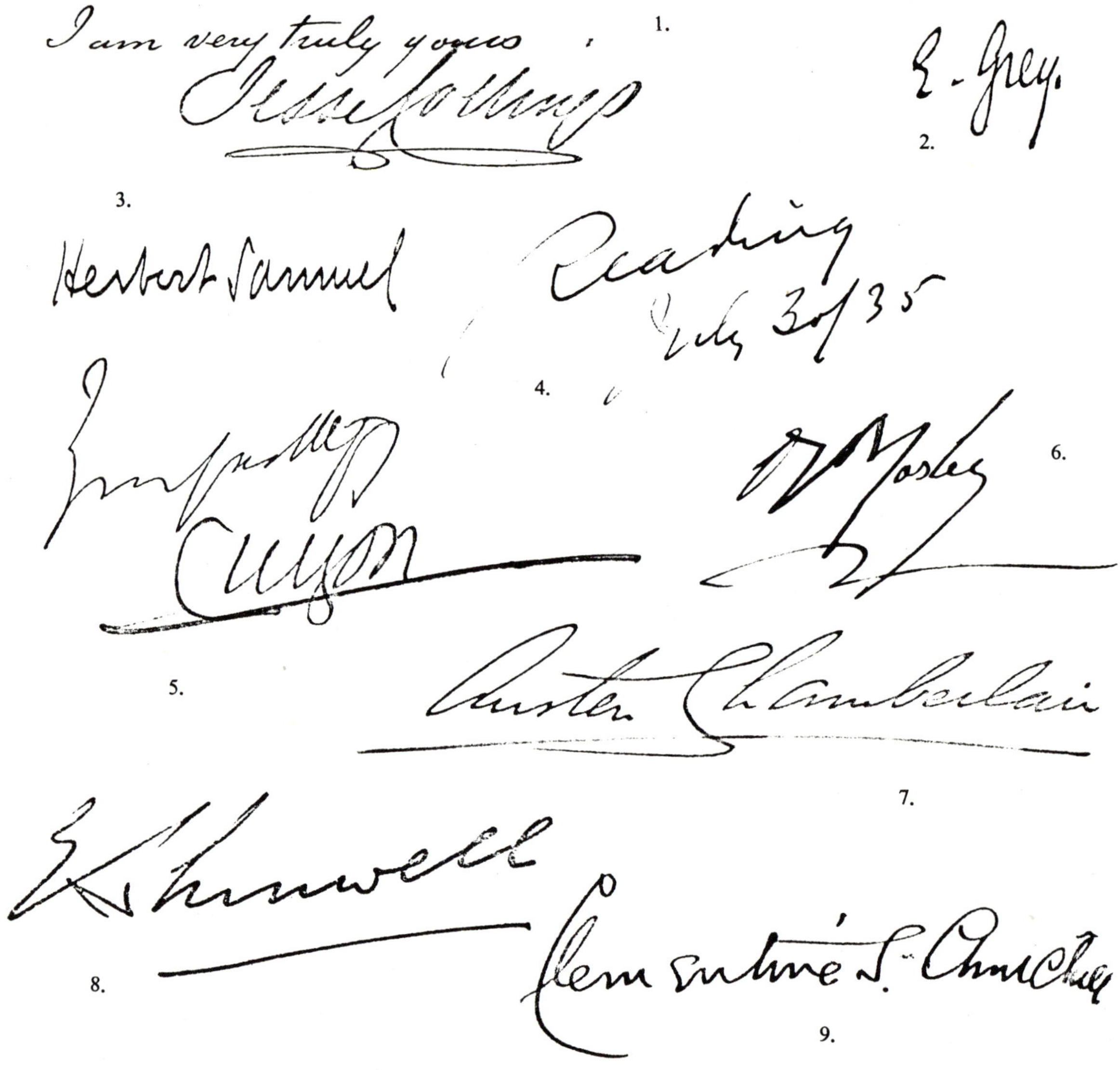

1. **Jesse Collings.** 1831–1920. Promoted allotments and small holdings ('three acres and a cow').
2. **Edward, Viscount Grey (of Fallodon).** 1862–1933. Foreign Minister.
3. **Herbert, Viscount Samuel.** 1870–1963. Liberal statesman.
4. **Rufus Isaacs, Marquis of Reading.** 1860–1935. Viceroy of India, Lord Chief Justice and Foreign Minister.
5. **George, Marquis Curzon.** 1859–1925. Viceroy of India and Foreign Minister.
6. **Sir Oswald Mosley.** 1896– . British Fascist leader.
7. **Sir Austen Chamberlain.** 1863–1937. Foreign Secretary. Won the 1925 Nobel Peace Prize for negotiating the Locarno Pact.
8. **Emanuel, Lord Shinwell.** 1884– . 'Elder Statesman' of the Labour Party.
9. **Clementine, Lady Churchill.** 1885– . Wife of Sir Winston Churchill. Created Baroness Spencer-Churchill, 1965.

MEN OF THE CHURCH: SOME ARCHBISHOPS OF CANTERBURY (1) SIXTEENTH- TO EIGHTEENTH-CENTURY

1.

2.

3.

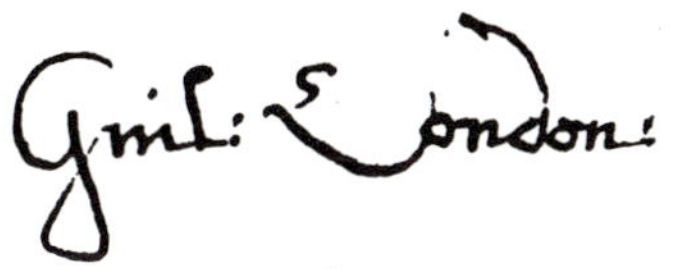

4.

5.

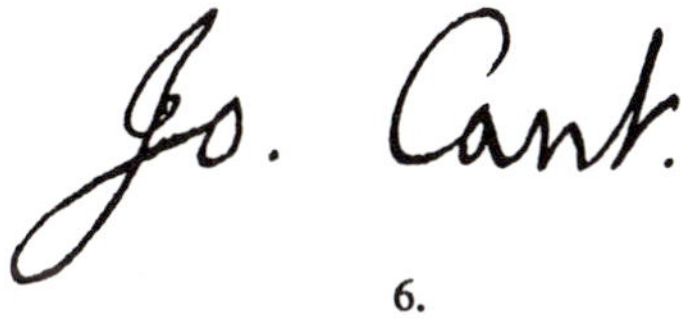

6.

7.

8.

N.B. All Archbishops of Canterbury sign 'Cant' or 'Cantuar' (Canterbury).

1. **Thomas Cranmer.** 1489–1556. Archbishop, 1533. Responsible for much of the Book of Common Prayer and other religious formularies; supported the accession of Lady Jane Grey rather than Mary I and was burned at the stake. He was Queen Elizabeth I's godfather. A rare autograph.
2. **John Whitgift.** 1530(?)–1604. Archbishop under Elizabeth I, 1583–1604.
3. **William Laud.** 1573–1645. Archbishop, 1633–45. A supporter of Charles I, imprisoned by Parliament and beheaded.
4. **William Juxon.** 1582–1663. Archbishop, 1660–3. Attended Charles I on the scaffold. Signed when Bishop of London.
5. **Thomas Tenison.** 1636–1715. Archbishop, 1694–1715.
6. **John Potter.** 1674(?)–1747. Archbishop, 1737–47. A distinguished theologian and scholar.
7. **Thomas Herring.** 1693–1757. Archbishop, 1747–57.
8. **Thomas Secker.** 1693–1768. Archbishop, 1758–68. Signed above when Bishop of Oxford.

MEN OF THE CHURCH: SOME ARCHBISHOPS OF CANTERBURY (2) NINETEENTH- AND TWENTIETH-CENTURY

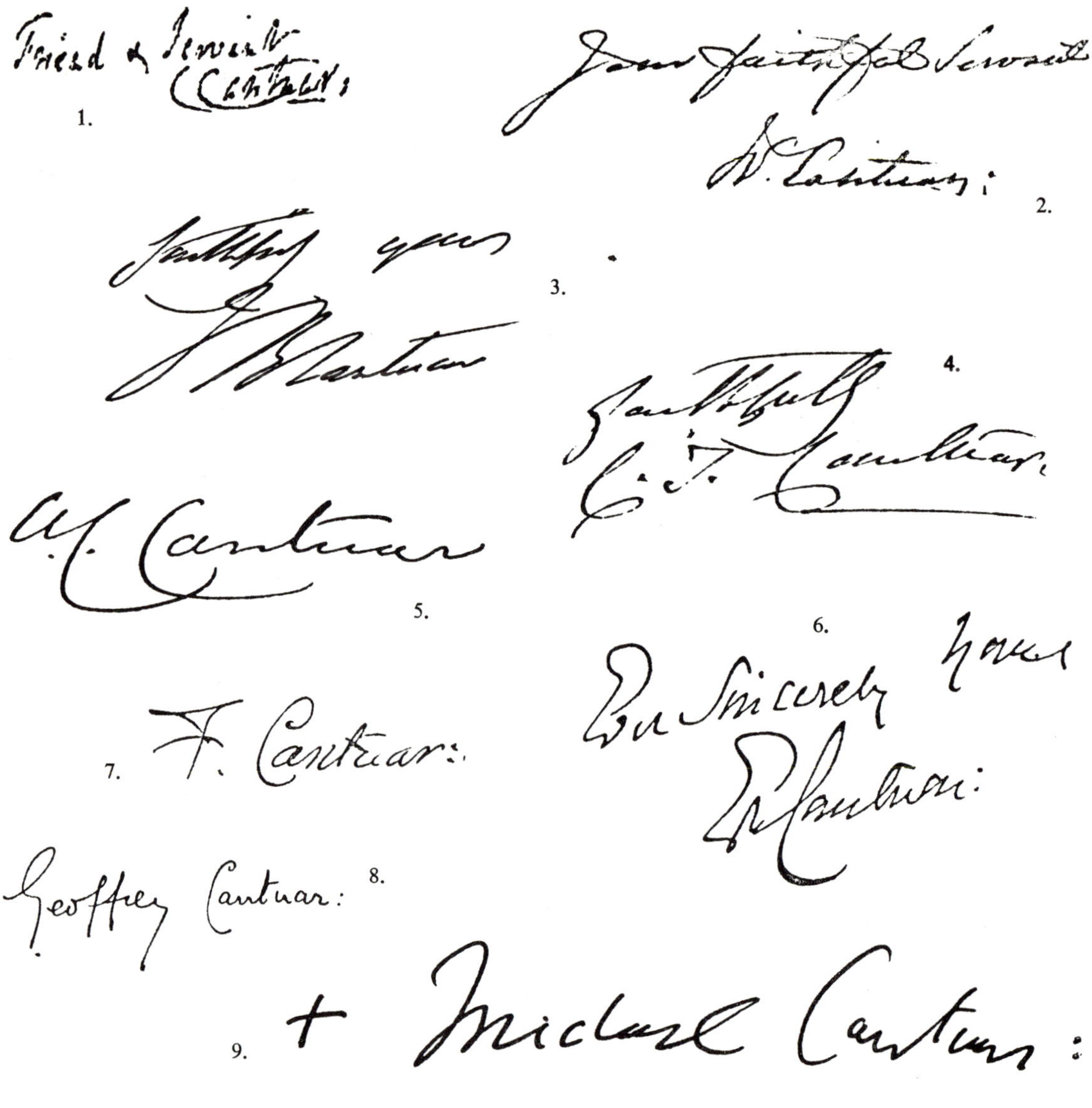

1. **Charles Manners-Sutton.** 1755–1828. Archbishop, 1805–28. Father of the Speaker of the same name (Viscount Canterbury): see page 73.
2. **William Howley.** 1766–1848. Archbishop, 1828–48.
3. **John Bird Sumner.** 1780–1862. Archbishop, 1848–62.
4. **Charles T. Longley.** 1794–1868. Archbishop, 1862–68.
5. **Archibald Campbell Tait.** 1811–82. Archbishop, 1869–82.
6. **Edward W. Benson.** 1829–96. Archbishop, 1882–96. The first Headmaster of Wellington (1858) and father of the three literary Benson brothers (see page 128).
7. **Frederick Temple.** 1821–1902. Archbishop, 1896–1902. His son William also became Archbishop of Canterbury.
8. **Geoffrey Francis, Lord Fisher of Lambeth.** 1887– . Archbishop, 1945–61. Earlier, Bishop of Chester, 1932–9, and of London, 1939–45.
9. **Arthur Michael Ramsey.** 1904– . Archbishop, 1961– . Formerly Bishop of Durham, 1952–6, and Archbishop of York, 1956–61.

MEN OF THE CHURCH: RELIGIOUS LEADERS, THEOLOGIANS AND PREACHERS (1)

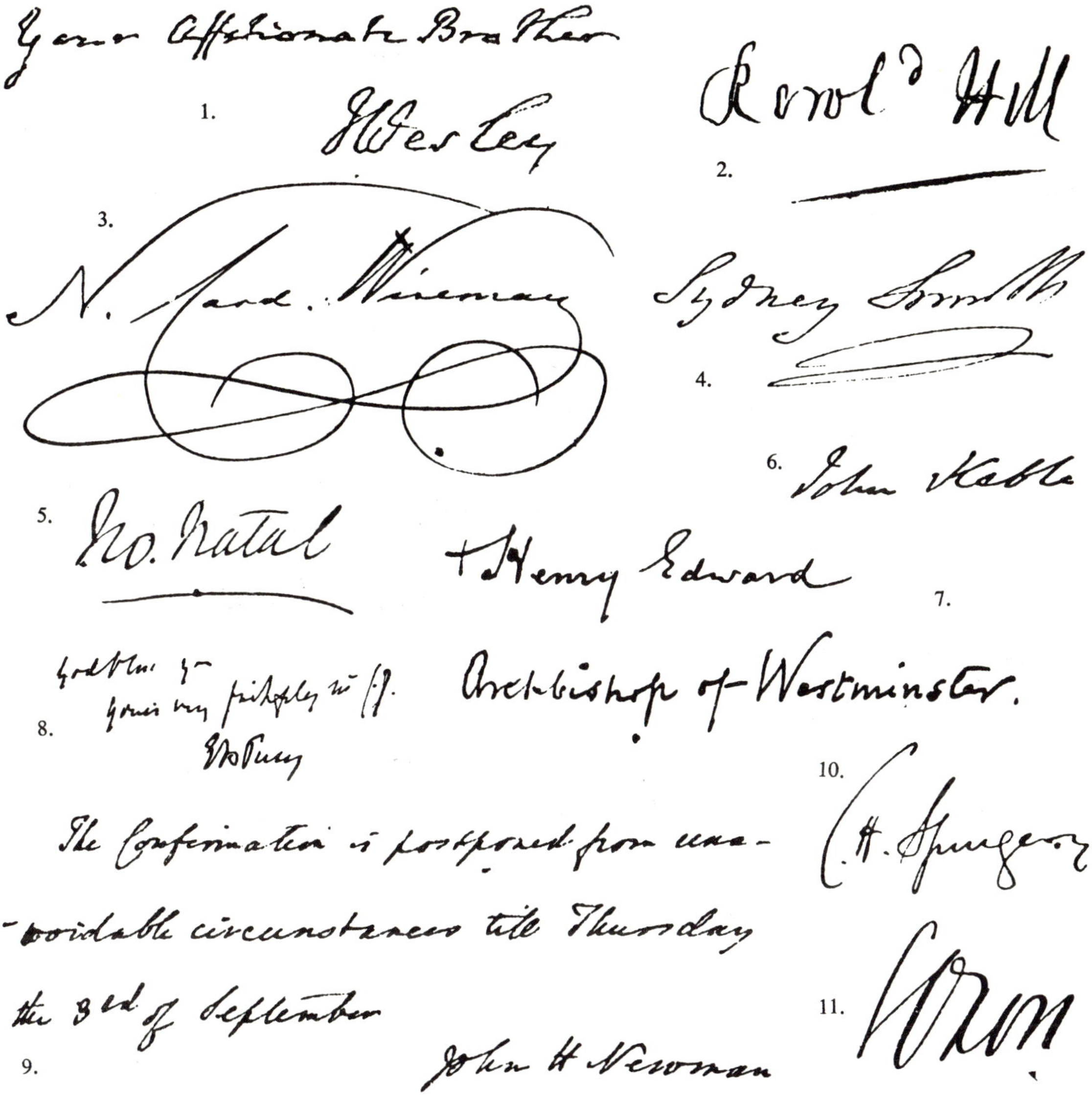

1. **John Wesley.** 1703–91. Evangelist and preacher. Founder of Methodism. A scarce and valuable autograph.
2. **Rowland Hill.** 1744–1833. Preacher. Sometimes confused with the postal reformer of the same name.
3. **Nicholas P. Wiseman.** 1802–65. Cardinal Archbishop of Westminster, 1850.
4. **Sydney Smith,** 1771–1845. Theologian, journalist and wit.
5. **John W. Colenso.** 1814–83. Controversial theologian. Bishop of Natal, where Colenso is named after him.
6. **John Keble.** 1792–1866. Theologian, a founder of the Oxford (Tractarian) Movement.
7. **Henry E. Manning.** 1808–92. Cardinal Archbishop of Westminster, 1865.
8. **Edward B. Pusey.** 1800–82. A Tractarian Movement leader. Laboured to reform Oxford University.
9. **John Henry Newman.** 1801–90. Cardinal, theologian and poet. An extended handwriting example is given above to avoid confusion with another J. H. Newman, a contemporary minor theologian.
10. **Charles H. Spurgeon.** 1834–92. Baptist preacher.
11. **Samuel Wilberforce.** 1805–73. 'Soapy Sam'. Bishop of Oxford (as in example) and Winchester.

MEN OF THE CHURCH: RELIGIOUS LEADERS, THEOLOGIANS AND PREACHERS (2)

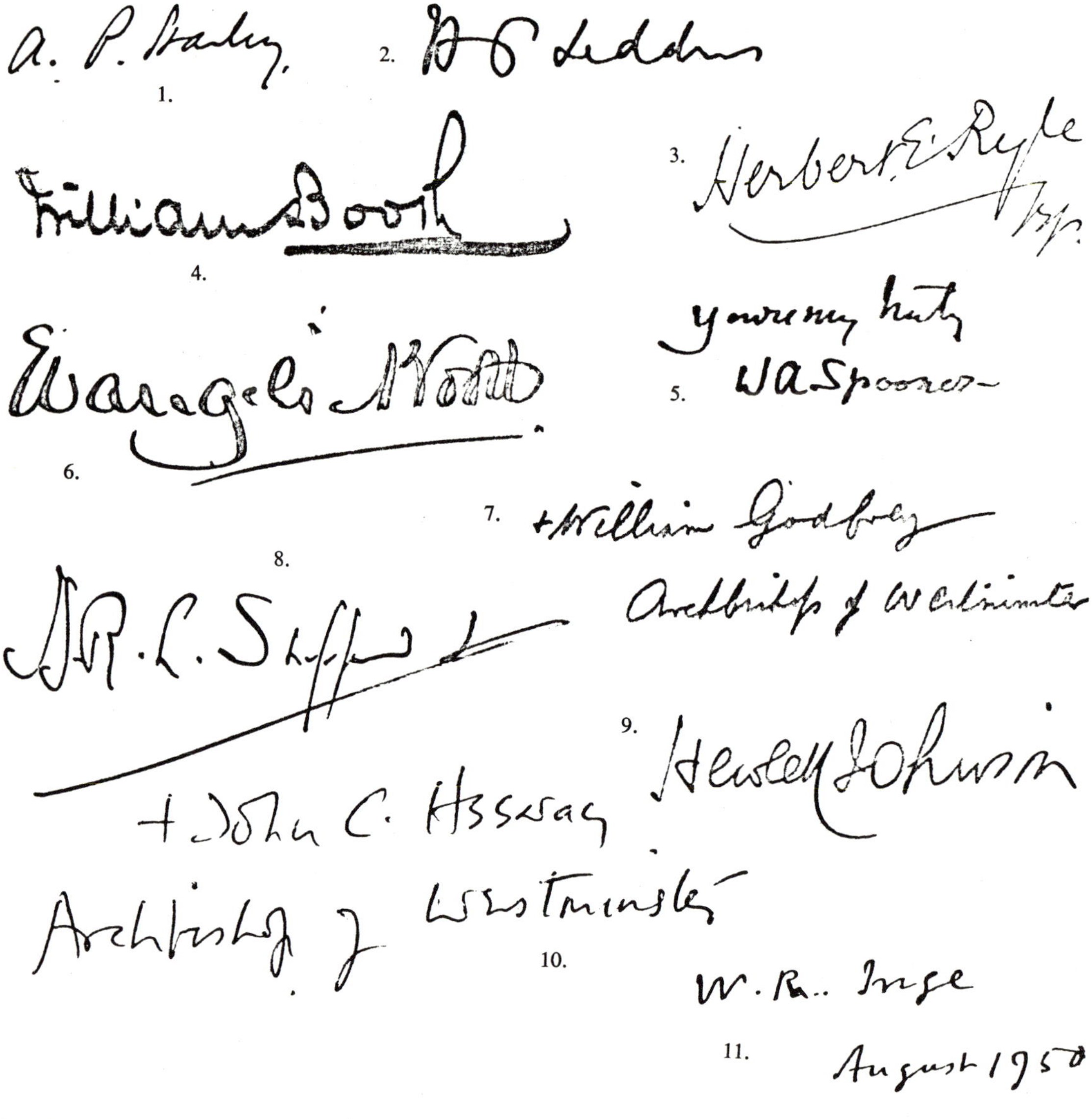

1. **Arthur P. Stanley.** 1815–81. Dean of Westminster and a major theological writer.
2. **Henry P. Liddon.** 1829–90. Theologian and an eloquent lecturer.
3. **Herbert E. Ryle.** 1856–1925. Theological writer, Bishop of Exeter and of Winchester, and Dean of Westminster.
4. **William Booth.** 1829–1912. Founder and 'General' of the Salvation Army.
5. **William A. Spooner.** 1844–1930. Theologian and educationalist, whose verbal errors gave rise to the term 'spoonerism'.
6. **Evangeline Booth.** 1865–1950. 'General' of the Salvation Army, daughter of William Booth, 4 above.
7. **William Godfrey.** 1889–1963. Cardinal Archbishop of Westminster.
8. **H. Richard L. Sheppard.** 1880–1937. 'Dick' Sheppard. Preacher and religious broadcaster.
9. **Hewlett Johnson.** 1874–1966. The 'Red Dean' of Canterbury.
10. **John C. Heenan.** 1905– Cardinal Archbishop of Westminster, 1963.
11. **William R. Inge.** 1860–1954. The 'Gloomy D.an' of St Paul's. A prolific theological writer.

MEN OF LAW: SIXTEENTH- TO EIGHTEENTH-CENTURY

1. 

2. 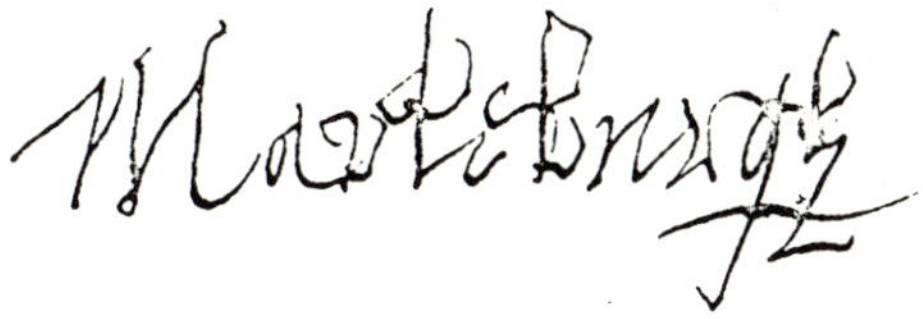

3. 

4. 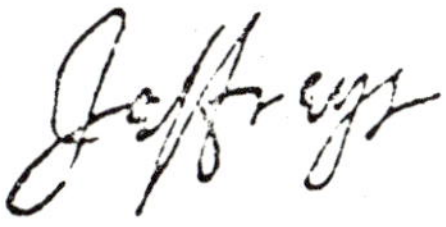

 5.

6.

7. 

8.

9.

N.B. Many great legal figures were also statesmen and thus may be found in the political sections.

1. **Edward, Lord Bruce of Kinloss.** 1549(?)–1611. Master of the Rolls.
2. **James Ley, Earl of Marlborough.** 1550–1629. Lord Chief Justice.
3. **Sir Thomas Jones.** (?)–1692. Chief Justice of Common Pleas.
4. **George, Lord Jeffreys.** 1648–89. Lord Chancellor. After Monmouth's rebellion he presided at the notorious 'Bloody Assize'. An important judicial autograph.
5. **William, Earl Cowper.** 1664(?)–1723. As Lord Chancellor under Queen Anne, he signs 'C' (Cancellarius) after his name.
6. **Philip Yorke, 1st Earl of Hardwicke.** 1690–1764. Lord Chancellor.
7. **William Murray, 1st Earl of Mansfield.** 1705–93. Lord Chief Justice.
8. **Sir J. Eardley-Wilmot.** 1709–92. Chief Justice of Common Pleas.
9. **Sir John Fielding.** (?)–1780. Blind from birth (hence his unusual signature). As London's Chief Magistrate, he was concerned (with his famous half-brother Henry Fielding) with organizing the Bow Street Runners, the predecessor of the Metropolitan Police Force.

1.

2.

3.

4.

6.

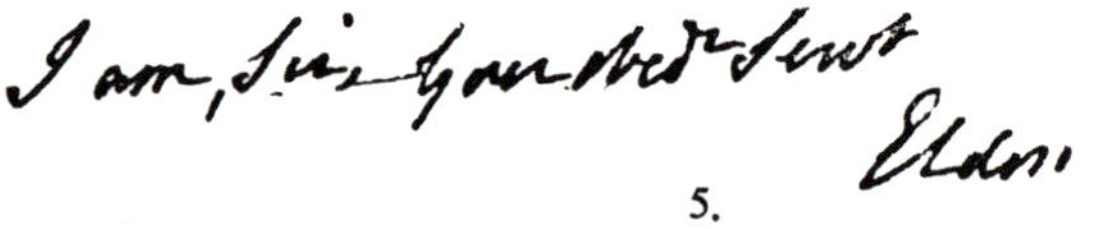

5.

8.

7.

9.

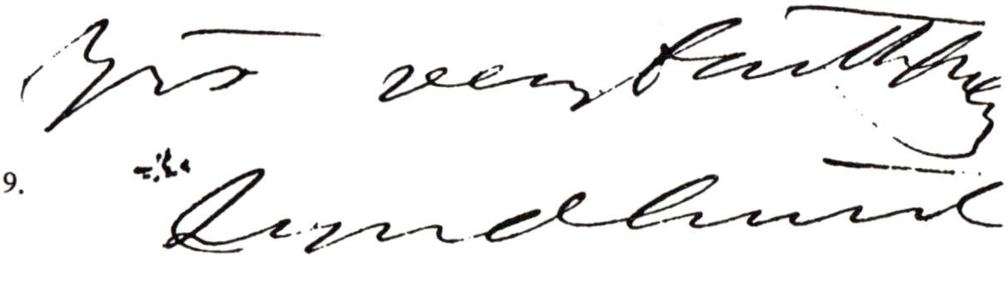

1. **Edward, Lord Thurlow.** 1731–1806. Lord Chancellor; opposed the independence of the American colonies.
2. **Alexander Wedderburn, Lord Loughborough (Earl Rosslyn).** 1733–1805. Lord Chancellor.
3. **William Scott, Lord Stowell.** 1745–1836. Judge and maritime lawyer. His autograph, though dissimilar, is sometimes confused with that of Sir Walter Scott.
4. **Edward Law, Baron Ellenborough.** 1750–1818. Lord Chief Justice.
5. **John Scott, 1st Earl of Eldon.** 1751–1838. Lord Chancellor and a very distinguished lawyer.
6. **Thomas, Lord Erskine.** 1750–1823. Lord Chancellor; probably the greatest forensic lawyer in our history.
7. **James Scarlett, Lord Abinger.** 1769–1844. Attorney-General under Canning.
8. **William (C.), Lord Plunket.** 1764–1854. Lord Chancellor of Ireland.
9. **John Singleton Copley, Lord Lyndhurst.** 1772–1863. Lord Chancellor. A brilliant defence lawyer, he was the son of the American painter of the same name who became a Royal Academician (see page 142).

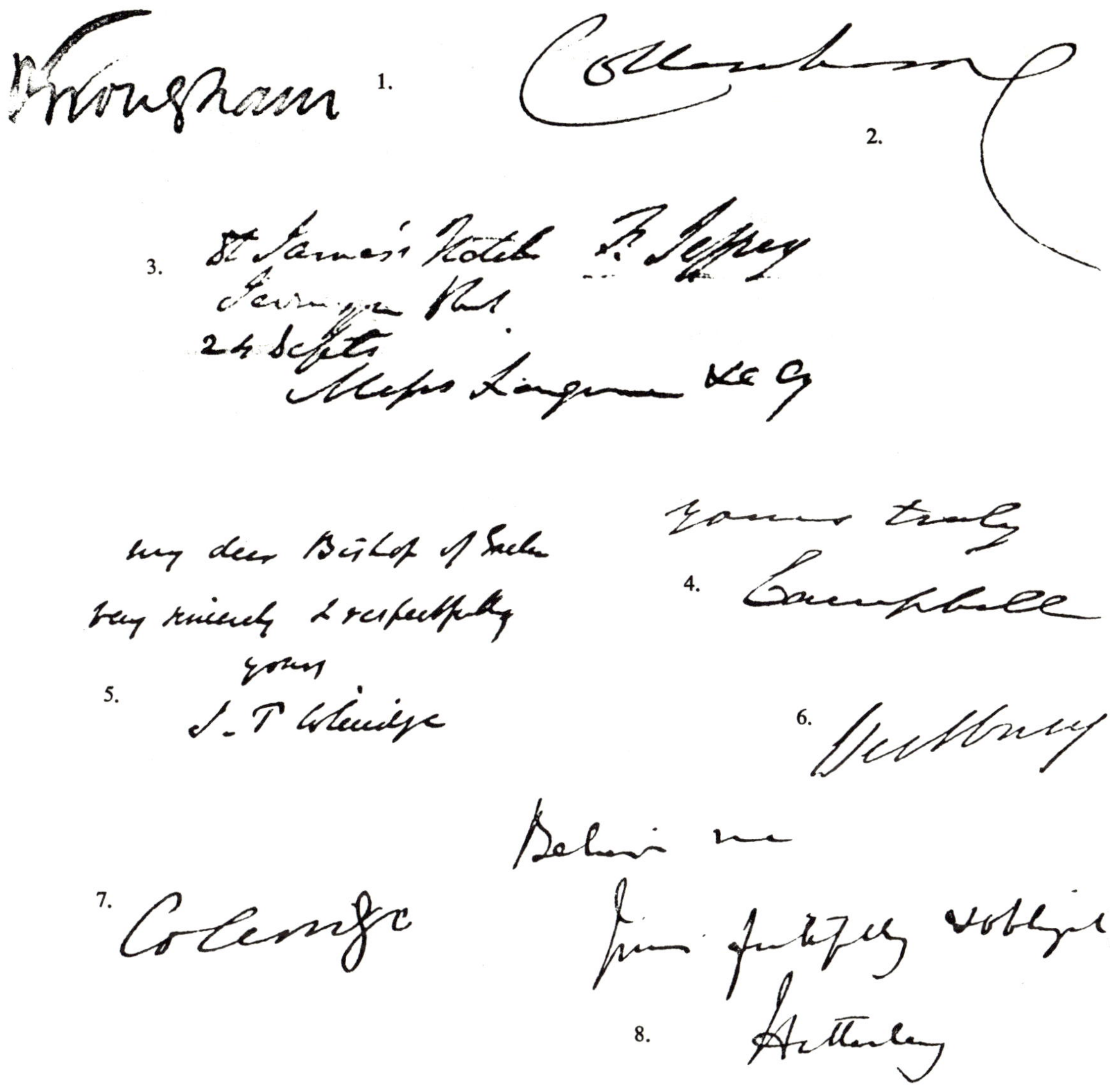

1. **Henry, Lord Brougham (and Vaux).** 1778–1868. Lord Chancellor, law reformer and brilliant orator, he was one of the most famous legal figures in our history.
2. **Charles C. Pepys, Earl of Cottenham.** 1781–1851. Twice Lord Chancellor.
3. **Francis, Lord Jeffrey.** 1773–1850. Scottish jurist and literary critic, famed for his critique, beginning 'This will never do', of Wordsworth's 'Excursion'.
4. **John, Lord Campbell.** 1779–1861. Lord Chancellor.
5. **Sir John Taylor Coleridge.** 1790–1876. Judge and writer. His autograph strongly resembles that of the poet Samuel Taylor Coleridge (see page 118).
6. **Richard Bethell, Lord Westbury.** 1800–73. Lord Chancellor.
7. **John (D.), Lord Coleridge.** 1821–94. Lord Chief Justice. Son of Sir J. T. Coleridge, 5 above.
8. **William Page Wood, Lord Hatherley.** 1801–81. Lord Chancellor.

1.

2.

3.

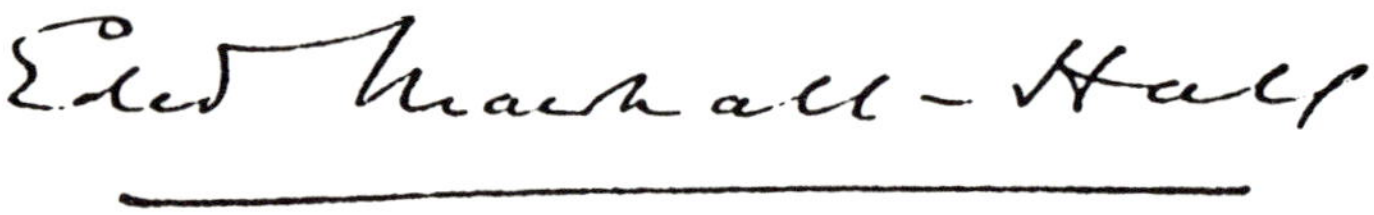

4.

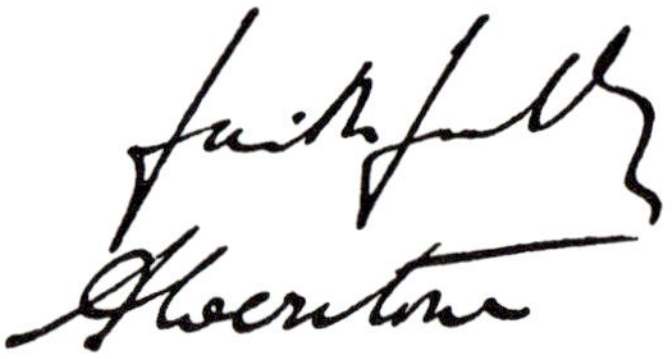

5.

6.

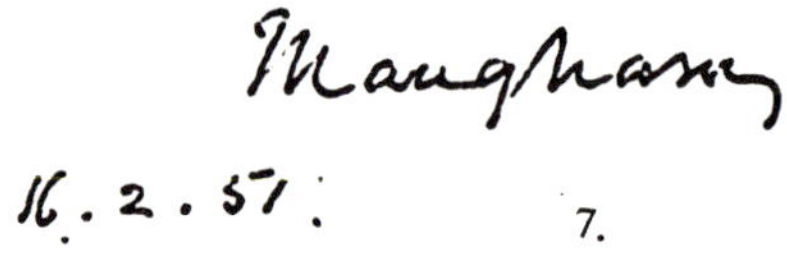

7.

8.

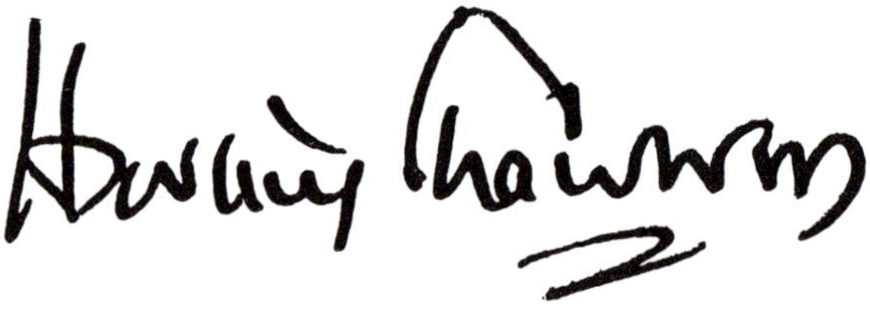

9.

1. **Roundell Palmer, 1st Earl of Selborne.** 1812–95. Twice Lord Chancellor.
2. **Hardinge S. Giffard, 1st Earl of Halsbury.** 1823–1921. Three times Lord Chancellor, he supervised the digest of the laws of England.
3. **Farrer, Lord Herschell.** 1837–99. Lord Chancellor.
4. **Sir Edward Marshall-Hall.** 1858–1927. One of the more notable criminal lawyers of his day.
5. **Richard E. Webster, Viscount Alverstone.** 1842–1915. Lord Chief Justice.
6. **Stanley (O.), Viscount Buckmaster.** 1861–1934. Lord Chancellor and Lord of Appeal.
7. **Frederic, Viscount Maugham.** 1866–1958. Lord Chancellor; brother of W. Somerset Maugham.
8. **David P. Maxwell Fyfe, Viscount Kilmuir.** 1900–67. Lord Chancellor; one of the principal prosecutors at the Nuremberg Trial.
9. **Hartley (W.), Lord Shawcross.** 1902– . Chief British prosecutor at Nuremberg Trial, he was subsequently appointed Attorney-General.

MEN OF ACTION: SIXTEENTH- TO EIGHTEENTH-CENTURY ADMIRALS

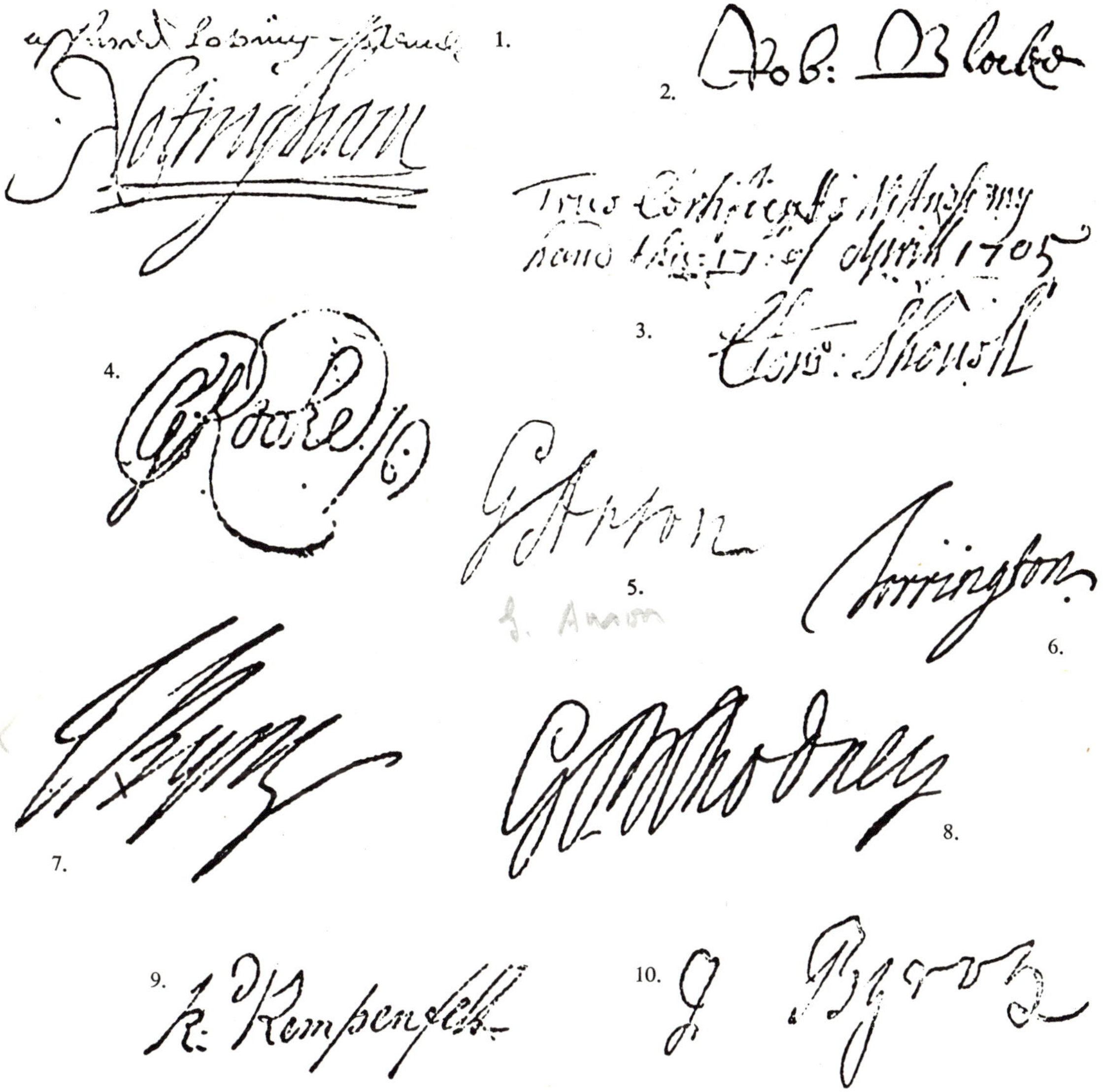

1. **Charles, Lord Howard of Effingham, Earl of Nottingham.** 1536–1624. Lord High Admiral. In command against the Spanish Armada. The signature only is in his writing.
2. **Robert Blake.** 1599–1657. The greatest of British Admirals, excepting Nelson.
3. **Sir Clowdesley Shovell.** 1650–1707. The (joint) captor of Barcelona (1705).
4. **Sir George Rooke.** 1650–1709. The captor of Gibraltar (1704).
5. **George, Lord Anson.** 1697–1762. Circumnavigator; won the battle of Cape Finisterre.
6. **George Byng, Viscount Torrington.** 1663–1733. Defeated the Spanish at Messina (1718).
7. **John Byng.** 1704–57. Son of Torrington, 6 above. For 'neglect of duty' in action off Minorca, shot on his own quarterdeck—'Pour encourager les autres', according to Voltaire.
8. **George, Lord Rodney.** 1719–92.
9. **Richard Kempenfelt.** 1718–82. 'Brave Kempenfelt' of Cowper's 'The Loss of the Royal George'.
10. **John Byron.** 1723–86. 'Foul Weather Jack'. Circumnavigator. Governor of Newfoundland.

MEN OF ACTION: MILITARY COMMANDERS OF THE SEVENTEENTH AND EIGHTEENTH CENTURIES

1.

2.

3.

4.

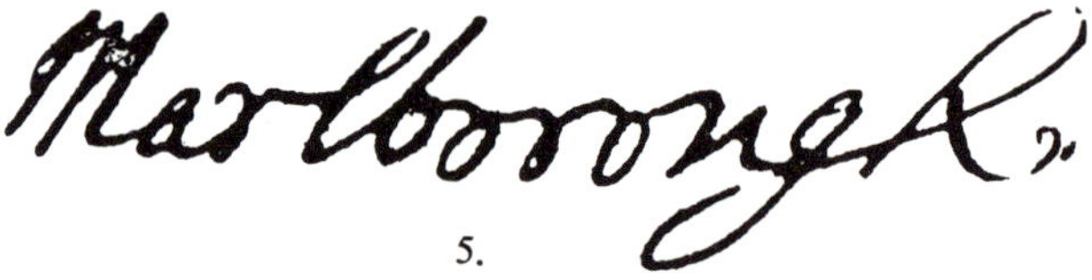

5.

6.

7.

8.

1. **Prince Rupert (of Bavaria).** 1619–82. 'The Mad Cavalier'. Royalist commander. Grandson of James I. A founder of the Hudson's Bay Company.
2. **Thomas, Lord Fairfax.** 1612–71. Commander-in-Chief of the Parliamentary forces.
3. **George Monck, Duke of Albemarle.** 1608–70. Both a general and an admiral.
4. **Meinhart, Duke of Leinster and Schomberg.** 1641–1719. British 'soldier of fortune' of German descent. Fought as a cavalry commander at the Boyne and Dettingen.

5 and 6. **John Churchill, Duke of Marlborough.** 1650–1722. Victor of Blenheim, Ramillies and Oudenarde. His wife, **Sarah Churchill, Duchess of Marlborough.** 1660–1744. Favourite of Queen Anne.

7. **John Dalrymple, 2nd Earl of Stair.** 1673–1747. Field-Marshal.
8. **George Wade.** 1673–1748. Field-Marshal. Famed for his construction of metalled military roads and stone bridges in the Scottish highlands.

1.

2.

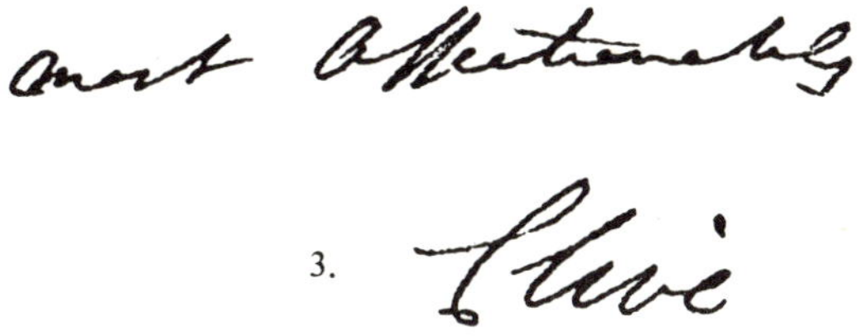

3.

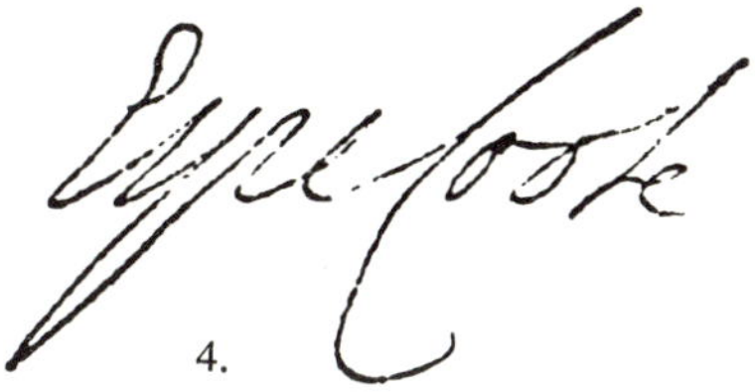

4.

5.

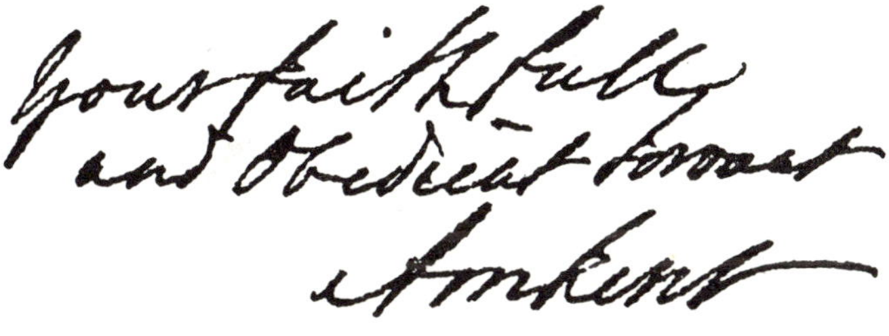

6.

7.

1. **John, Earl Ligonier.** 1680–1770. Field-Marshal. Commander-in-Chief of the Army, 1757.
2. **James Wolfe.** 1727–59. Major-General. Killed whilst leading his troops in the capture of Quebec. A rare and highly sought-after autograph.
3. **Robert, Lord Clive.** 1725–74. 'Clive of India'. The victor of Plassey. Soldier and administrator. A scarce autograph.
4. **Sir Eyre Coote.** 1726–83. The conqueror of Hyder Ali.
5. **Jeffrey, Lord Amherst.** 1717–97. Field-Marshal. Governor-General of British North America (1761) and Governor of Virginia (1763).
6. **Charles, 1st Marquis Cornwallis.** 1738–1805. British commander in the American Civil War, he capitulated at Yorktown in 1781. More successful as Governor-General and Commander-in-Chief in India.
7. **John Manners, Marquis of Granby.** 1721–70. Commander-in-Chief during the Seven Years War.

1.

2.

3.

4.

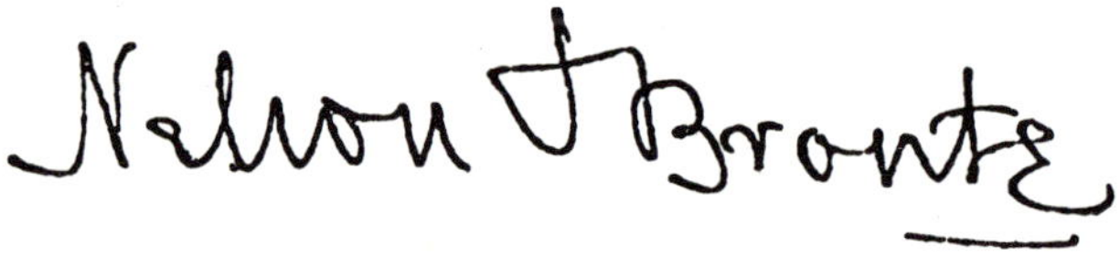

5.

6.

7.

8.

1. **Sir Peter Parker.** 1721–1811. Patron of Nelson.
2. **Sir Hyde Parker.** 1739–1807. It was his signal at Copenhagen which Nelson affected not to see by putting his telescope to his blind eye (1801). Both his father and his son were also called Hyde Parker and care should be taken not to confuse these.
3. **Richard, Earl Howe.** 1726–99. Victor of the 'Glorious First of June' (1794).
4. **Horatio, Viscount Nelson.** 1758–1805. Nelson's signature includes his Neapolitan title, Duke of Bronte, and is written with his left hand. Before the loss of his right arm (1797) his writing sloped the other way.
5. **Cuthbert, Lord Collingwood.** 1750–1810. Took command at Trafalgar after Nelson's death.
6. **Sir Thomas Masterman Hardy.** 1769–1839. Nelson's flag captain, to whom he addressed his dying words 'Kiss me [Kismet?], Hardy'.
7. **John Jervis, Earl of St Vincent.** 1735–1823.
8. **Adam, Viscount Duncan.** 1731–1804.

1.

2.

3.

4.

5.

6.

7.

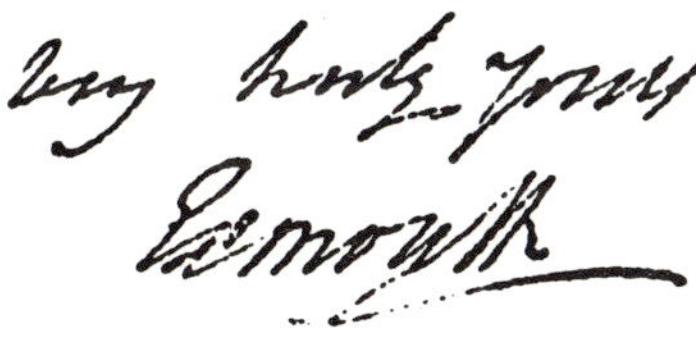

8.

1. **Sir Alexander Hood, Viscount Bridport.** 1727–1814.
2. **Alan, Lord Gardner.** 1742–1809.
3. **Samuel, Viscount Hood.** 1724–1816. Occupied Toulon and captured Corsica (1794).
4. **George K. Elphinstone, Viscount Keith.** 1746–1823.
5. **James, Baron Gambier.** 1756–1833. Defeated the French in the Basque (Aix) Roads (1809). Governor-General of Newfoundland, 1802–4. His signature is easily confused with that of his uncle, who bore the same name and was also an admiral (1723–89).
6. **Sir (W.) Sidney Smith.** 1764–1840. Remembered for his defence of Acre against the French, 1799.
7. **Edward Pellew, Viscount Exmouth.** 1757–1833.
8. **Thomas, Lord Cochrane, 10th Earl of Dundonald.** 1775–1860. In command of their respective navies, he fought successively for the independence of Chile, Peru and Greece. Signed 'Dundonald' from 1831.

1.

2.

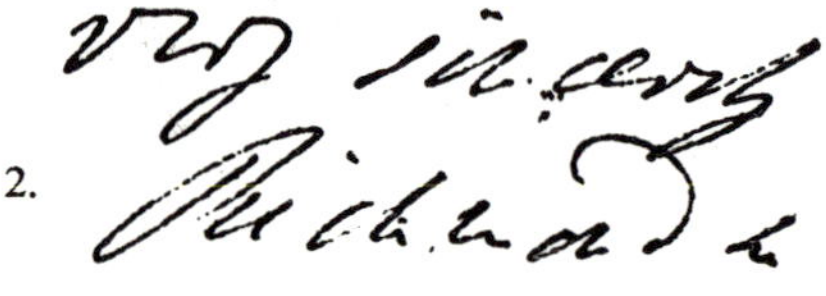

3.

4.

5.

6.

7.

8.

1. **Francis Rawdon-Hastings, Marquis Hastings, Earl of Moira.** 1754–1826. Soldier and adminstrator in India. Signed 'Moira' 1793–1817.
2. **Charles Lennox, 4th Duke of Richmond.** 1764–1819. Soldier and Governor-General of British North America (1818). Gave the famous 'Waterloo Ball' on the eve of Quatre Bras (1815).
3. **Rowland, Viscount Hill.** 1744–1833. Not to be confused with the founder of penny postage nor the theologian. See pages 74, 81.
4. **Sir John Moore.** 1761–1809. Killed at Coruña. The subject of Charles Wolfe's poem 'The Burial of Sir John Moore'.
5. **Sir Stapleton Cotton, Viscount Combermere.** 1773–1865.
6. **Sir Benjamin D'Urban.** 1777–1849. Durban, S. Africa, named after him.
7. **Henry, Viscount Hardinge.** 1785–1856. Succeeded Wellington as Commander-in-Chief.
8. **Arthur Wellesley, Duke of Wellington.** 1769–1852. Victor of Waterloo. Often signed with his initial only, as in the postscript beneath his full signature in the example above.

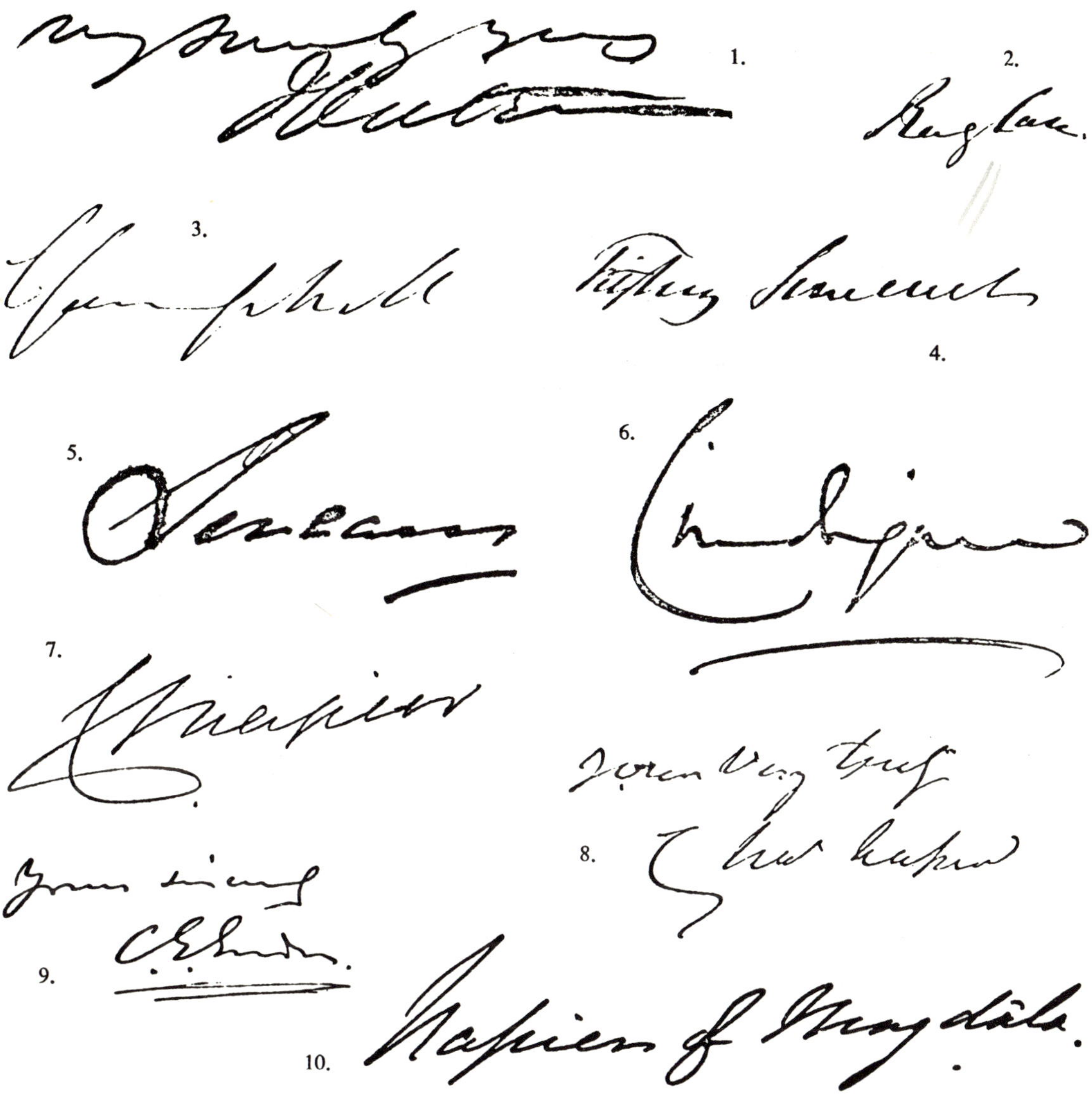

1. **Sir James Outram.** 1803–63. 'The Bayard of India'. Relieved and defended Lucknow.

2 and 4. **Fitzroy Somerset, Baron Raglan.** 1788–1855. Commander-in-Chief in the Crimea. Variant signatures.

3. **Colin Campbell, Lord Clyde.** 1792–1863. Held the 'thin red line' at Balaklava and effected the final relief of Lucknow. Signed 'Clyde' after 1858.

5. **George Bingham, Earl of Lucan.** 1800–88. As commander of the cavalry, gave the order for the Charge of the Light Brigade at Balaklava, 1854.

6. **James Brudenell, Earl of Cardigan.** 1797–1868. Led the Charge of the Light Brigade, Balaklava, 1854.

7. **General Sir Charles Napier.** 1782–1853. Conquered the Sind.

8. **Admiral Sir Charles Napier.** 1786–1860. Signature inserted here for comparison with that of the General, 7 above, with whom he is constantly confused.

9. **Charles George Gordon.** 1833–85. Known as 'Gordon of Khartoum' and 'Chinese Gordon'.

10. **Robert, Lord Napier (of Magdala).** 1810–90.

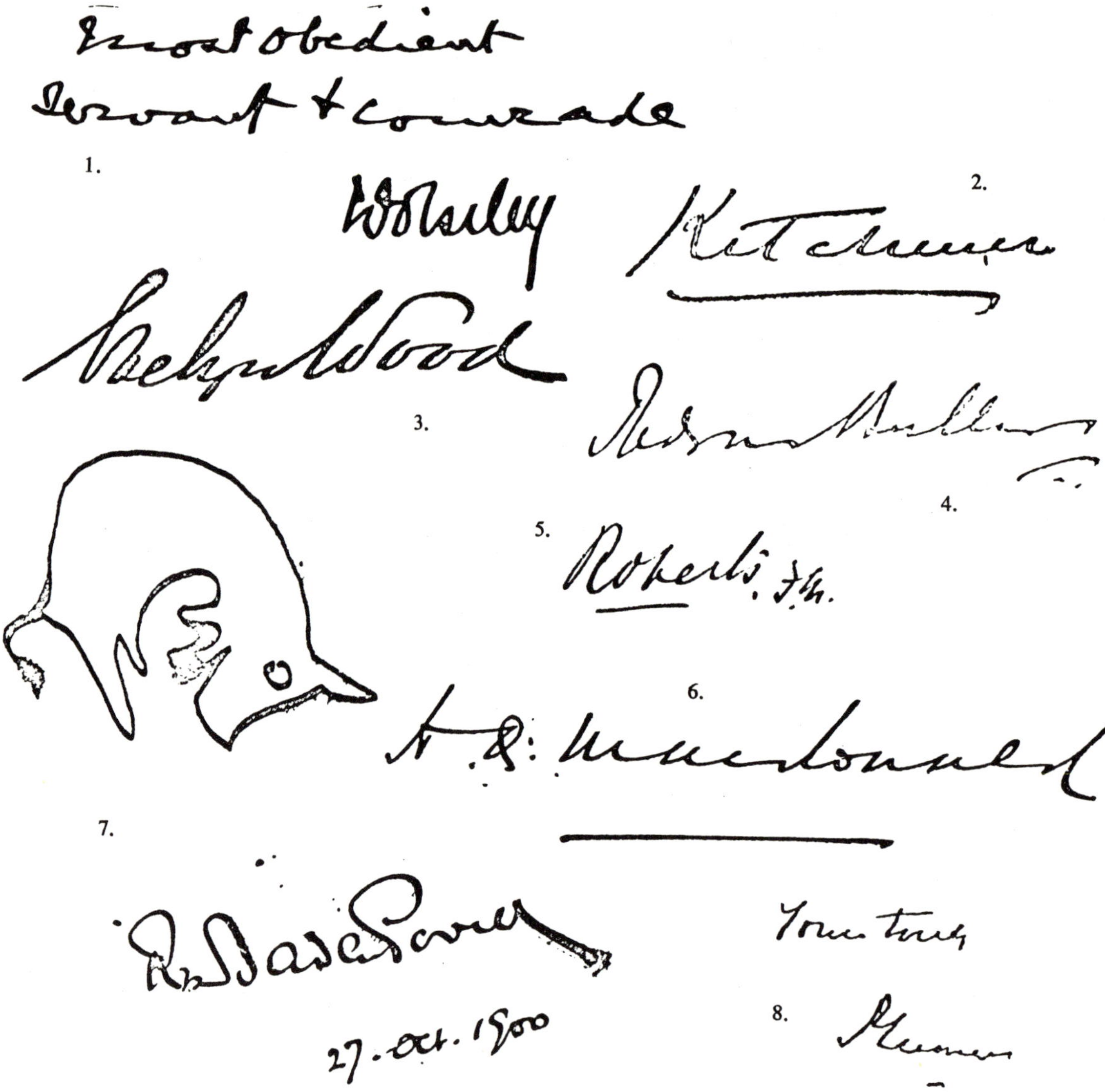

1. **Garnet, Viscount Wolseley.** 1833–1913. Field-Marshal. Commander-in-Chief of the British Army, 1900. His writing differs noticeably from his (upright) signature.
2. **Herbert, Earl Kitchener.** 1850–1916. Succeeded Roberts as Commander-in-Chief in S. Africa.
3. **Sir (H.) Evelyn Wood.** 1838–1919. Adjutant-General and Field-Marshal.
4. **Sir Redvers Buller.** 1839–1908. Commander-in-Chief in S. Africa, 1899–1900. Raised the Siege of Ladysmith.
5. **Frederick, Earl Roberts.** 1832–1914. Field-Marshal. Succeeded Buller as Commander-in-Chief in S. Africa and relieved Kimberley.
6. **Sir Hector MacDonald.** 1853–1903. 'Fighting Mac'.
7. **Robert, Lord Baden Powell.** 1857–1941. Defender of Mafeking and founder (1908) of the Boy Scouts. Baden Powell drew this pig, blindfold, five months after the relief of Mafeking.
8. **Herbert, Lord Plumer.** 1857–1932. Field-Marshal. Led the Matabele Relief Force to Mafeking. Subsequently Governor of Malta and High Commissioner of Palestine.

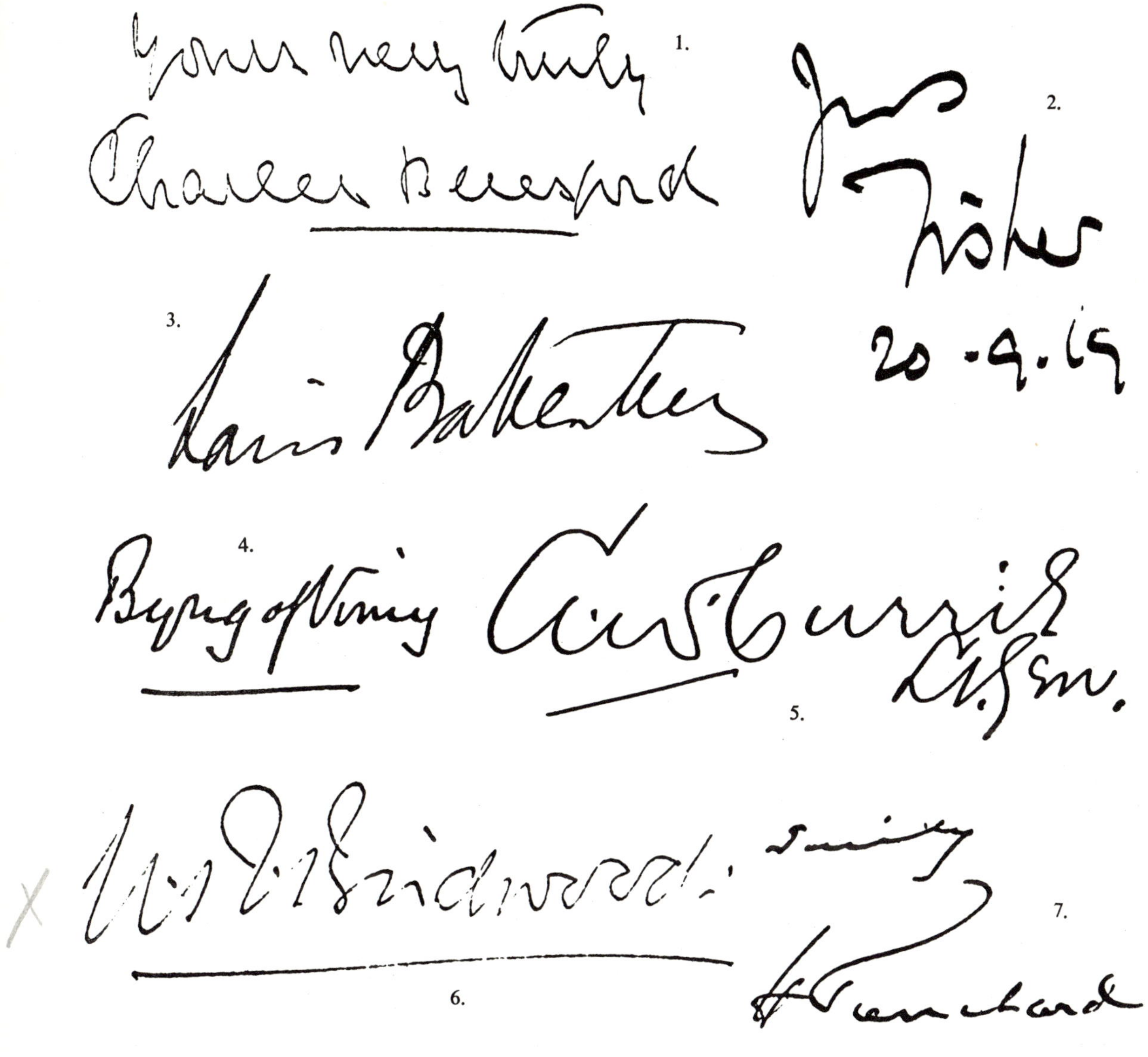

1. **Admiral Lord (Charles) Beresford.** 1846–1919.
2. **Admiral of the Fleet Lord (John) Fisher.** 1841–1920. First Sea Lord.
3. **Admiral of the Fleet Prince Louis of Battenberg, Marquis of Milford Haven.** 1854–1921. First Sea Lord, 1912–14. Father of Earl Mountbatten of Burma.
4. **Field-Marshal Viscount (Julian) Byng of Vimy.** 1862–1935. Commanded the Canadian Army Corps. Governor-General of Canada, 1921–6.
5. **General Sir Arthur W. Currie.** 1875–1933. Canadian soldier. Commanded the Canadians at Hill 70.
6. **Field-Marshal Lord (William) Birdwood.** 1865–1951. Commanded the Australian and New Zealand Army (ANZAC). Later became Master of Peterhouse, Cambridge.
7. **Marshal of the R.A.F. Viscount (Hugh) Trenchard.** 1873–1956. The 'Father of the R.A.F.', he was the first general officer to command the Royal Flying Corps in the field.

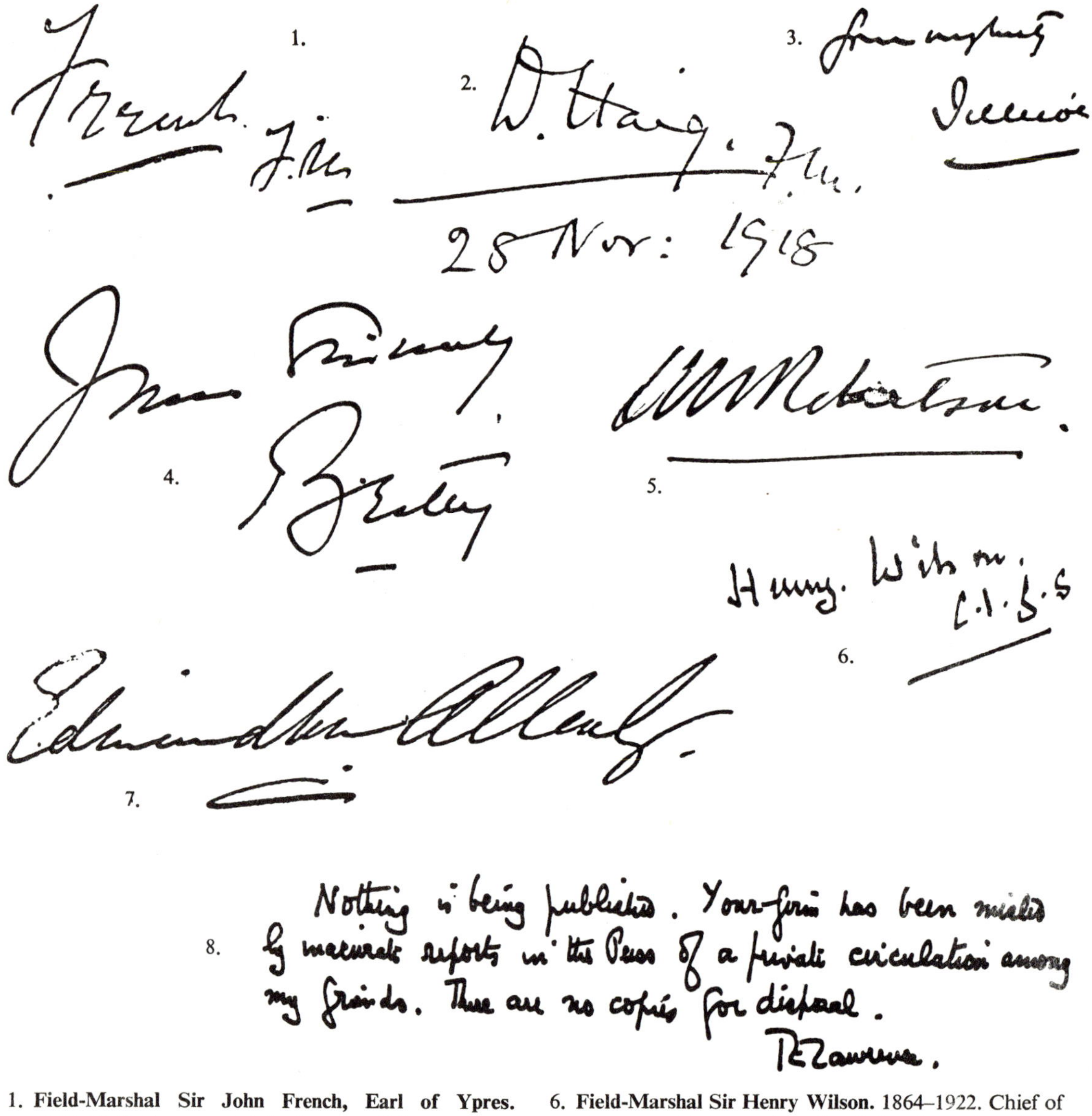

1. **Field-Marshal Sir John French, Earl of Ypres.** 1852–1925. Commanded the first expeditionary force.
2. **Field-Marshal Earl (Douglas) Haig.** 1861–1928. Commanded the British Forces in France.
3. **Admiral of the Fleet Earl (John R.) Jellicoe.** 1859–1935. Commander at Jutland. Governor-General of New Zealand, 1920–4.
4. **Admiral of the Fleet Earl (David) Beatty.** 1871–1936. Commanded the Grand Fleet in succession to Jellicoe.
5. **Field-Marshal Sir William Robertson.** 1860–1933. Chief of the Imperial General Staff. The first private soldier to rise to Field-Marshal.
6. **Field-Marshal Sir Henry Wilson.** 1864–1922. Chief of the Imperial General Staff, 1918. Assassinated by the Irish Sinn Fein.
7. **Field-Marshal Viscount (Edmund) Allenby.** 1861–1936. Captured Jerusalem and Damascus from the Turks.
8. **Colonel Thomas E. Lawrence.** 1888–1935. 'Lawrence of Arabia'. See discussion of his autograph on page 32.

1.

2.

3.

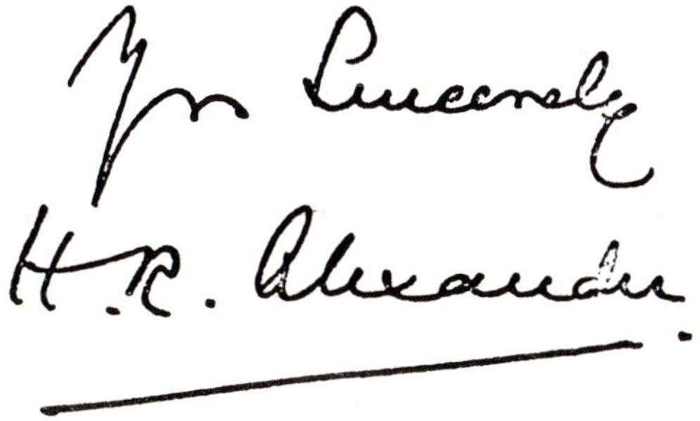

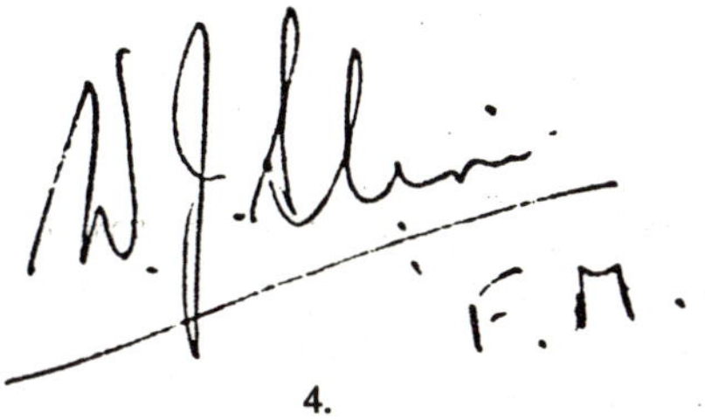

4.

5.

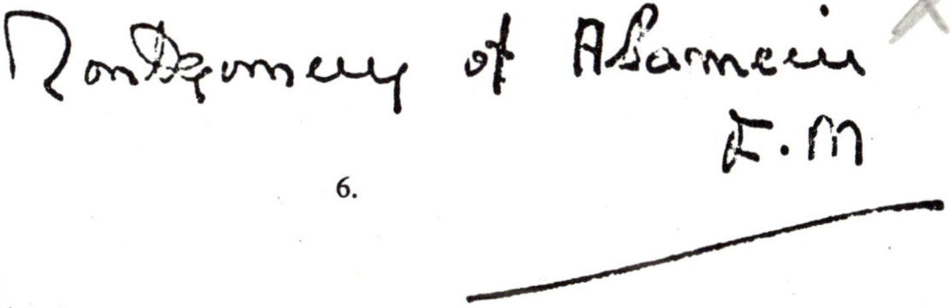

6.

7.

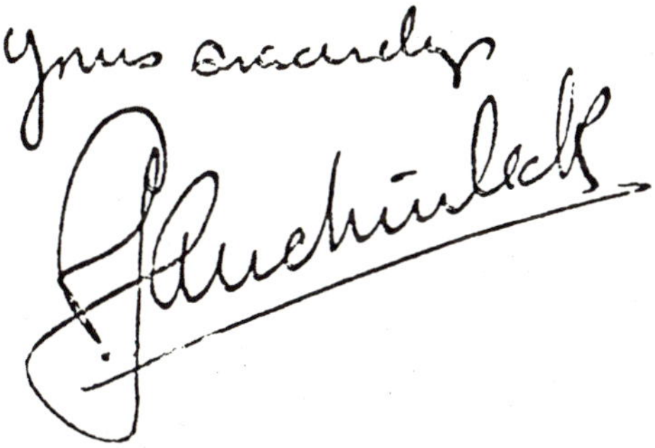

8.

1. **Field-Marshal Viscount Gort (John Vereker).** 1886–1946. Commanded the first expeditionary force. Subsequently Governor of Gibraltar and Malta.
2. **Field-Marshal Viscount Alanbrooke.** 1883–1963. Chief of the Imperial General Staff.
3. **Field-Marshal Earl (Harold R.) Alexander.** 1891–1969. Allied Commander-in-Chief in Italy. Governor-General of Canada, 1946–52. He signed 'Alexander of Tunis' from 1946.
4. **Field-Marshal Viscount (William) Slim.** 1891– . Commanded the 14th ('Forgotten') Army in Burma. Governor-General of Australia, 1953.
5. **Field-Marshal Earl (Archibald) Wavell.** 1883–1950. Supreme Commander in India and Burma. Viceroy of India.
6. **Field-Marshal Viscount (Bernard L.) Montgomery of Alamein.** 1887– . 'Monty'. Commanded the 8th Army and the Allied Armies in Northern France.
7. **Field-Marshal Sir Claude Auchinleck.** 1884– . 'The Auk'. Commander-in-Chief in India.
8. **Field-Marshal Sir Thomas A. Blamey.** 1884–1951. The first Australian Field-Marshal. Received the Japanese surrender in 1945.

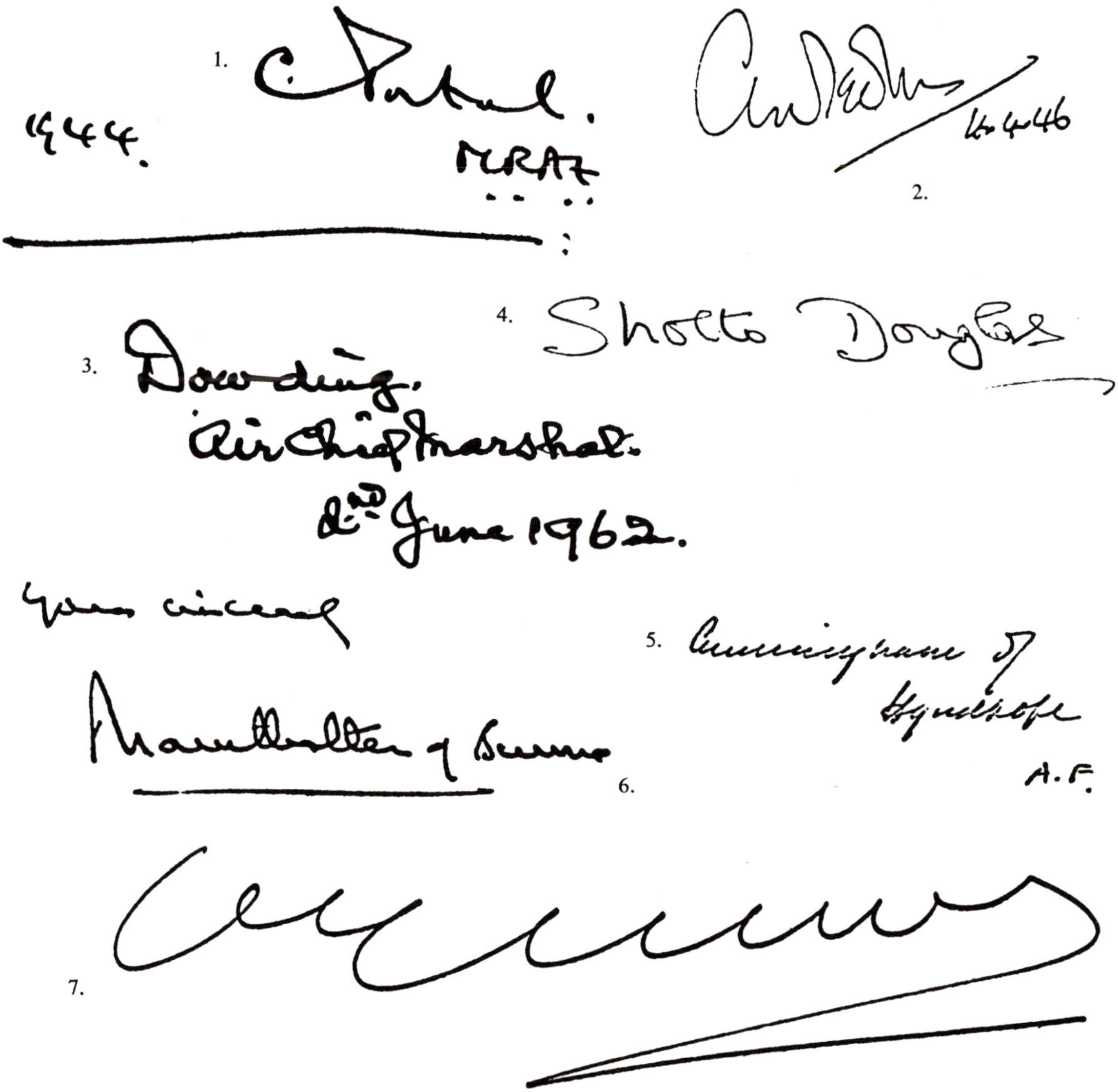

1. **Marshal of the R.A.F. Viscount (Charles F. A.) Portal.** 1893– . Chief of Air Staff.
2. **Marshal of the R.A.F. Lord (Arthur W.) Tedder.** 1890–1967. Deputy Supreme Commander to General Eisenhower.
3. **Air Chief Marshal Lord (Hugh C. T.) Dowding.** 1882–1970. As head of Fighter Command he was the architect of victory in the Battle of Britain, Aug.–Sept. 1940.
4. **Marshal of the R.A.F. Lord (Sholto) Douglas.** 1893–1969. Commander-in-Chief, Fighter and Coastal Commands.
5. **Admiral of the Fleet Viscount (Andrew) Cunningham (of Hyndhope)** 1883–1963. First Sea Lord.
6. **Admiral of the Fleet Earl (Louis) Mountbatten of Burma.** 1900– . Supreme Commander, S.E. Asia. After the war, last Viceroy of India and Chief of the Naval and Defence Staffs.
7. **Lieutenant-General Sir John Bagot Glubb.** 1897– . 'Glubb Pasha'. Commander of the Arab Legion; the 'second Lawrence of Arabia'.

PIONEERS AND BENEFACTORS: PHILANTHROPISTS AND REFORMERS (1)

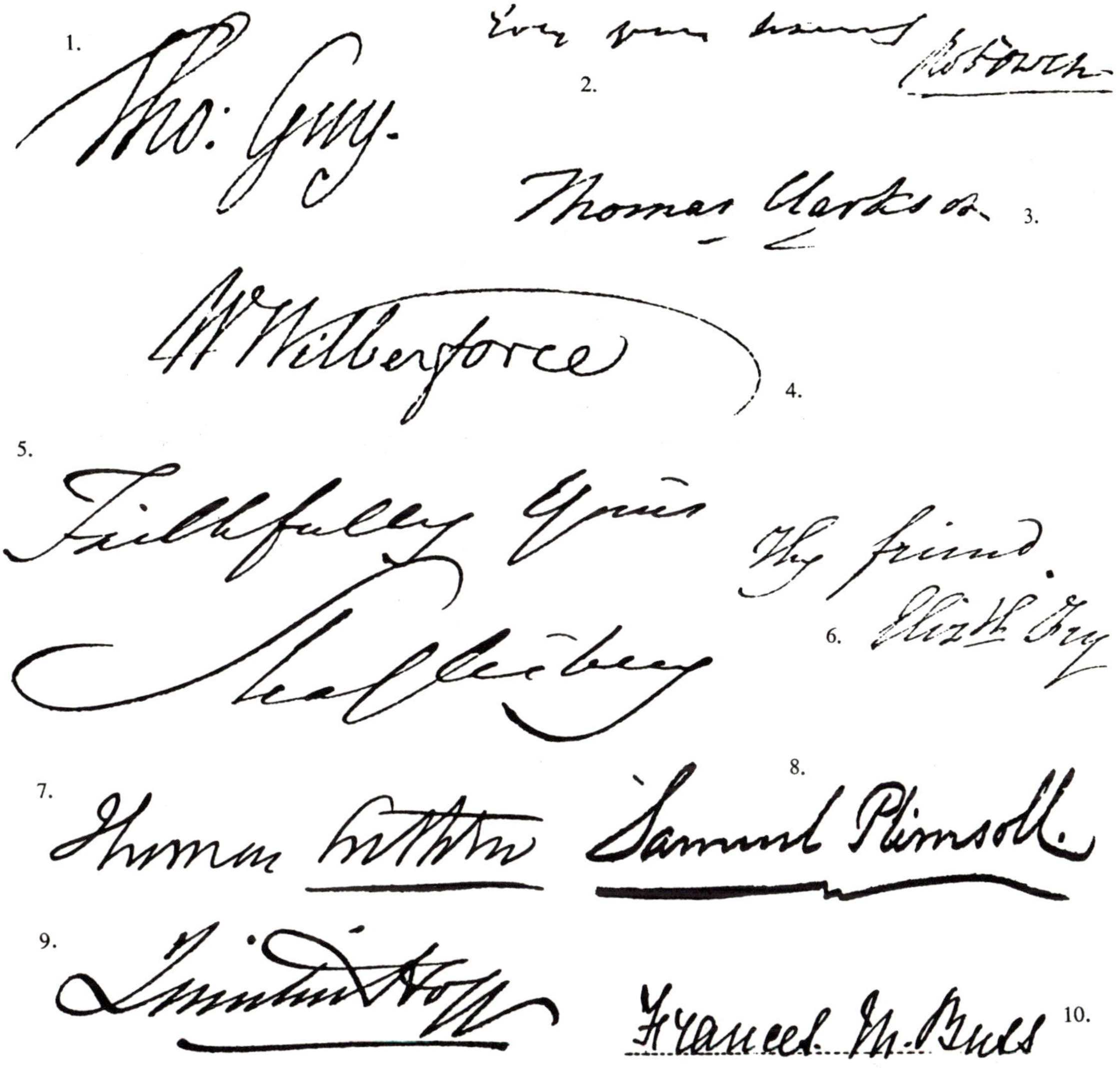

1. **Thomas Guy.** 1644–1724. Philanthropist. Founded Guy's Hospital.
2. **Robert Owen.** 1771–1858. Social reformer. Pioneer of co-operatives. Signed 'Rob' or 'Robert' equally frequently.
3. **Thomas Clarkson.** 1760–1846. Slave Trade abolitionist.
4. **William Wilberforce.** 1759–1833. With Clarkson, 3 above, the leading Slave Trade abolitionist.
5. **Anthony Ashley Cooper, 7th Earl of Shaftesbury.** 1801–85. Factory and social reformer (Shaftesbury Homes).
6. **Elizabeth Fry.** 1780–1845. Celebrated Quaker prison reformer.
7. **Thomas Guthrie.** 1803–73. Philanthropist. 'The Apostle of Ragged Schools'.
8. **Samuel Plimsoll.** 1824–98. 'The Sailor's Friend'. Remembered for his instigation of the safety line on ships, the Plimsoll line.
9. **Quintin Hogg.** 1845–1903. Founder of the Polytechnic.
10. **Frances M. Buss.** 1827–94. Schoolmistress and pioneer of higher education for women. Immortalized in the rhyme 'Miss Buss and Miss Beale/Cupid's darts do not feel . . .'.

PIONEERS AND BENEFACTORS: PHILANTHROPISTS AND REFORMERS (2)

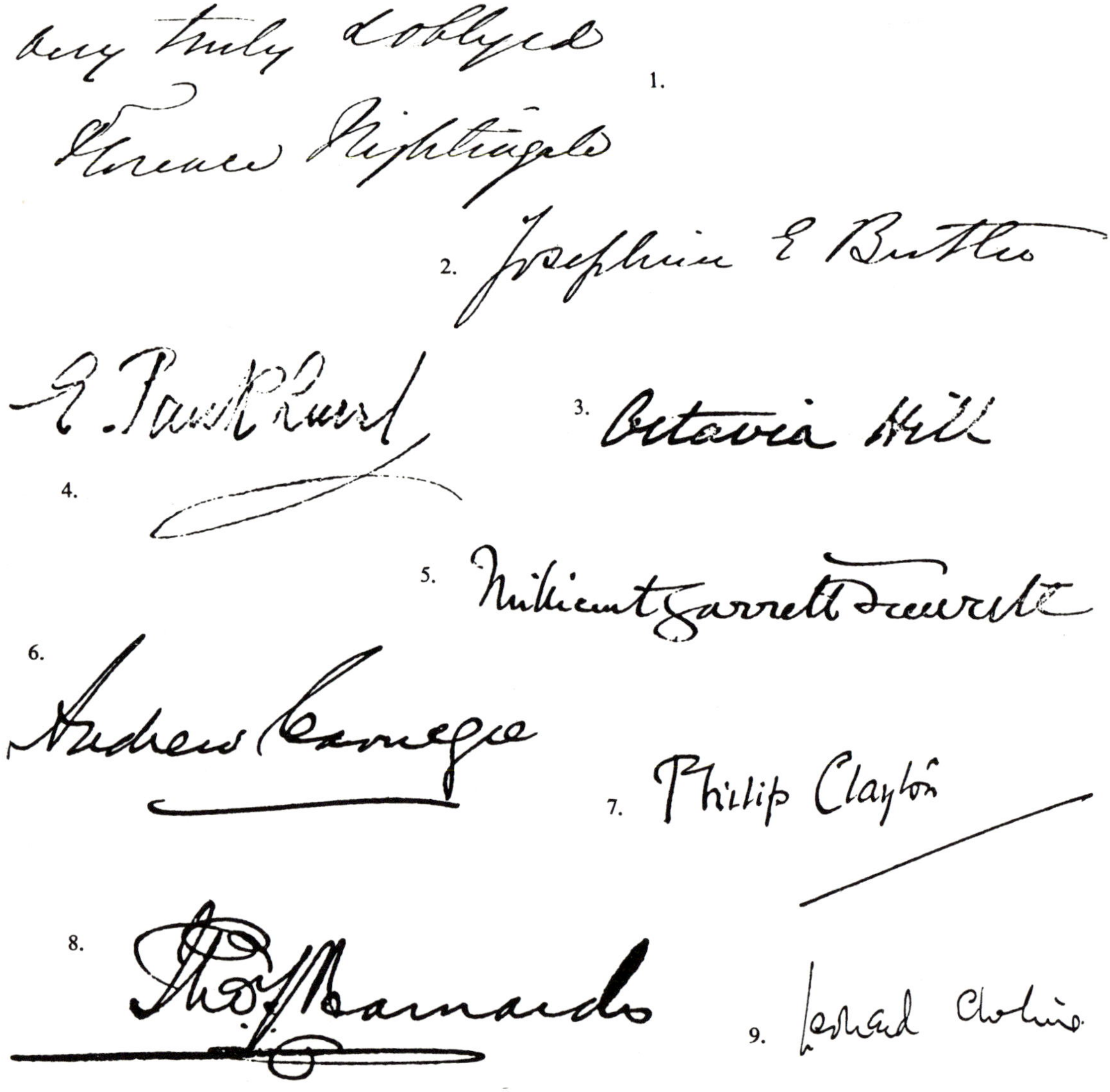

1. **Florence Nightingale.** 1820–1910. Hospital reformer. Florence Nightingale's handwriting in pencil, a medium she frequently employed, was much more upright than this ink example, but her signature can always be identified by the characteristic capital 'F'.
2. **Josephine E. Butler.** 1828–1906. Social reformer and feminist.
3. **Octavia Hill.** 1838–1912. Housing reformer and pioneer of slum clearance.
4. **Emmeline Pankhurst.** 1857–1928. Leader of the women's suffrage movement.
5. **Dame Millicent Garrett Fawcett.** 1847–1929. A leading suffragette. Campaigned for higher education for women.
6. **Andrew Carnegie.** 1835–1918. Scottish millionaire philanthropist. Endowed libraries and universities throughout Britain and the U.S.
7. **Rev. Philip T. B. Clayton.** 1885– . 'Tubby' Clayton, founder of 'Toc H'.
8. **Dr Thomas J. Barnardo.** 1845–1905. Founder of the Barnardo Homes for destitute children.
9. **Group Captain G. Leonard Cheshire, V.C.** 1917– . War hero and founder of the Cheshire Homes for the sick.

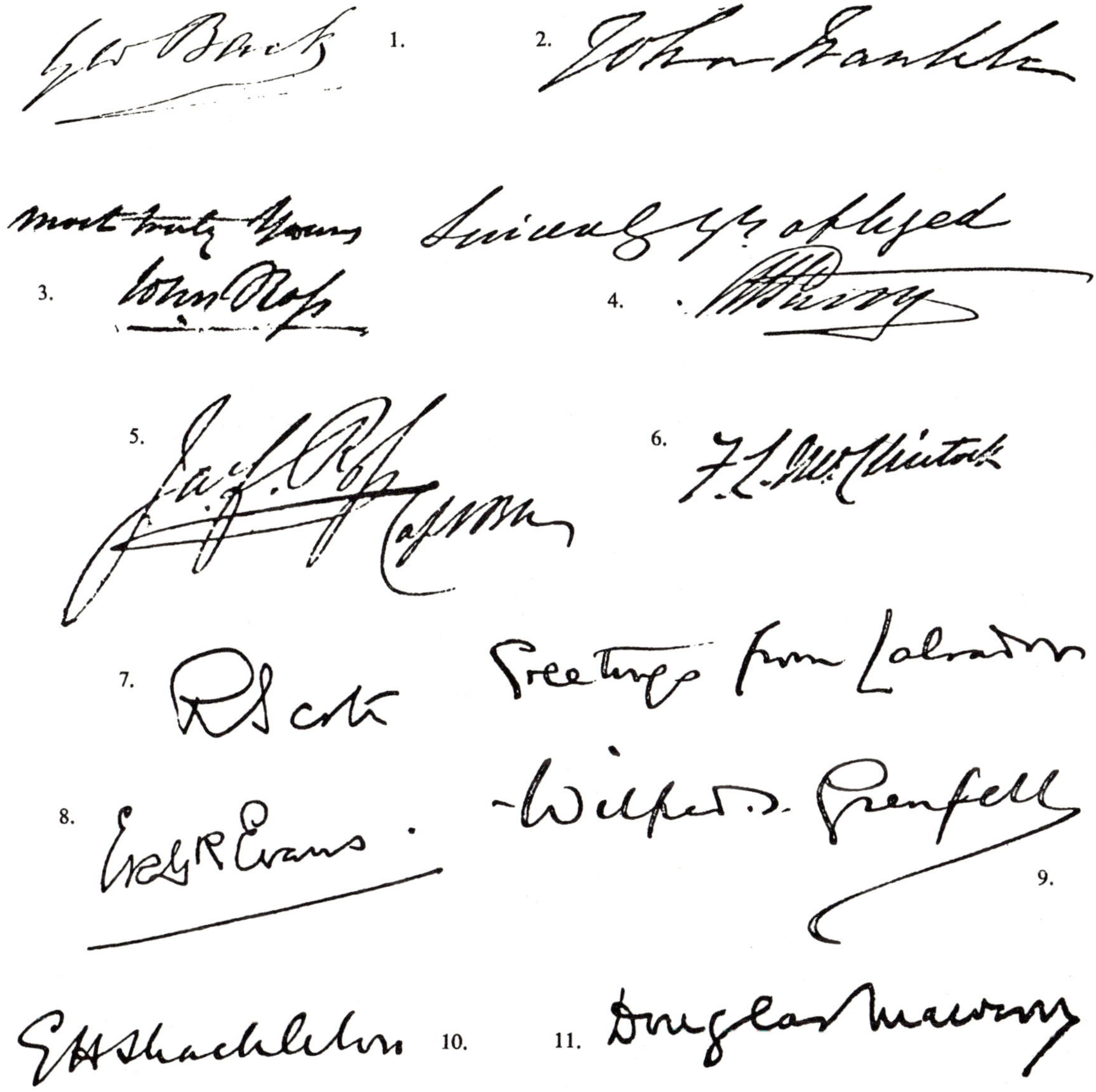

1. **Admiral Sir George Back.** 1796–1878. Arctic navigator.
2. **Sir John Franklin.** 1786–1847. Arctic explorer, lost in search of the North-West Passage.
3. **Admiral Sir John Ross.** 1777–1856. Arctic explorer.
4. **Admiral Sir William E. Parry.** 1790–1855. Commanded five Arctic expeditions.
5. **Admiral Sir James Clark Ross.** 1800–62. Arctic explorer; nephew of Sir John, 3 above. Discovered the North magnetic pole.
6. **Admiral Sir F. Leopold McClintock.** 1819–1907. Arctic navigator.
7. **Captain Robert F. Scott.** 1868–1912. 'Scott of the Antarctic.' Perished whilst returning from the South Pole.
8. **Admiral Edward R. G. R. Evans, Lord Mountevans.** 1881–1957. 'Evans of the Broke', served in the *Discovery* Antarctic expedition, 1900–4.
9. **Sir Wilfred T. Grenfell.** 1865–1940. Medical missionary in Labrador.
10. **Sir Ernest H. Shackleton.** 1874–1922. An intrepid Antarctic explorer, he died there on his third expedition.
11. **Sir Douglas Mawson.** 1882–1958. Led Australasian expeditions to the Antarctic.

PIONEERS AND BENEFACTORS: EXPLORERS IN AFRICA AND ELSEWHERE

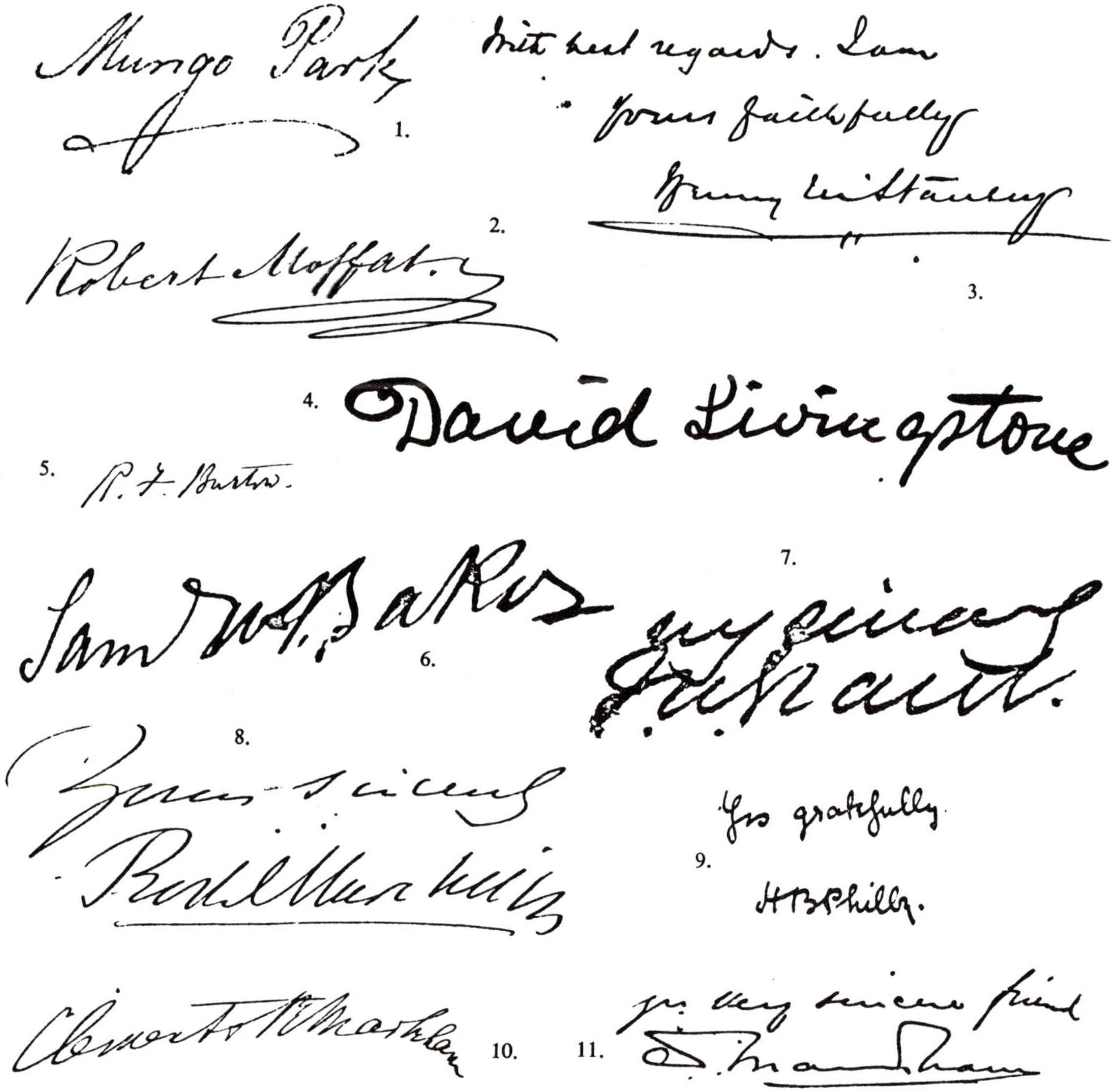

1. **Mungo Park.** 1771–1806. Explored the Niger. A scarce signature.
2. **Robert Moffat.** 1795–1883. Missionary-explorer in Bechuanaland. Livingstone's father-in-law.
3. **Sir Henry M. Stanley.** 1841–1904. Explorer in Africa who 'found' Livingstone and established the Congo Free State.
4. **David Livingstone.** 1813–73. Discoverer of the Victoria Falls, Lake Nyasa, etc.
5. **Sir Richard F. Burton.** 1821–90. Explorer in Africa. Translated the *Arabian Nights*.
6. **Sir Samuel W. Baker.** 1821–93. Explored the sources of the Nile.
7. **James Augustus Grant.** 1827–92. Explored the sources of the Nile.
8. **Sir Roderick I. Murchison.** 1792–1871. Explorer and geologist.
9. **H. St John B. Philby.** 1885–1960. Explorer in Arabia. An early example of his signature.
10. **Sir Clements R. Markham.** 1830–1916. Geographer and explorer in Peru, Abyssinia, etc.
11. **Admiral Sir Albert H. Markham.** 1841–1918. Arctic explorer. Brother and biographer of Sir C. Markham, 10 above.

1. **Samuel Franklin Cody.** 1862–1913. His flight of 1,390 feet at Farnborough, 16th October 1908, is accepted as the first in Britain. A Texan, naturalized British.
2. **Sir Keith (M.) Smith.** 1890–1955. An Australian, he made the first Britain–Australia flight, with his brother, in 1919.
3. **Claude Grahame-White.** 1879–1959. Held the first British certificate of proficiency in aviation and ran Britain's first flying school.
4. **J. T. C. Moore, Lord Brabazon of Tara.** 1884–1964. Held the first British flying licence.
5. **Amy Johnson.** 1903–41. Her signature is often found in her married name, Mollison.
6. **Sir Alan J. Cobham.** 1894– . Celebrated for his 'flying circus'.
7. **Sir Geoffrey de Havilland.** 1882–1965. Pioneer aircraft designer and aviator.
8. **Sir Alliott Verdon-Roe.** 1877–1958. Pioneer aircraft designer.
9. **Sir Frederick Handley Page.** 1885–1962. Pioneer aircraft designer.
10. **Group Captain John Cunningham.** 1917– . War-time flying 'ace'. Now a leading test pilot.

1. **Frederick G. Burnaby.** 1842–85. Soldier and pioneer balloonist, famed for his winter ride across the Russian steppes.
2. **Edward Whymper.** 1840–1911. Mountaineer, artist and explorer. First to climb Matterhorn.
3. **(H. C.) John, Lord Hunt.** 1910– . Leader of the first successful Everest expedition, 1953.
4. **Tenzing Norkay.** 1914– . Nepalese (Sherpa) mountaineer. First, with Hillary, 5 below, to climb Everest.
5. **Sir Edmund Hillary.** 1919– . New Zealand mountaineer and Antarctic explorer. With Tenzing, 4 above, first to climb Everest.
6. **Odette M. C. Hallowes, G.C.** 1912– . 'Odette', the heroic British agent with the French Resistance in World War II. Signed above in her second married surname.
7. **Douglas R. S. Bader.** 1910– . Heroic legless fighter pilot of World War II..
8. **Sir Francis Chichester.** 1901– . Pioneer aviator and yachtsman. Achieved the first true circumnavigation of the world by a single-handed yacht rounding the three Capes, 1966–7.

1.

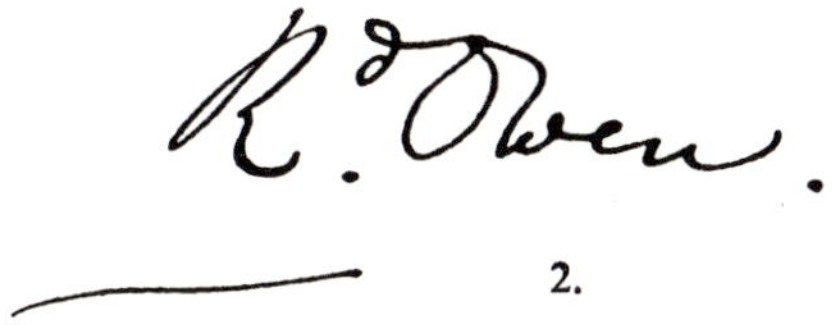

2.

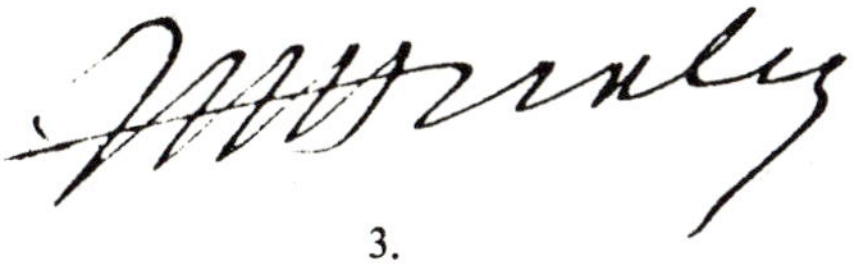

3.

4.

5.

6.

7.

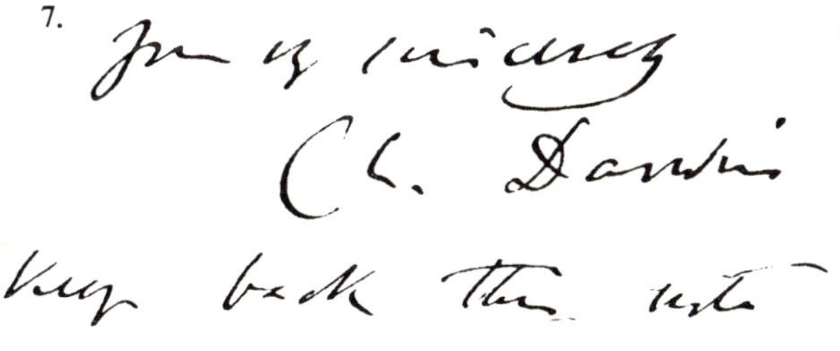

8.

1. **Sir Joseph Banks.** 1744–1820. Botanist. He accompanied Captain Cook's expedition round the world and was President of the Royal Society for 41 years.
2. **Sir Richard Owen.** 1804–92. Zoologist and comparative anatomist.
3. **Thomas (H.) Huxley.** 1825–95. One of the greatest of all British biologists. His signature is not easily identifiable.
4. **Sir William Henry Flower.** 1831–99. Natural History Director of the British Museum.
5. **Sir Francis Galton.** 1822–1911. Anthropologist and explorer. Founded the science of eugenics and pioneered fingerprint identification.
6. **Sir Joseph Dalton Hooker.** 1817–1911. Botanist. Succeeded his father, Sir William, as Director at Kew.
7. **Charles R. Darwin.** 1809–82. Celebrated for his *Origin of Species*. Darwin's irregular autograph is valuable and highly sought-after.
8. **Edward Forbes.** 1815–54. Manx naturalist and geologist. Professor of Natural History at Edinburgh.

SCIENTISTS AND SCHOLARS: SEVENTEENTH- TO NINETEENTH-CENTURY SURGEONS AND PHYSICIANS

1.

2.

4.

3.

5.

6.

7.

8.

1. **Sir Edmund King.** 1629–1709. Medical researcher and writer. Physician to Charles II.
2. **John Abernethy.** 1764–1831. One of the most distinguished surgeons in British history.
3. **Sir Astley Cooper.** 1768–1841. Surgeon and anatomist. Although this example is otherwise typical, Astley Cooper often used a rounded capital 'A'.
4. **Sir Charles Bell.** 1774–1842. Scottish anatomist and surgeon. A major authority on the nervous system.
5. **Robert Liston.** 1794–1847. Surgeon, famous for the 'Liston' splint. Note the difference in the height of his signature to that of his handwriting.
6. **Sir Benjamin C. Brodie.** 1783–1862. Surgeon. Not to be confused with his son, who discovered graphitic acid.
7. **Sir William Jenner.** 1815–98. Physician, the first to differentiate between typhus and typhoid.
8. **Sir James Young Simpson.** 1811–70. Scottish obstetrician and pioneer gynaecologist. Discoverer of the anaesthetic properties of chloroform (1847).

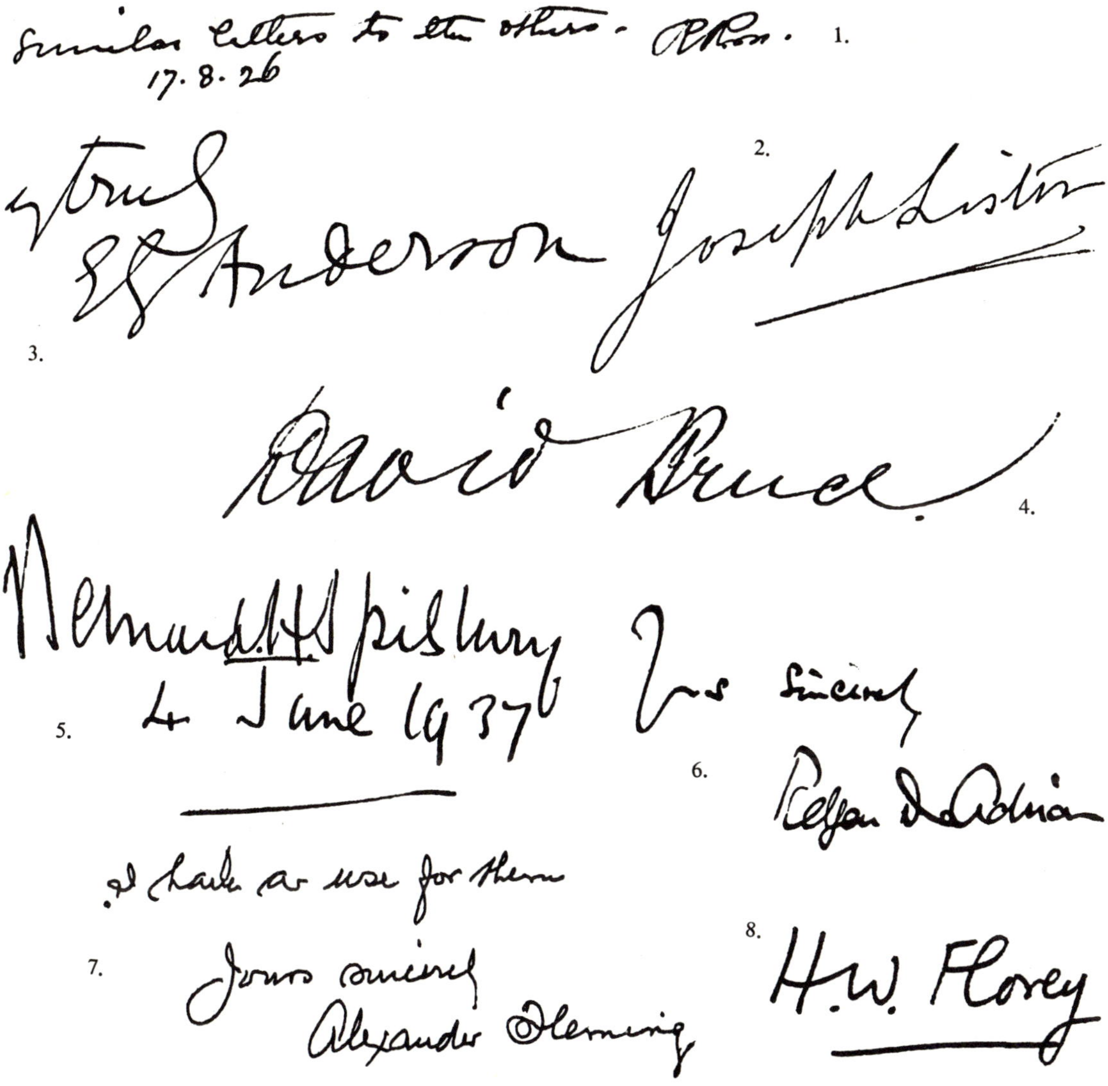

1. **Sir Ronald Ross.** 1857–1932. Discovered the mosquito cycle in malaria. Won 1902 Nobel Prize.
2. **Lord (Joseph) Lister.** 1827–1912. Pioneered antiseptic surgery.
3. **Elizabeth Garrett Anderson.** 1836–1917. One of the first woman doctors, she was also the first woman mayor (of Aldeburgh, 1908) in Britain.
4. **Sir David Bruce.** 1855–1931. Australian-born military physician. Discovered that the carrier of sleeping sickness is the tsetse fly.
5. **Sir Bernard H. Spilsbury.** 1877–1947. As Home Office pathologist and an unrivalled expert in forensic medicine, he gave evidence at many famous murder trials.
6. **Lord (Edgar D.) Adrian.** 1889– . Physiologist and Master of Trinity, Cambridge. Won 1932 Nobel Prize.
7. **Sir Alexander Fleming.** 1881–1955. Discovered penicillin. Won 1945 Nobel Prize.
8. **Lord (Howard W.) Florey.** 1898–1968. Australian pathologist. Developed penicillin, for which he shared the 1945 Nobel Prize with Fleming.

SCIENTISTS AND SCHOLARS: MATHEMATICIANS, PHILOSOPHERS AND LOGICIANS

1.

2.

3.
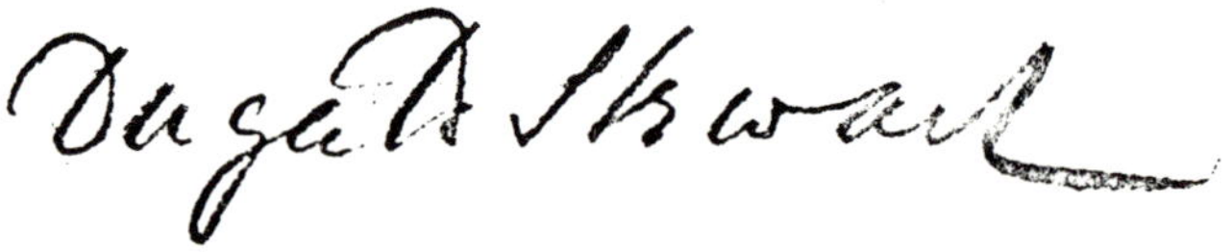

4.
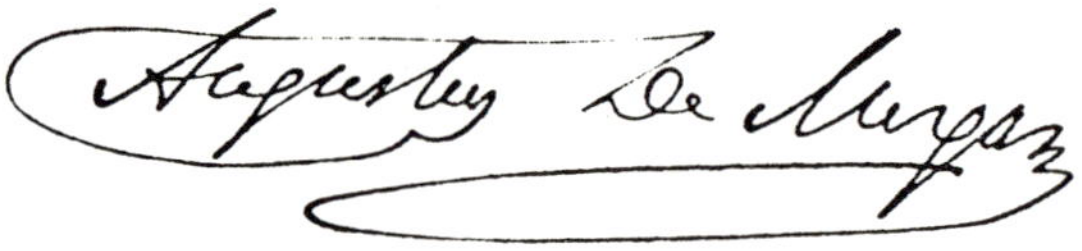

5.

7.
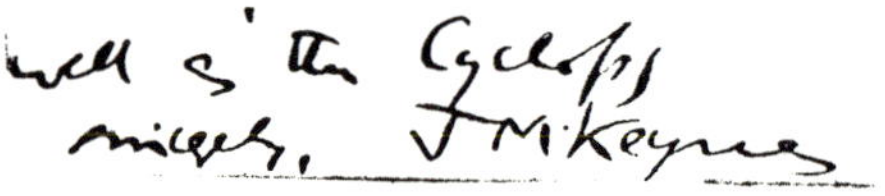

6.
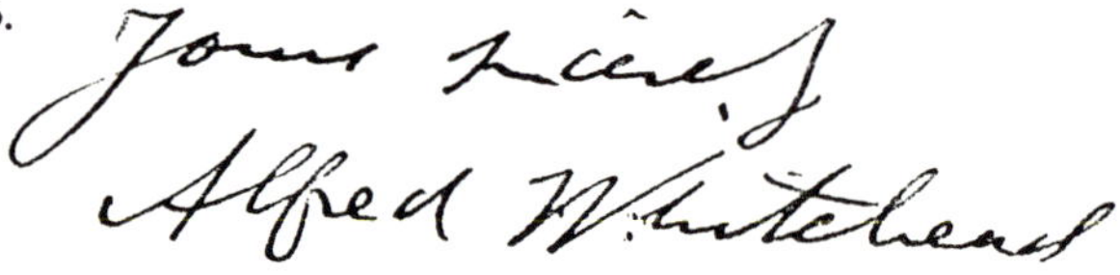

8.

9.
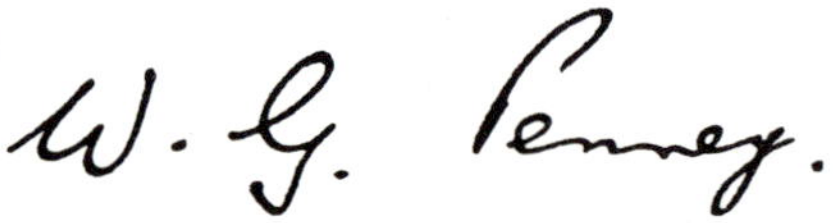

1. **Sir Isaac Newton.** 1642–1727. Established the law of gravitation. An example of his flowing hand. Newton's signature also took a very different form, tall and more upright with the capital letters totally unlike those shown above.
2. **Sir John Leslie.** 1766–1832. Natural philosopher and mathematician.
3. **Dugald Stewart.** 1753–1828. Philosopher and mathematician.
4. **Augustus de Morgan.** 1806–71. Mathematician and logician.
5. **William Thomson, Lord Kelvin.** 1824–1907. Physicist, mathematician and inventor.
6. **Alfred North Whitehead.** 1861–1947. A professor of mathematics in London, he also taught philosophy at Harvard.
7. **John Maynard, Lord Keynes.** 1883–1946. Economist and logician.
8. **Bertrand (A. W.), 3rd Earl Russell.** 1872–1970. Equally renowned as philosopher and mathematician, he has been called 'the greatest logician since Aristotle'. Won 1950 Nobel Prize for Literature.
9. **William (G.), Lord Penney.** 1909– . Physicist and leading British atomic weapons research scientist.

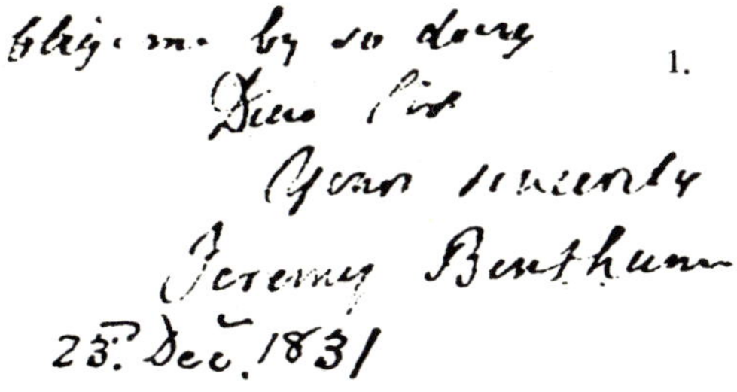
1.

2.

3.
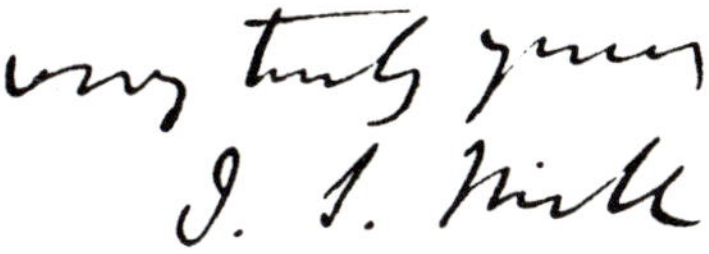

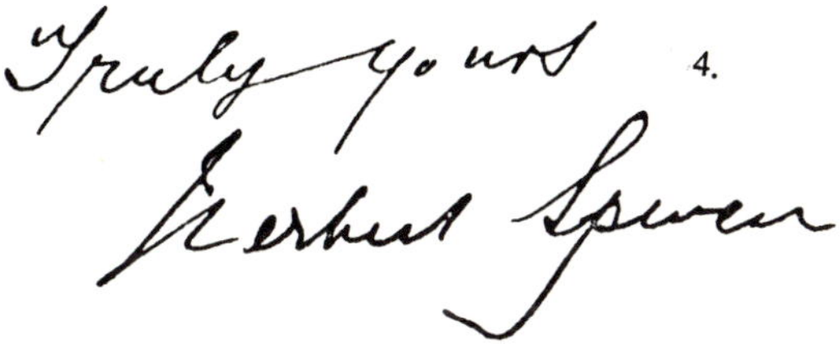
4.

5.

6.

7.
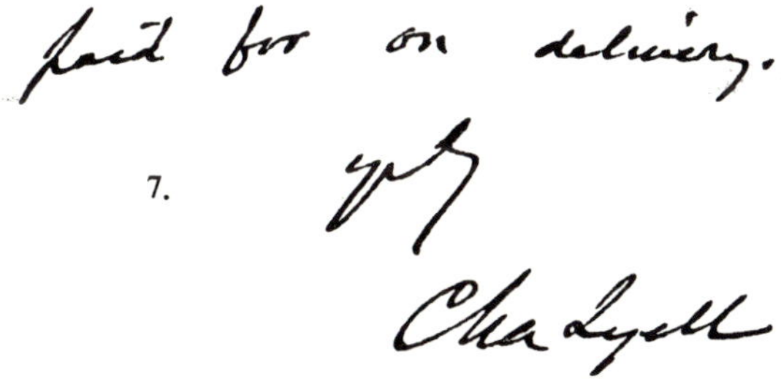

8.
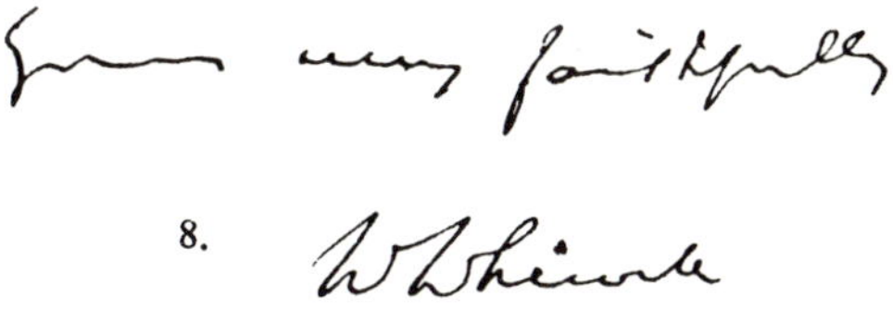

1. **Jeremy Bentham.** 1748–1832. Jurist and philosopher. The exponent of Utilitarian ethics. His skeleton, dressed in his own clothes, is preserved at University College, London, which he founded.
2. **Sir John Bowring.** 1792–1872. Scholar, diplomat and linguist (with a knowledge of over 200 languages). Associate of Bentham.
3. **John Stuart Mill.** 1806–73. Philosopher and political economist.
4. **Herbert Spencer.** 1820–1903. Philosopher.
5. **Sir James Mackintosh.** 1765–1832. Scottish philosopher, judge and writer.
6. **John Playfair.** 1748–1819. Professor of Natural Philosophy at Edinburgh, he was also a mathematician and geologist.
7. **Sir Charles Lyell.** 1797–1875. Geologist. As well as numerous works on geology, he wrote two books on America.
8. **William Whewell.** 1794–1866. Mineralogist, moral theologist and classical scholar. Master of Trinity, Cambridge.

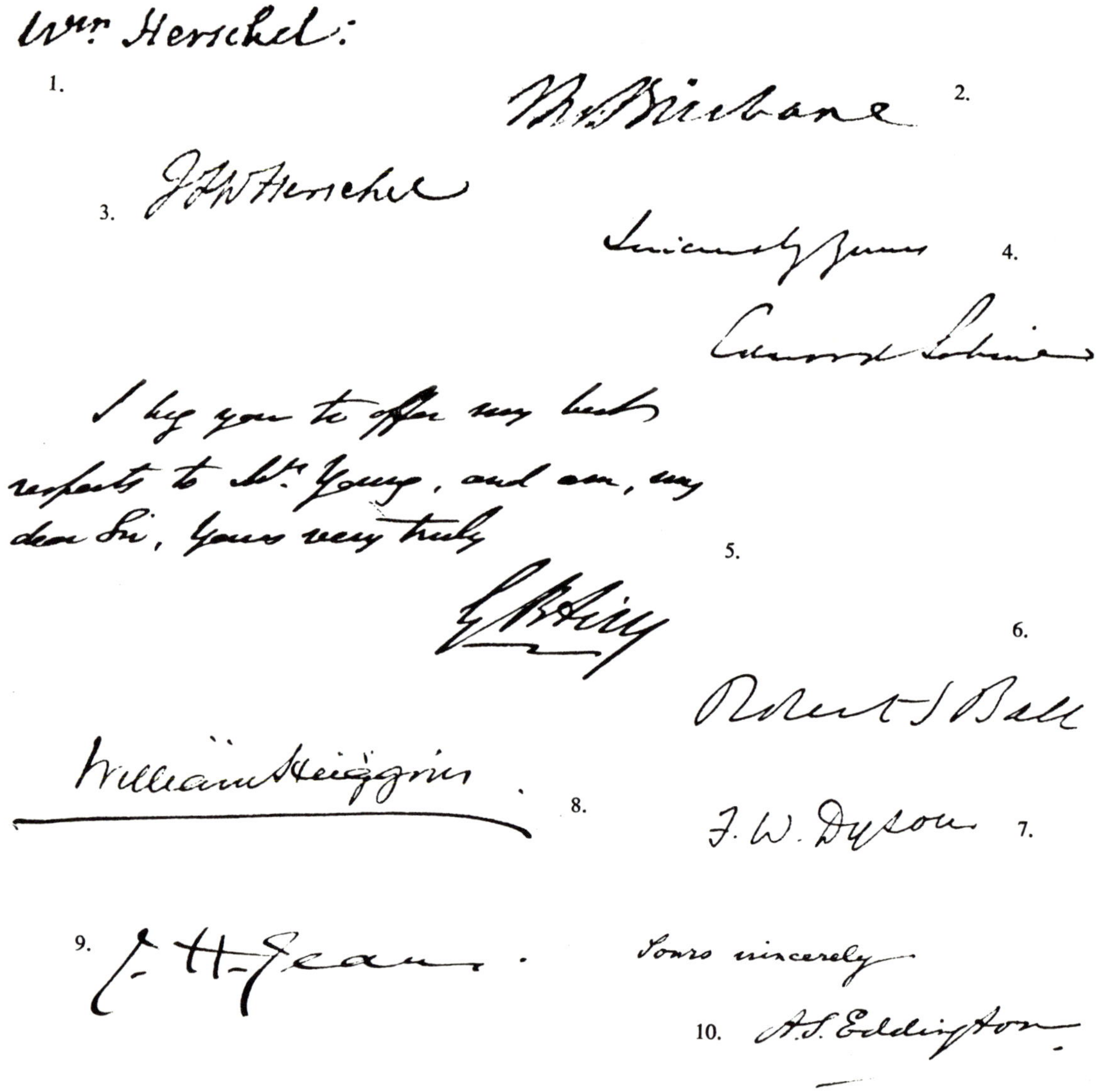

1. **Sir F. William Herschel.** 1738–1822. Astronomer to George III. Discovered Uranus and the period of rotation of Saturn.
2. **Sir Thomas M. Brisbane.** 1773–1860. Governor of New South Wales, he catalogued, in Australia, 7,385 stars. Brisbane, Queensland, named after him.
3. **Sir John F. W. Herschel.** 1792–1871. Son of William, 1 above.
4. **Sir Edward Sabine.** 1788–1883. Astronomer with Ross and Parry in the Arctic. Known for his researches on terrestrial magnetism.
5. **Sir George B. Airy.** 1801–92. Astronomer Royal for 45 years.
6. **Sir Robert S. Ball.** 1840–1913. Royal Astronomer for Ireland.
7. **Sir Frank W. Dyson.** 1868–1939. Astronomer Royal, 1910–33.
8. **Sir William Huggins.** 1824–1910. Co-inventor of the stellar spectroscope, he determined the velocity of stars.
9. **Sir James H. Jeans.** 1877–1946. Also a distinguished mathematical physicist.
10. **Sir Arthur S. Eddington.** 1882–1944. Director of the observatory at Cambridge.

1.

2.
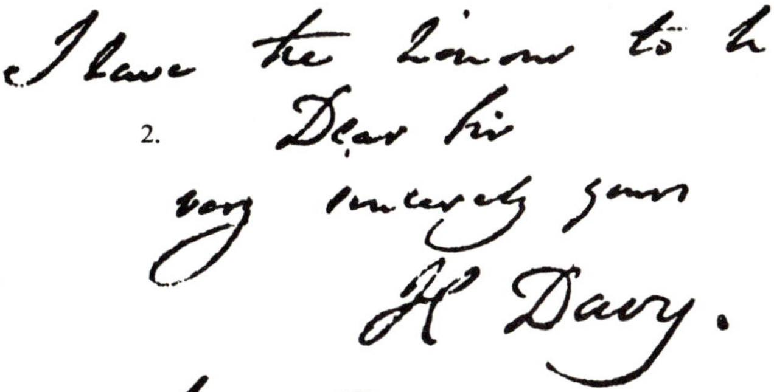

3.
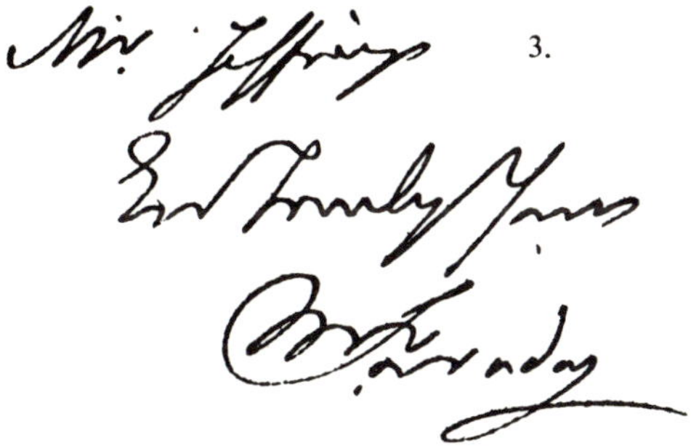

4.

6.

5.

7.
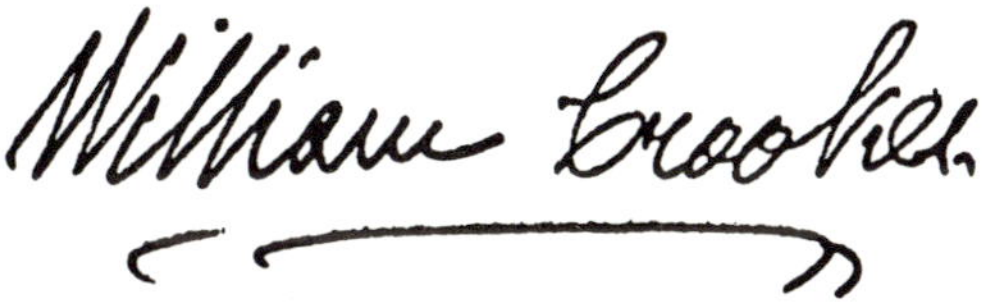

8.

9.
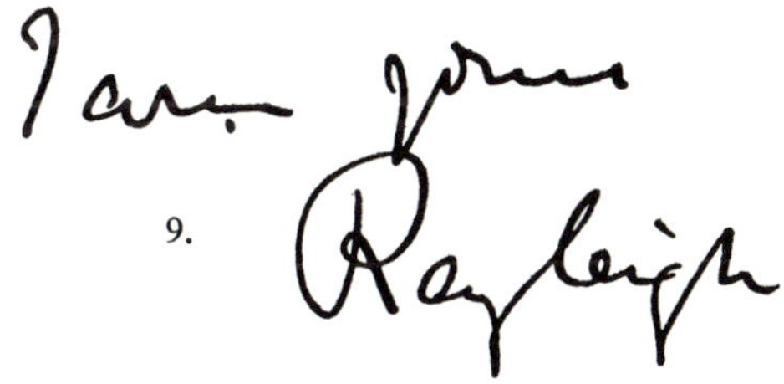

1. **Joseph Priestley.** 1733–1804. Chemist and controversial clergyman. Arguably the discoverer of oxygen.
2. **Sir Humphry Davy.** 1778–1829. Discovered sodium and potassium and invented the miners' safety lamp.
3. **Michael Faraday.** 1791–1867. Responsible for numerous electro-chemical discoveries, he was also a distinguished natural philosopher.
4. **John Tyndall.** 1820–93. Physicist and natural philosopher.
5. **Thomas Graham.** 1805–69. Chemist and physicist. His autograph should not be confused with that of General Sir Thomas Graham.
6. **Sir David Brewster.** 1781–1868. Physicist. Invented the kaleidoscope.
7. **Sir William Crookes.** 1832–1919. Chemist. Discovered thallium and invented the radiometer.
8. **Sir James Dewar.** 1842–1923. Co-discoverer (with Abel) of cordite. Invented the vacuum flask.
9. **Robert J. S. Strutt, 4th Lord Rayleigh.** 1875–1947. Physicist. His signature is sometimes confused with that of his father (see page 112).

NOBEL PRIZEWINNERS

1.

2.

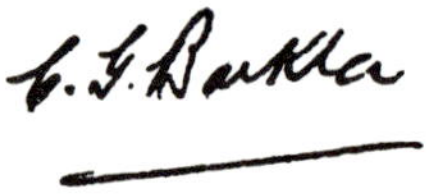

3.

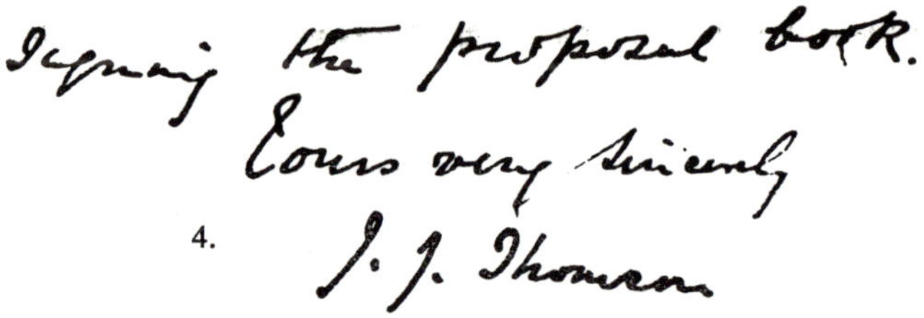

4.

5.

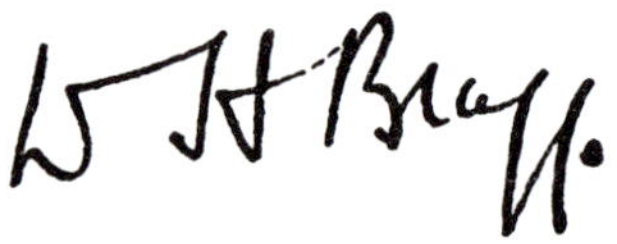

6.

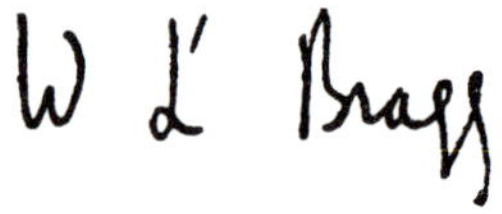

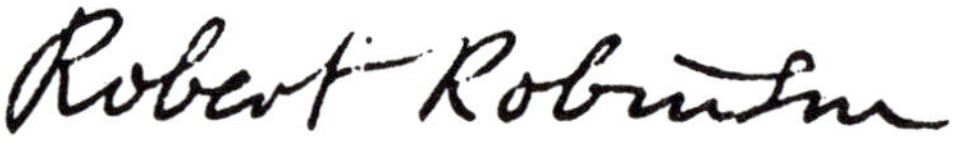

7.

8.

1. **Sir William Ramsay.** 1852–1916. Chemist. Co-discoverer (with Rayleigh, 2 below) of argon. Nobel Prize, 1904.
2. **John W. Strutt, 3rd Lord Rayleigh.** 1842–1919. Co-discoverer (with Ramsay) of argon. Nobel Prize, 1904.
3. **Charles G. Barkla.** 1877–1944. Physicist. Researched into X-rays. Nobel Prize, 1917.
4. **Sir Joseph J. Thomson.** 1856–1940. Physicist and Master of Trinity, Cambridge. Nobel Prize, 1906.
5. **Sir William H. Bragg.** 1862–1942. Physicist, noted for his work on X-rays and crystals. Shared the 1915 Nobel Prize with his son, 6 below.
6. **Sir W. Lawrence Bragg.** 1890– . Physicist. See note on his father, 5 above.
7. **Sir Robert Robinson.** 1886– . Nobel Prize for Chemistry, 1947.
8. **Sir James Chadwick.** 1891– . Physicist. Discovered the neutron. Nobel Prize, 1935.

1.

2.

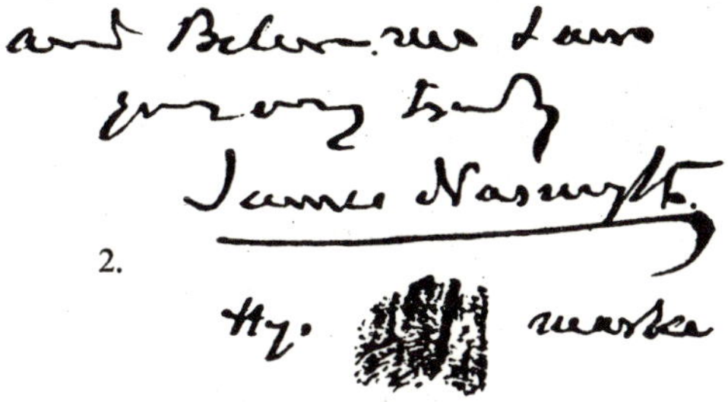

3.

4.

5.

6.

7.

8.

1. **James Watt.** 1736–1819. Invented the steam engine. Watt's scarce signature usually has a flourish beneath it but in the original letter from which this is taken he left no room at the foot of the page.
2. **James Nasmyth.** 1808–90. Invented the steam-hammer and the pile-driver.
3. **Sir William Congreve.** 1772–1828. Inventor of the Congreve rocket.
4. **W. Henry Fox Talbot.** 1800–77. Pioneer in photography. Invented photogenic drawing (subsequently the Talbotype process). Published the first photographically illustrated book, *Pencil of Nature*, 1844.
5. **Admiral Sir Francis Beaufort.** 1774–1857. Hydrographer. Invented the Beaufort Scale of wind force.
6. **Charles Babbage.** 1792–1871. A mathematical genius, he constructed one of the earliest calculating machines.
7. **George Stephenson.** 1781–1848. Invented the locomotive. His unusual autograph is highly sought-after.
8. **Alexander Graham Bell.** 1847–1922. Invented the telephone. Scottish-born, he became an American citizen.

1.

2.

3.

4.

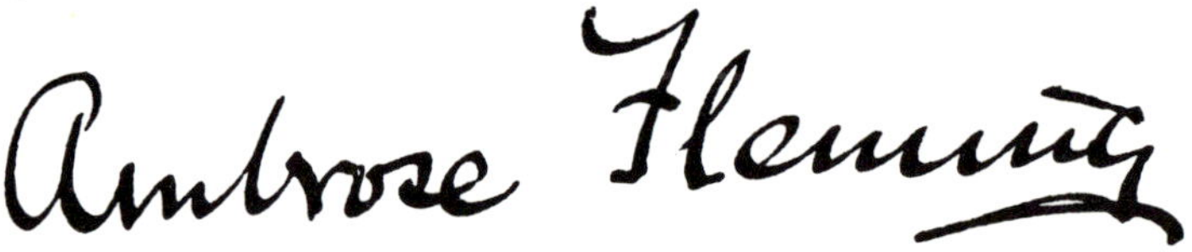

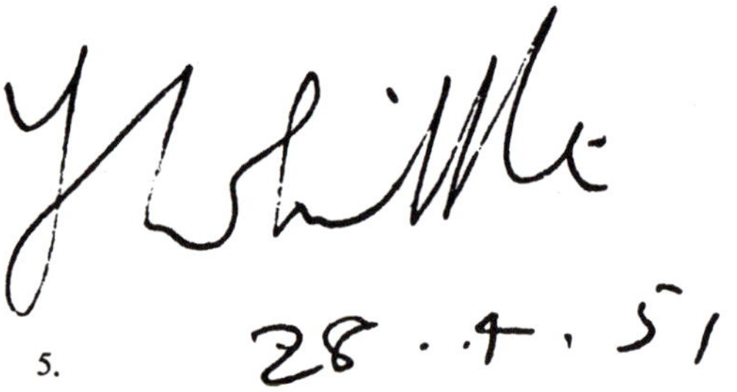

5.

6.

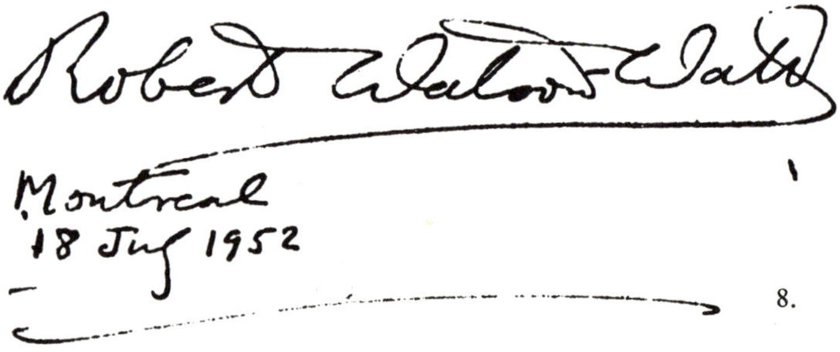

7.

8.

1. **Sir Hiram S. Maxim.** 1840–1916. American-born inventor of the Maxim (machine) gun; became a naturalized British citizen.
2. **John Boyd Dunlop.** 1840–1921. Invented the pneumatic tyre.
3. **John Logie Baird.** 1888–1946. Television inventor.
4. **Sir (J.) Ambrose Fleming.** 1849–1945. Invented the thermionic valve and devised the electron tube.
5. **Sir Frank Whittle.** 1907–   Developed the jet engine for aircraft.
6. **Louis Brennan.** 1852–1932. Invented the dirigible torpedo.
7. **Sir Barnes (N.) Wallis.** 1887–   . Inventor of geodetic constructions and the 'bouncing bomb'; leading designer of the R100 airship.
8. **Sir Robert Watson-Watt.** 1892–   . Pioneered the development and use of radar.

SCIENTISTS AND SCHOLARS: ANTIQUARIES, ARCHAEOLOGISTS AND ENGINEERS

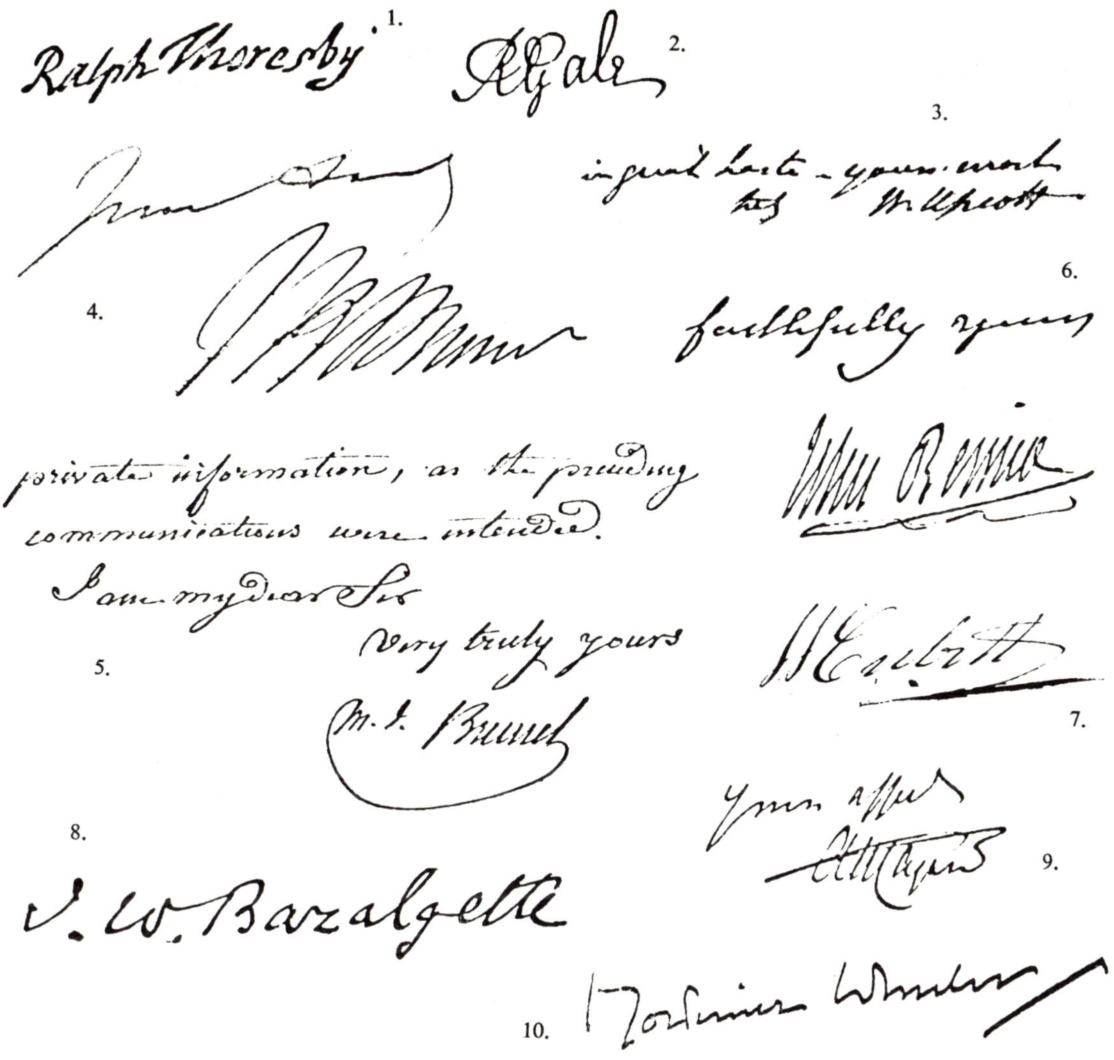

1. **Ralph Thoresby.** 1658–1725. Controversial antiquary and topographer.
2. **Roger Gale.** 1672–1744. Antiquary, topographer and numismatist.
3. **William Upcott.** 1779–1845. Antiquary. Built up a famous autograph collection.
4. **Isambard Kingdom Brunel.** 1806–59. Engineer. Designed the 'Great Western', the first steamship to cross the Atlantic.
5. **Sir Marc Isambard Brunel.** 1769–1849. Built the Thames Tunnel. Born in France, he worked as an architect in New York before settling in England. Father of I. K. Brunel, 4 above.
6. **John Rennie.** 1761–1821. Bridge and dockyard builder. Planned London Bridge (completed by his son, Sir John Rennie).
7. **Sir William Cubitt.** 1785–1861. Chief engineer of the South-Eastern railway.
8. **Sir Joseph W. Bazalgette.** 1819–91. The engineer of London's drainage system and the Thames embankment.
9. **Sir Austin Henry Layard.** 1817–94. Archaeologist and diplomat. Excavated Nineveh.
10. **Sir (R. E.) Mortimer Wheeler.** 1890–   . Archaeologist. Former Keeper of the London Museum.

LITERARY FIGURES: A SEVENTEENTH- AND EIGHTEENTH-CENTURY MISCELLANY

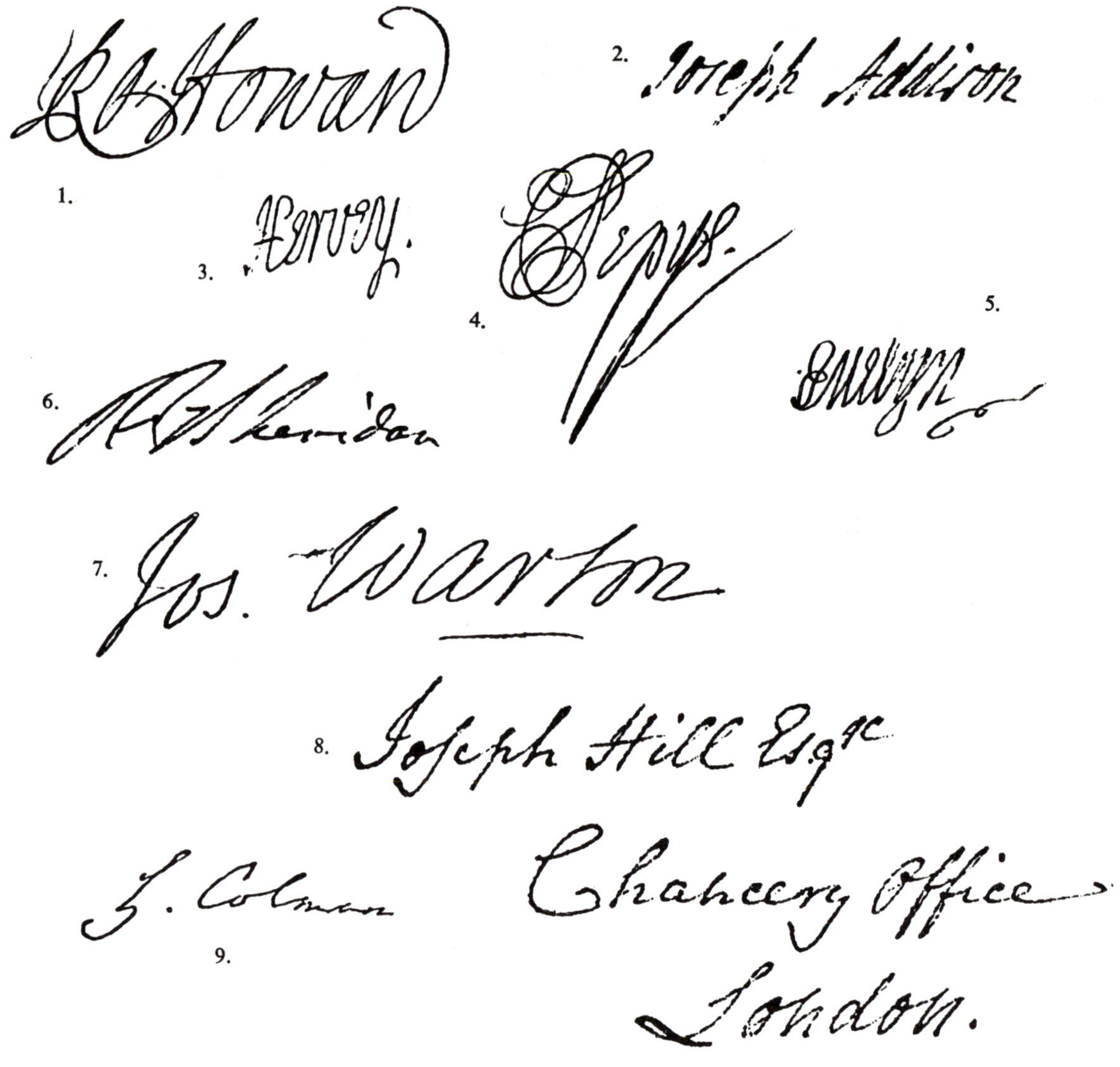

1. **Sir Robert Howard.** 1626–98. Restoration dramatist. Collaborated with Dryden. A public figure, his signature appears on State documents.
2. **Joseph Addison.** 1672–1719. Essayist. His signature is sometimes found on State documents.
3. **John, Lord Hervey.** 1696–1743. Pamphleteer and memoir writer.
4. **Samuel Pepys.** 1633–1703. Pepys's signature appears sometimes on documents of the Admiralty, of which he was Secretary.
5. **John Evelyn.** 1620–1706. Autographically more rare than his fellow diarist, Pepys.
6. **Richard Brinsley Sheridan.** 1751–1816. Dramatist.
7. **Joseph Warton.** 1722–1800. Critic. Friend of Johnson.
8. **William Cowper.** 1731–1800. As another William Cowper (see page 174) had a signature very similar to that of the poet, a handwriting example is safest for identification purposes in this case. The original is a letter cover, in Cowper's holograph, postmarked 'Olney', where he lived.
9. **George Colman 'The Elder'.** 1732–94. His son ('the Younger'), who was also a dramatist, used a totally dissimilar signature.

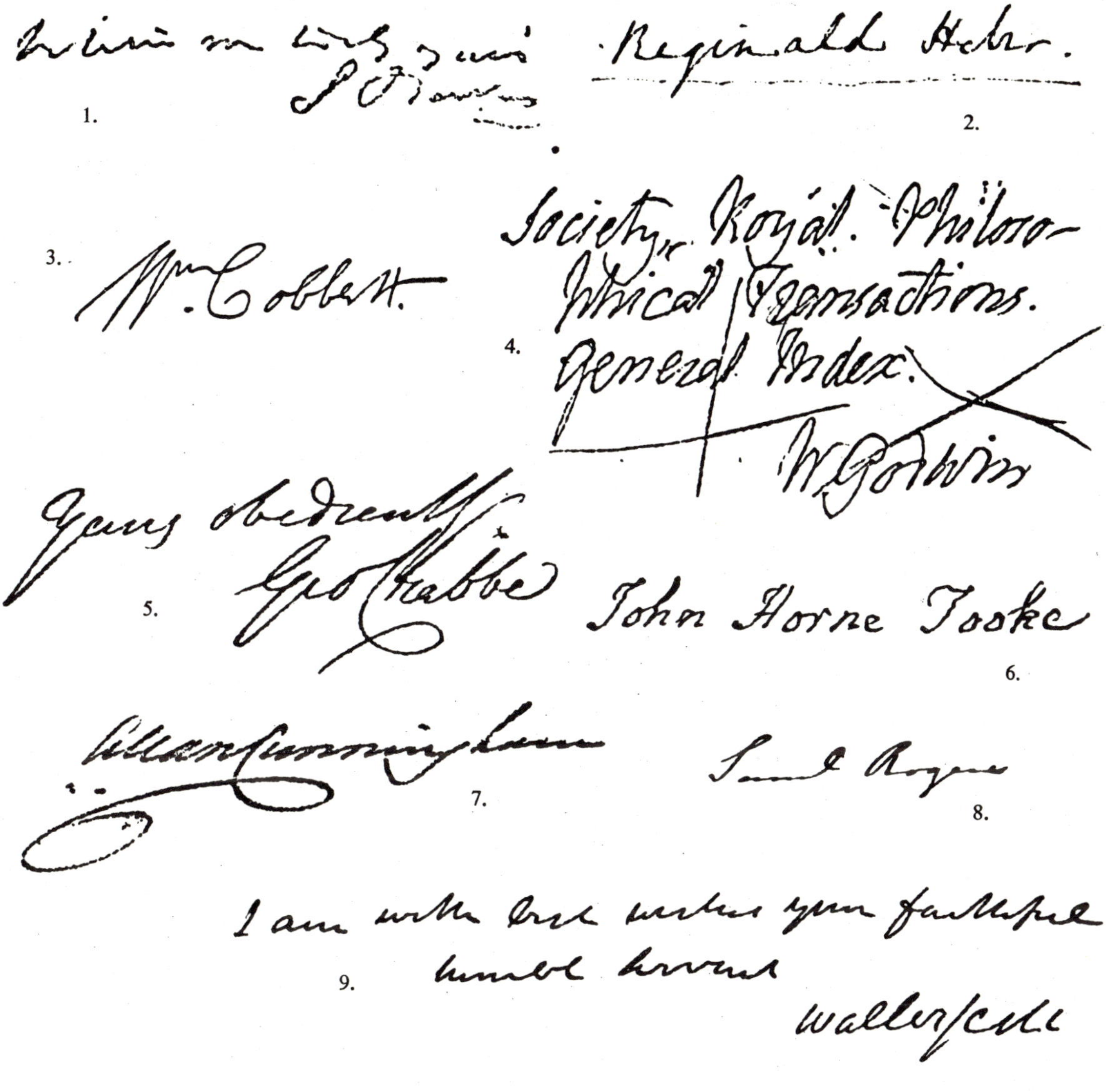

1. **Samuel Parr.** 1747–1825. The short extract above is typical of Parr's virtually illegible writing.
2. **Reginald Heber.** 1783–1826. Bishop of Calcutta. Wrote the hymns *From Greenland's Icy Mountains*, *Holy, Holy, Holy*.
3. **William Cobbett.** 1763–1835. A Radical and a reformer, he spent many years in America.
4. **William Godwin.** 1756–1836. Shelley's father-in-law.
5. **George Crabbe.** 1754–1832. This poet's signature is sometimes confused with that of his son of the same name.
6. **John Horne Tooke.** 1736–1812. Being on a subscription form for one of his works, the signature above is more carefully written than his usual one.
7. **Allan Cunningham.** 1784–1842. Poet and miscellaneous writer.
8. **Samuel Rogers.** 1763–1855. 'Melodious Rogers'. He refused the Poet Laureateship.
9. **Sir Walter Scott.** 1771–1832. Scott also frequently signed just 'W. Scott'.

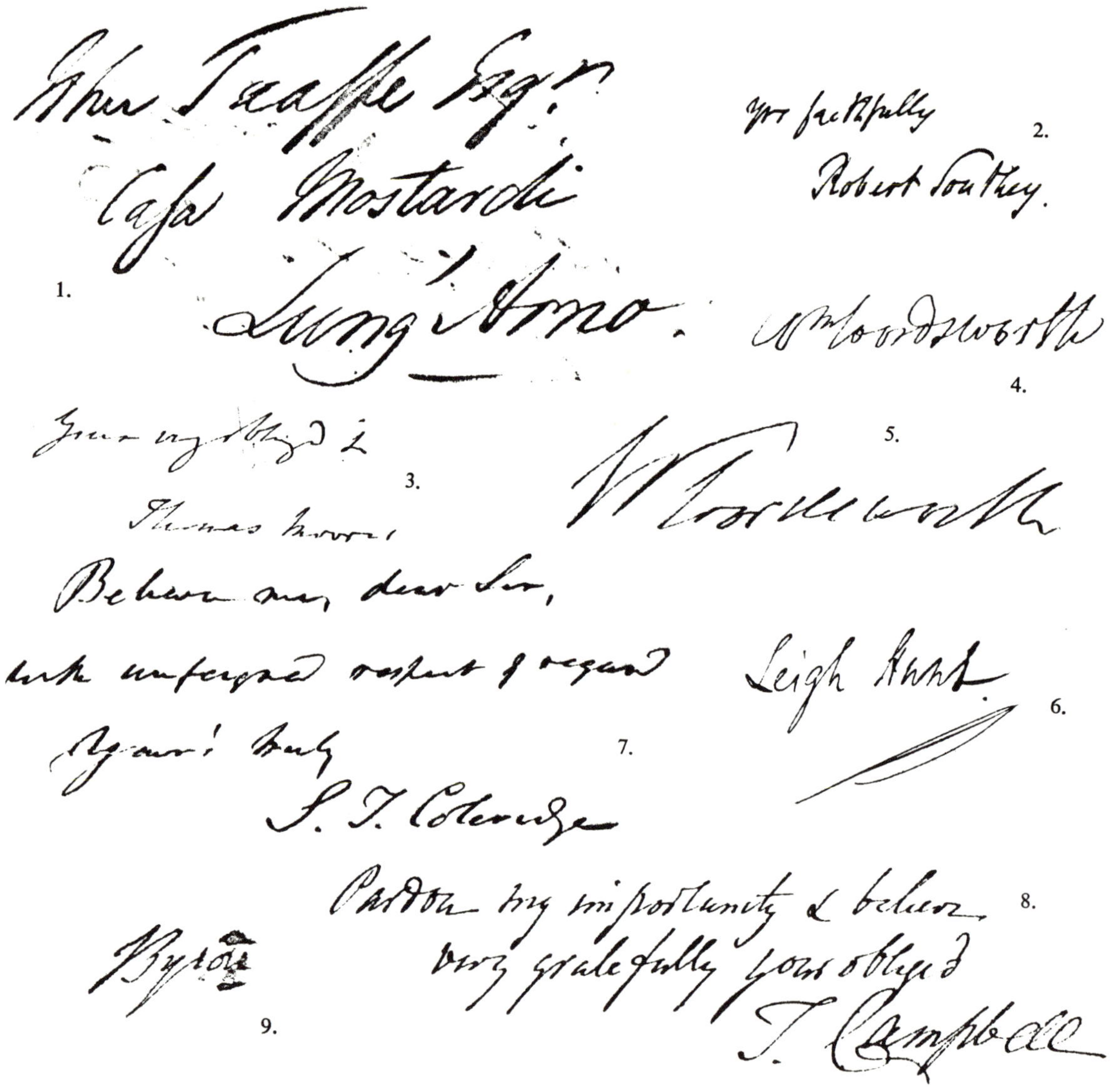

1. **Percy Bysshe Shelley.** 1792–1822. Holograph cover. See remarks about this item on page 28.
2. **Robert Southey.** 1774–1843.
3. **Thomas Moore.** 1779–1852. 'The Bard of Erin'.
4. and 5. **William Wordsworth.** 1770–1850. Variant signatures.
6. **(James H.) Leigh Hunt.** 1784–1859.
7. **Samuel Taylor Coleridge.** 1772–1834. From the three-line holograph example above, it should be possible to avoid confusion between the very similar signatures of the poet and his nephew, the judge (see page 85).
8. **Thomas Campbell.** 1777–1844. He sometimes wrote in a more upright (but otherwise similar) hand.
9. **George Gordon, Lord Byron.** 1788–1824. Byron's signature varied considerably, being usually more flamboyant than this example, which is a franking signature on a holograph envelope (1813) addressed to (Bishop) Samuel Butler.

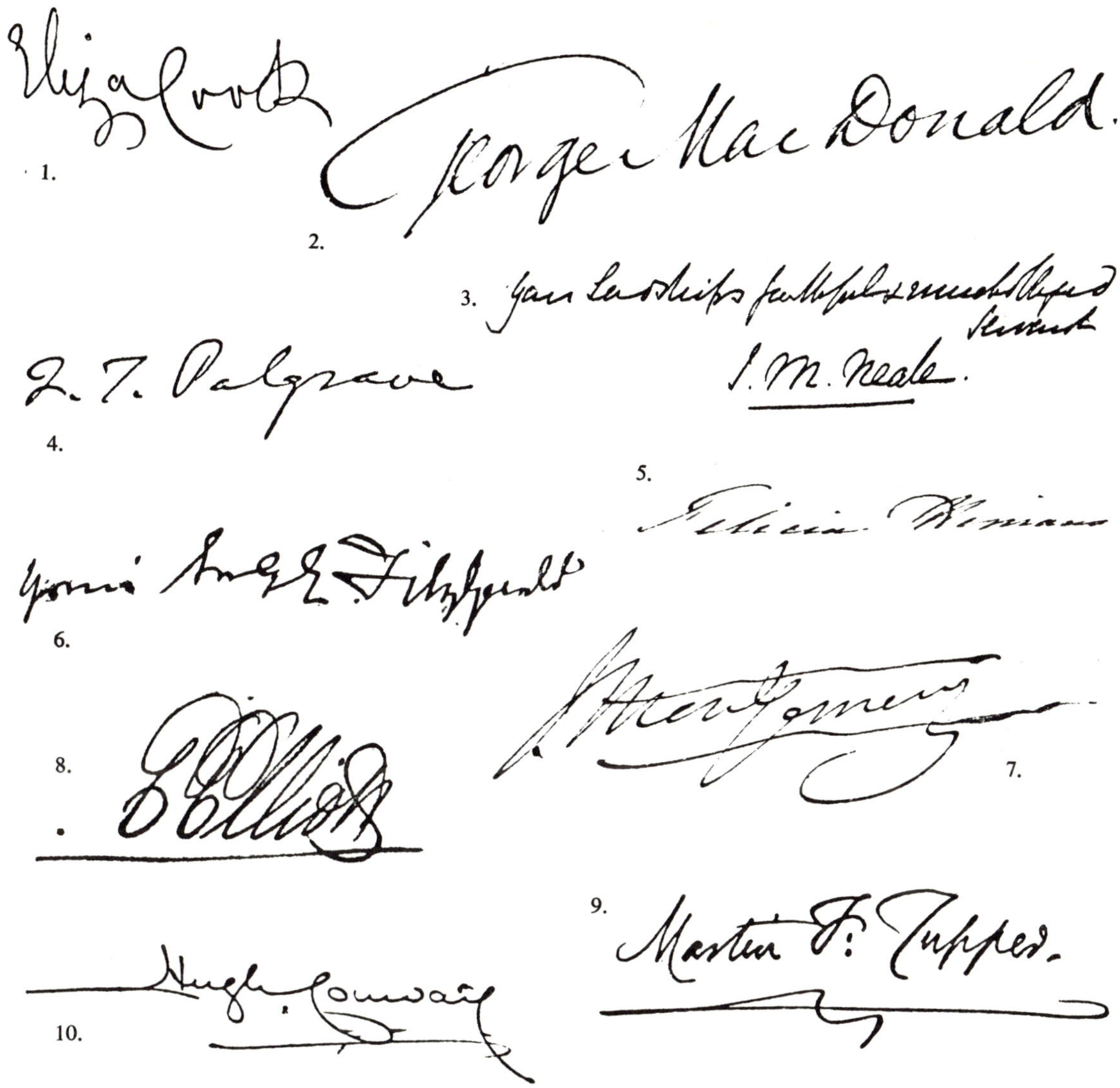

1. **Eliza Cook.** 1818–89.
2. **George MacDonald.** 1824–1905. As much a novelist as a poet, he wrote many charming stories for children.
3. **John Mason Neale.** 1818–66. Hymn writer. Responsible for one-eighth of *Hymns Ancient and Modern.*
4. **Francis Turner Palgrave.** 1824–97. Editor of the famous anthology *The Golden Treasury.*
5. **Felicia Hemans.** 1793–1835. Best remembered for 'The boy stood on the burning deck . . .'.
6. **Edward FitzGerald.** 1809–83. Famed for his translation of the *Rubáiyát of Omar Khayyám.*
7. **James Montgomery.** 1771–1854. Also a hymn writer.
8. **Ebenezer Elliott.** 1781–1849. The 'Corn Law Rhymer'.
9. **Martin F. Tupper.** 1810–89.
10. **'Hugh Conway' (F. J. Fargus).** 1847–85. Also a writer of melodrama, he took his pseudonym from the frigate *Conway*, on which he had served.

1.

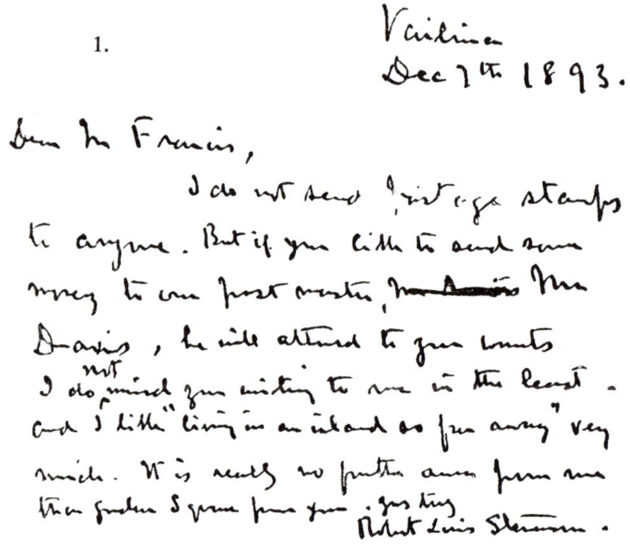
Vailima
Dec 7th 1893.

Dear Mr Francis,

I do not send postage stamps to anyone. But if you like to send some money to our post master, Mr Davis, he will attend to your wants. I do not mind your writing to me in the least — and I like "living on an island so far away" very much. It is really no further away from me than London is from you. Yours truly

Robert Louis Stevenson.

2.

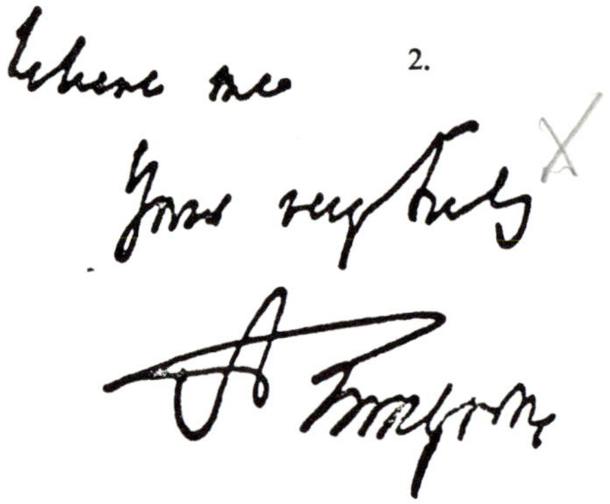

3.

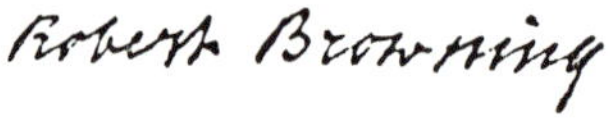

4.

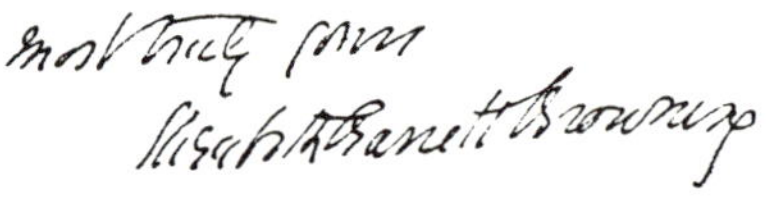

5.

6.

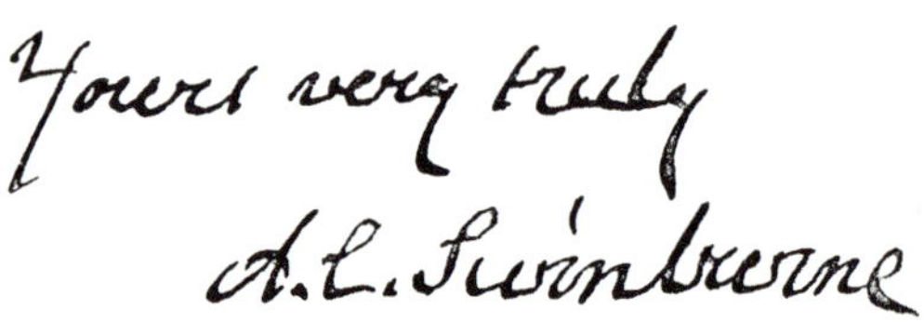

7.

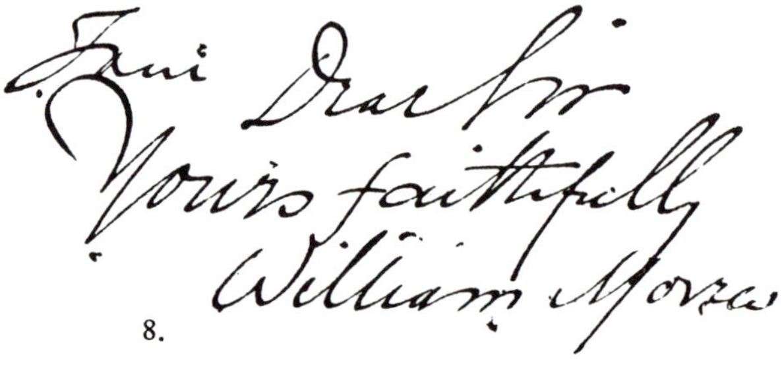

8.

1. **Robert Louis Stevenson.** 1850–94. Equally famous as a novelist. His handwriting is not always as minute as this example, written in the last year of his life.
2. **Alfred, Lord Tennyson.** 1809–92. Poet Laureate. See remarks on Tennyson's autograph on page 41.
3. **Robert Browning.** 1812–89.
4. **Elizabeth Barrett Browning.** 1806–61. Her autograph is more scarce and valuable than that of her husband Robert, 3 above.
5. **Christina G. Rossetti.** 1830–94.
6. **Dante Gabriel Rossetti.** 1828–82. Equally famous as a painter: Pre-Raphaelite. Brother of Christina, 5 above.
7. **Algernon C. Swinburne.** 1837–1909.
8. **William Morris.** 1834–96. Equally famous as an architect, painter and craftsman.

FOUR LITERARY FAMILIES

1.

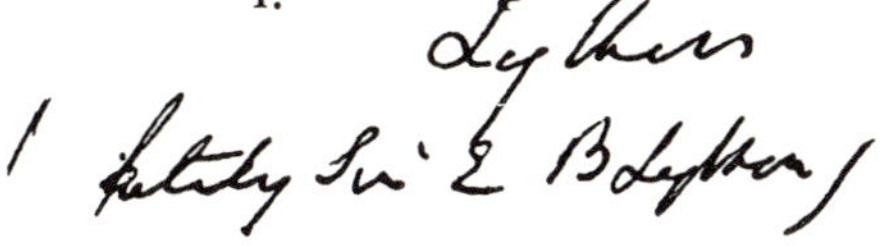

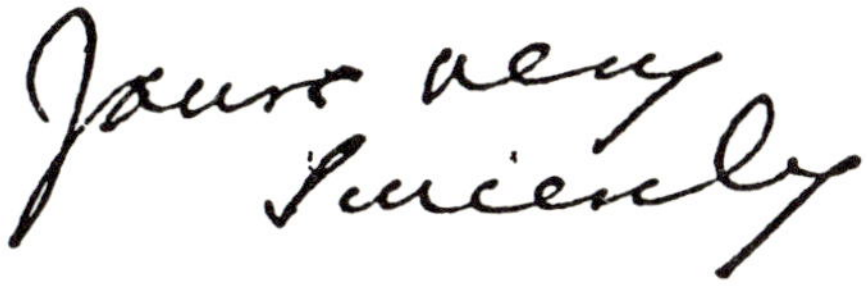

2.

3.

4.

5.

6.

7.

8.

1. **Edward George Lytton Bulwer, 1st Baron Lytton.** 1803–73. Novelist, poet, essayist and Colonial Secretary.
2. **Edward Robert Bulwer, 1st Earl of Lytton.** 1831–91. Poet (pseudonym 'Owen Meredith') and Viceroy of India. Constantly confused with his father, 1 above. Comparison of the writing of the two men should establish their separate identities.
3. **Thomas Crofton Croker.** 1798–1854. Irish folklorist.
4. **John Wilson Croker.** 1780–1857. Historian and essayist, his signature is frequently found on documents of the Admiralty, of which he was Secretary.
5. **James Martineau.** 1805–1900. Theologian.
6. **Harriet Martineau.** 1802–76. Sister of James, 5 above. Miscellaneous writer (travel books, philosophical works, etc.).
7. **Samuel Carter Hall.** 1800–89. Irish editor (of *John Bull* etc.), and prolific miscellaneous writer.
8. **Anna Maria Hall.** 1800–81. Wife of S. C. Hall, 7 above. Novelist and writer on Irish life.

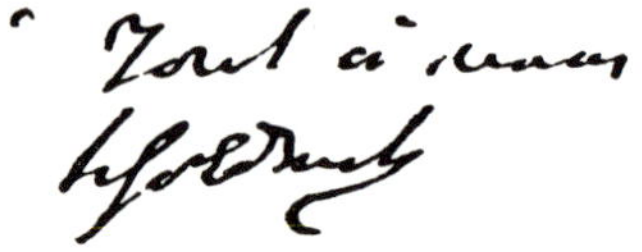

1.

2.

3.

4.

5.

6.

7.

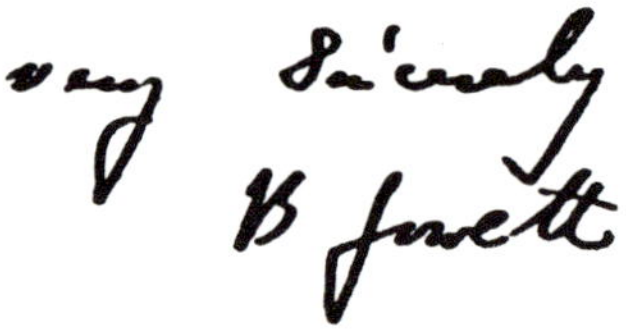

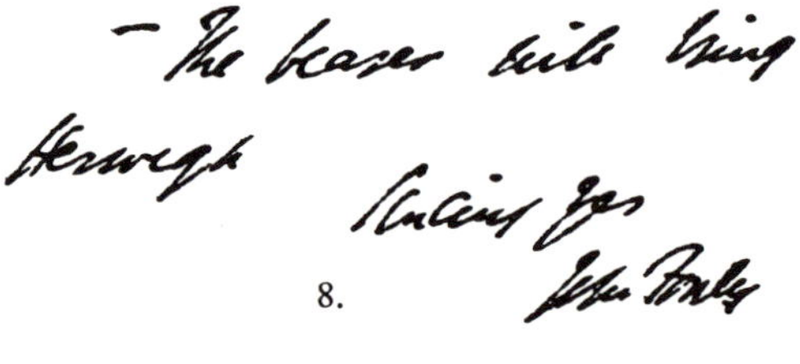

8.

1. **Lewis Goldsmith.** 1763(?)–1846. Political writer.
2. **Caroline E. S. Norton.** 1808–77. Poet and writer on social reform. Sheridan's granddaughter, celebrated for her beauty and wit.
3. **Douglas W. Jerrold.** 1803–57. Journalist, dramatist and wit.
4. **Agnes Strickland.** 1796–1874. Historian and poet.
5. **Sir Thomas Noon Talfourd.** 1795–1854. Judge, critic and dramatist.
6. **Amelia Opie.** 1769–1853. Quaker authoress, wife of the painter John Opie. Her signature is usually smaller than the example above and with a rounded capital 'A'. This signature, coming from a receipt, is altogether much more studied and carefully executed than her normal one.
7. **Benjamin Jowett.** 1817–93. Classical scholar and translator. Master of Balliol College, Oxford.
8. **John Forster.** 1812–76. Biographer, historian and journalist.

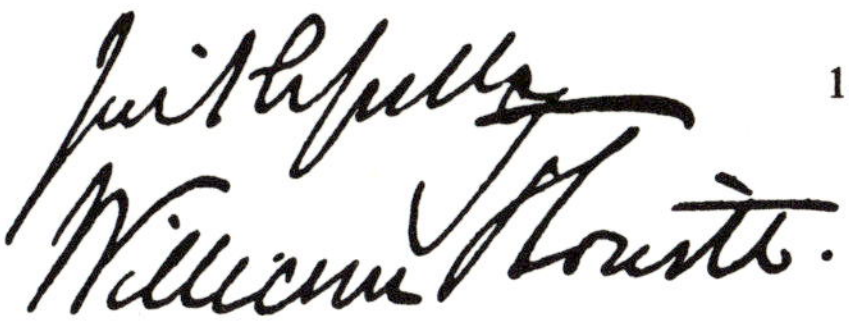
1.

2.

3.

4.
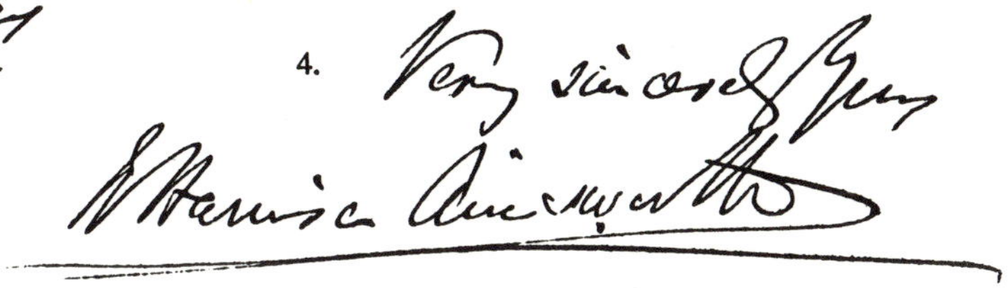

5.

6.

7.
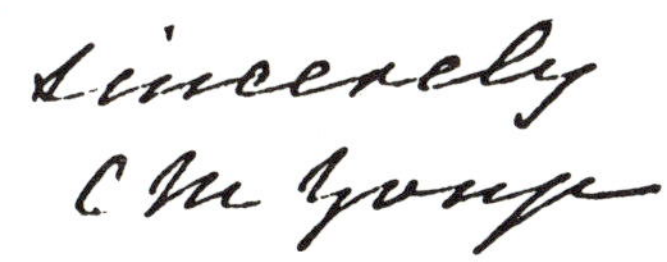

8.

1. **William Howitt.** 1792–1879. Miscellaneous writer and reformer.
2. **George Augustus Sala.** 1828–95. Satirist, novelist and travel writer.
3. **John Churton Collins.** 1848–1908. Critic and editor of English classics. The example above, from a closely written letter, is a little smaller than his normal handwriting.
4. **(William) Harrison Ainsworth.** 1805–82. Journalist and novelist. Friend of Dickens and Cruikshank.
5. **Samuel Smiles.** 1812–1904. Surgeon, biographer (of George Stephenson and other engineers) and writer on social reform (*Self Help*, 1857).
6. **Ebenezer Cobham Brewer.** 1810–97. Compiler of reference works, best known for his *Dictionary of Phrase and Fable*.
7. **Charlotte M. Yonge.** 1823–1901. Novelist, translator and historian.
8. **John Addington Symonds.** 1840–93. Critic, biographer and translator.

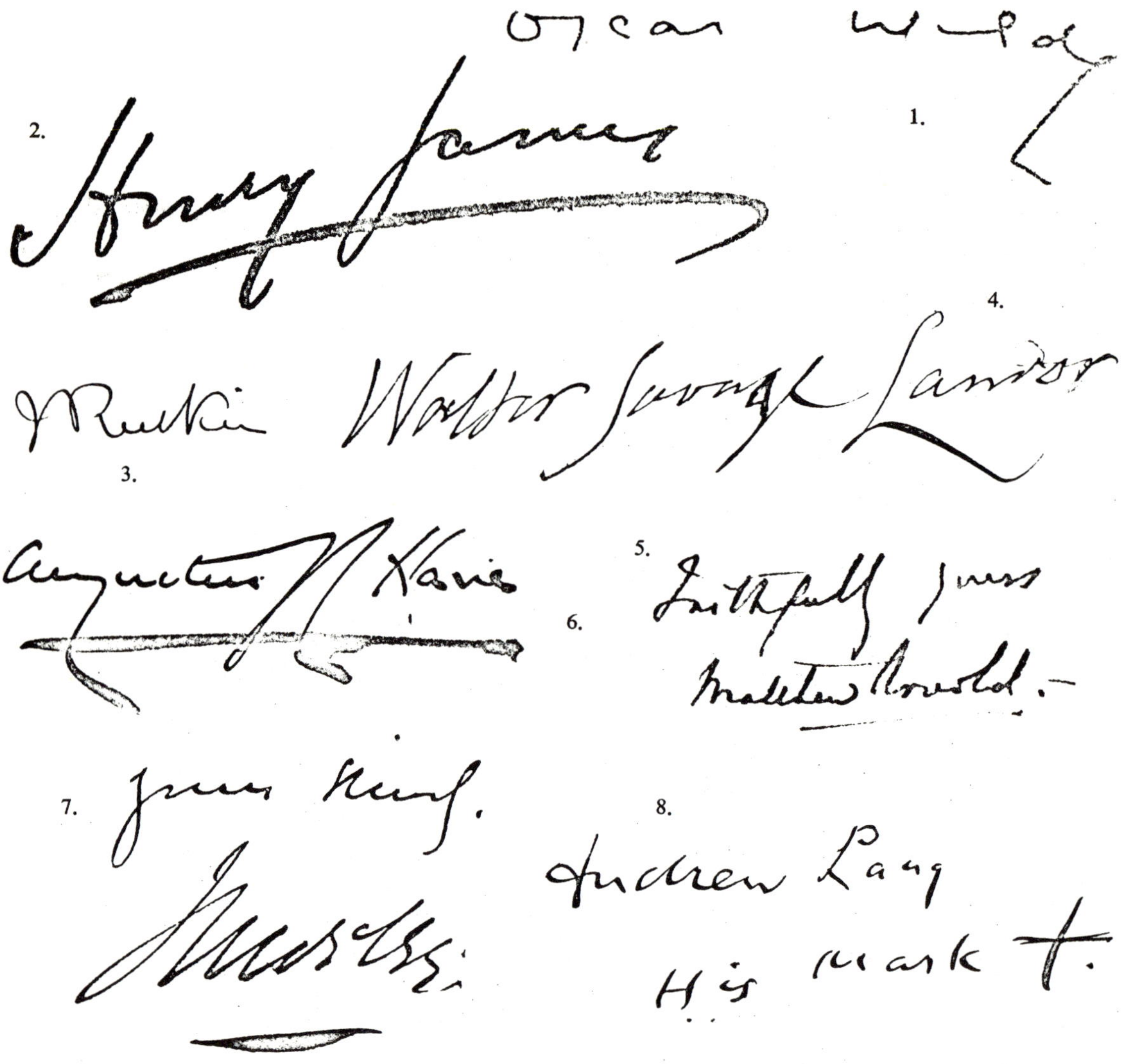

1. **Oscar Wilde.** 1854–1900. Irish dramatist and poet. A highly sought-after literary autograph.
2. **Henry James.** 1843–1916. Novelist. American by birth, he became a naturalized British subject. See discussion of confusion of his signature and those of two other persons of the same name on page 38.
3. **John Ruskin.** 1819–1900. Art critic and writer on social and economic reform.
4. **Walter Savage Landor.** 1775–1864. Poet and writer of 'conversations'.
5. **Matthew Arnold.** 1822–1888. Poet and critic.
6. **Augustus (J. C.) Hare.** 1834–1903. Topographical writer.
7. **John, Viscount Morley.** 1838–1923. Journalist, critic, biographer and politician.
8. **Andrew Lang.** 1844–1912. Scholar, folklorist and poet.

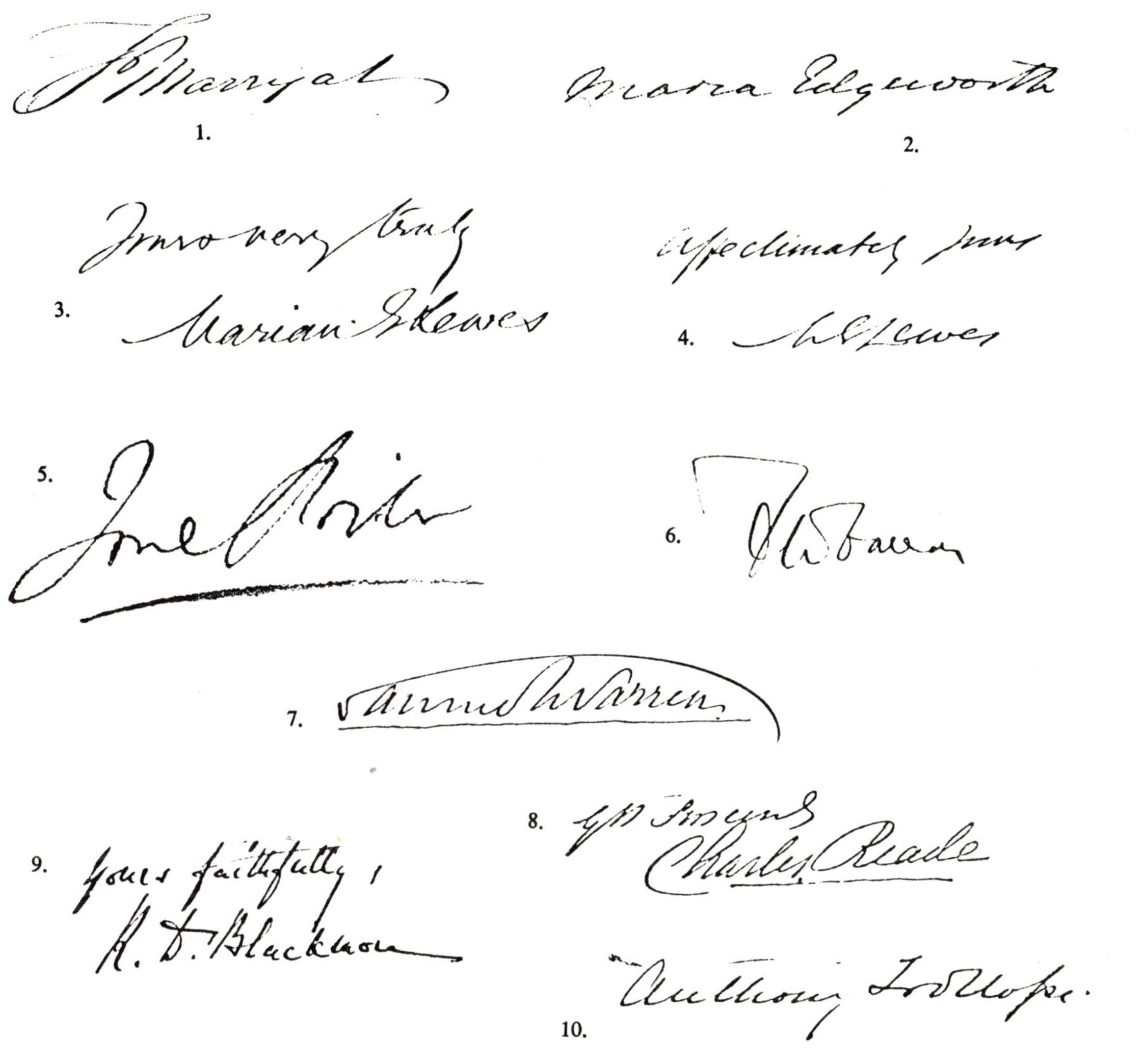

1. **Frederick Marryat.** 1792–1848. Naval captain and writer of sea stories.
2. **Maria Edgeworth.** 1767–1849.
3 and 4. **Marian Evans ('George Eliot').** 1819–80. Variant signatures, both using the surname 'Lewes' which she assumed in 1854 when she began to live with G. H. Lewes, the litterateur. She very seldom used her real name after that date and her pseudonym signature is very scarce.
5. **Jane Porter.** 1776–1850. Author of *The Scottish Chiefs*.
6. **Frederick W. Farrar.** 1831–1903. Dean of Canterbury and author of school stories, including *Eric, or Little by Little.*
7. **Samuel Warren.** 1807–77. Author of *Ten Thousand a Year.*
8. **Charles Reade.** 1814–84. Author of *The Cloister and the Hearth.*
9. **Richard D. Blackmore.** 1825–1900.
10. **Anthony Trollope.** 1815–82.

1.

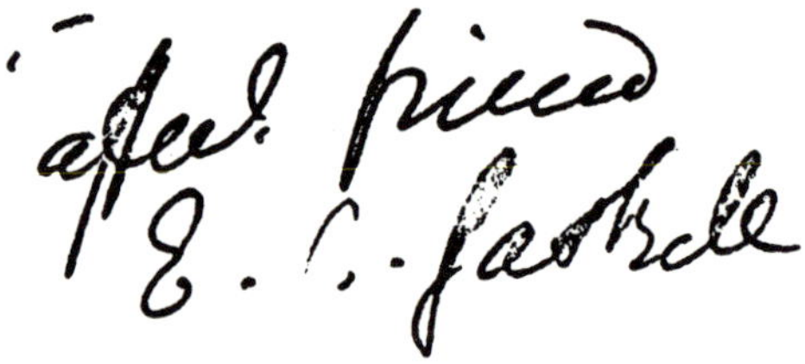
2.

3.

4.

5.

6.

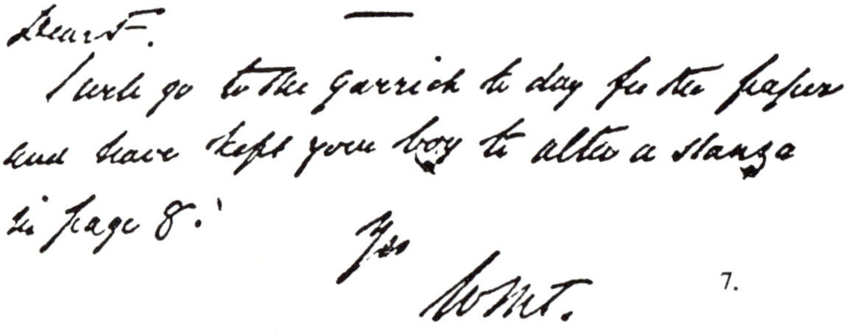
7.

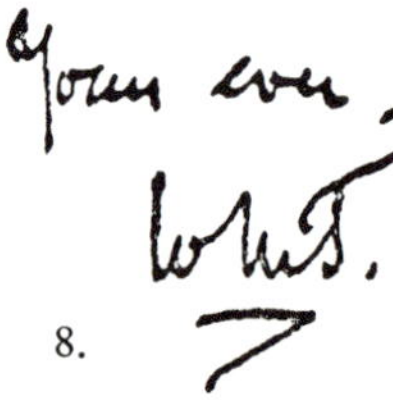
8.

1. **Charles Dickens.** 1812–70. The original is in the light blue ink which he used fairly regularly in later life. His signature varied considerably and when he was younger it was larger and more upright. The number of flourishes beneath it is seldom more than in this example (1866). The unusual capital 'C' is typical.
2. **Elizabeth C. Gaskell.** 1810–65. Author of *Cranford.*
3. **W. Wilkie Collins.** 1824–89.
4. **Charles Kingsley.** 1819–75.
5. **Charles Lutwidge Dodgson ('Lewis Carroll').** 1832–98. His signature as 'Lewis Carroll' is scarce. Many of his letters are in purple ink.
6. **Thomas Hughes.** 1822–96. Judge by profession. Author of *Tom Brown's Schooldays.*
7 and 8. **William Makepeace Thackeray.** 1811–63. Examples of his slanting and upright styles; see page 38.

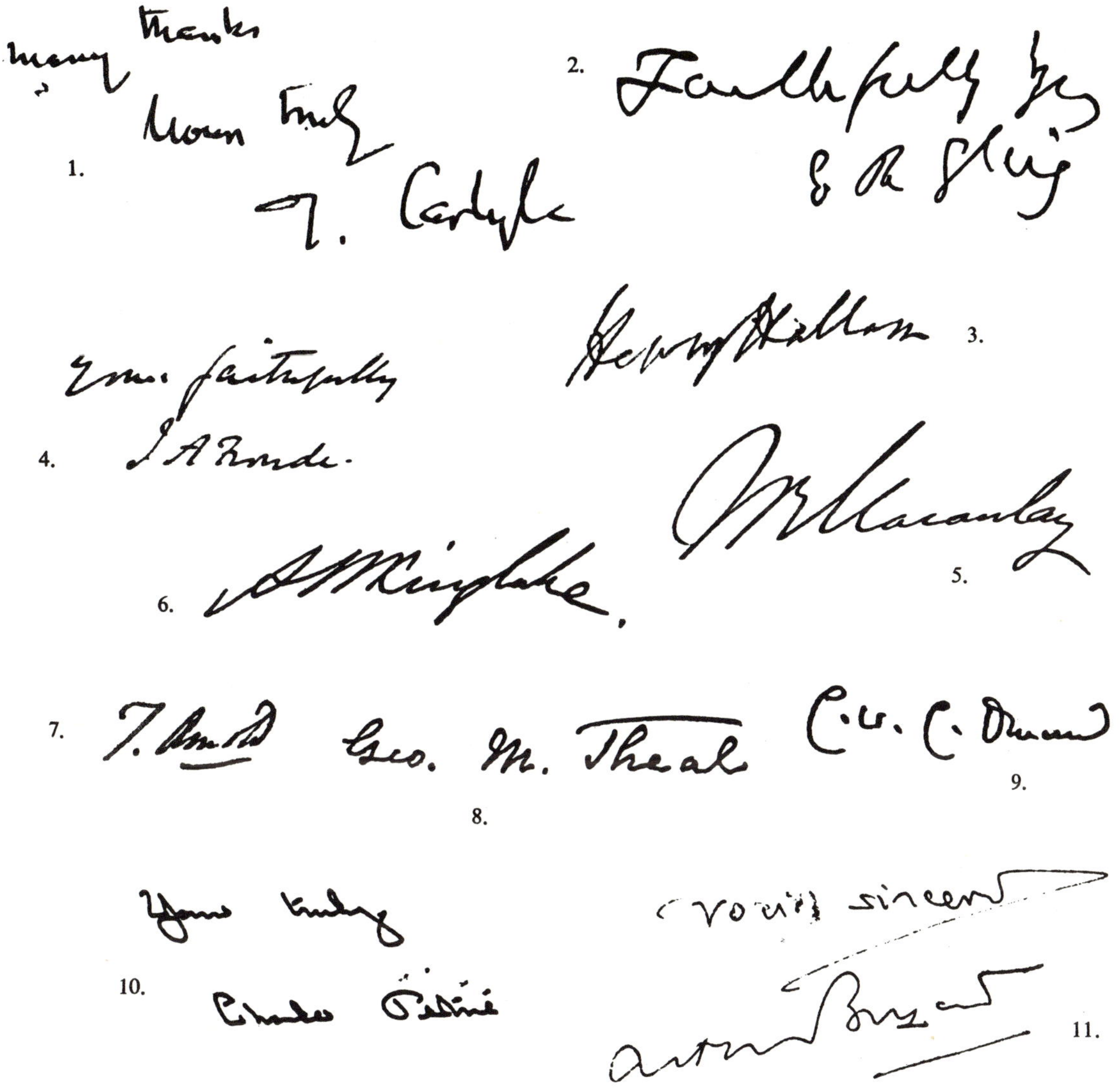

1. **Thomas Carlyle.** 1795–1881. Carlyle's signature is currently much sought-after.
2. **George R. Gleig.** 1796–1888. Scottish military historian. Also a novelist and biographer.
3. **Henry Hallam.** 1777–1859.
4. **James Anthony Froude.** 1818–94.
5. **Thomas Babington, Lord Macaulay.** 1800–59. Equally famous as a poet. Also a statesman and Minister of War under Melbourne.
6. **Alexander W. Kinglake.** 1809–91. *History of the War in the Crimea* is his greatest work.
7. **Thomas Arnold.** 1795–1842. Headmaster of Harrow and immortalized thus in Hughes's *Tom Brown's Schooldays*.
8. **George McCall Theal.** 1837–1919. Canadian-born historian of S. Africa.
9. **Sir Charles W. Chadwick Oman.** 1860–1946. Historian of the Peninsular War, etc.
10. **Sir Charles A. Petrie.** 1895– . One of our leading historians.
11. **Sir Arthur Bryant.** 1899– . Historian and man-of-letters.

ERRATUM—Page 127, Note 7. For "Harrow" read "Rugby"

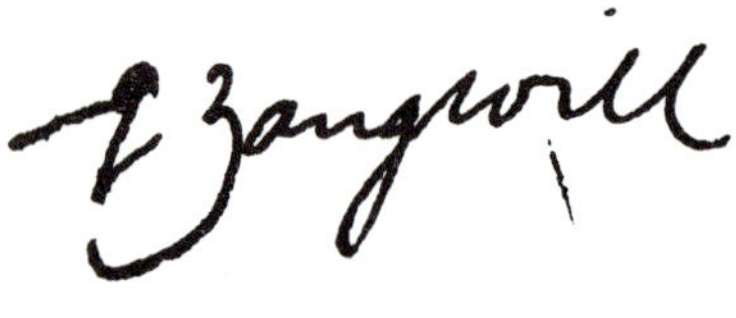

1.

2.

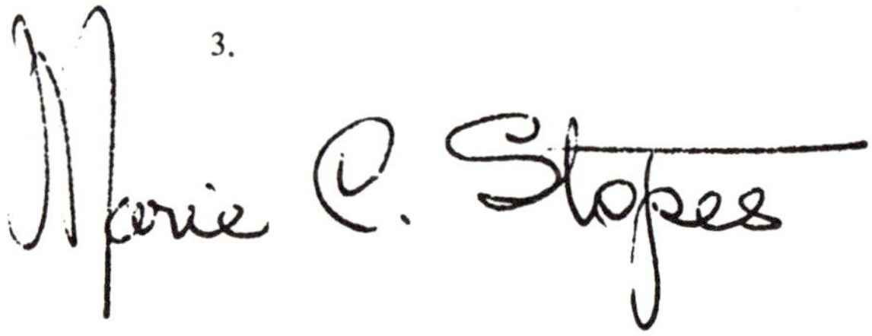

3.

4.

5.

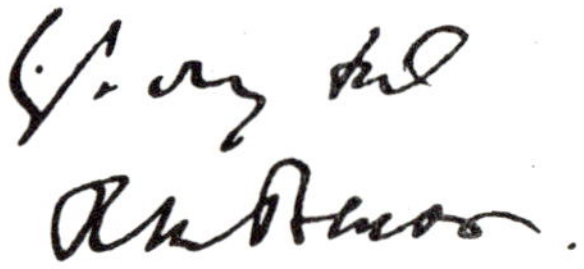

6.

7.

8.

1. **Israel Zangwill.** 1864–1926. Jewish playwright, essayist, novelist and poet.
2. **H. Havelock Ellis.** 1859–1939. Pioneer writer on the psychology of sex.
3. **Marie C. Stopes.** 1880–1958. Writer on birth control and sex in married life. Also a poet, an authority on Japanese drama and a university (Manchester) lecturer on palaeontology.
4. **Sir Walter Besant.** 1836–1901. Novelist, biographer and social reformer.
5. **Annie Besant.** 1847–1933. Theosophical writer. Sister-in-law of Sir Walter Besant, 4 above.
6. **Robert Hugh Benson.** 1871–1914. Catholic novelist and preacher.
7. **Arthur C. Benson.** 1862–1925. Literary biographer and poet.
8. **Edward Frederick Benson.** 1867–1940. Novelist and scholar. Brother of R. H. and A. C. Benson, 6 and 7 above. All three were sons of Archbishop Edward Benson of Canterbury (see page 80).

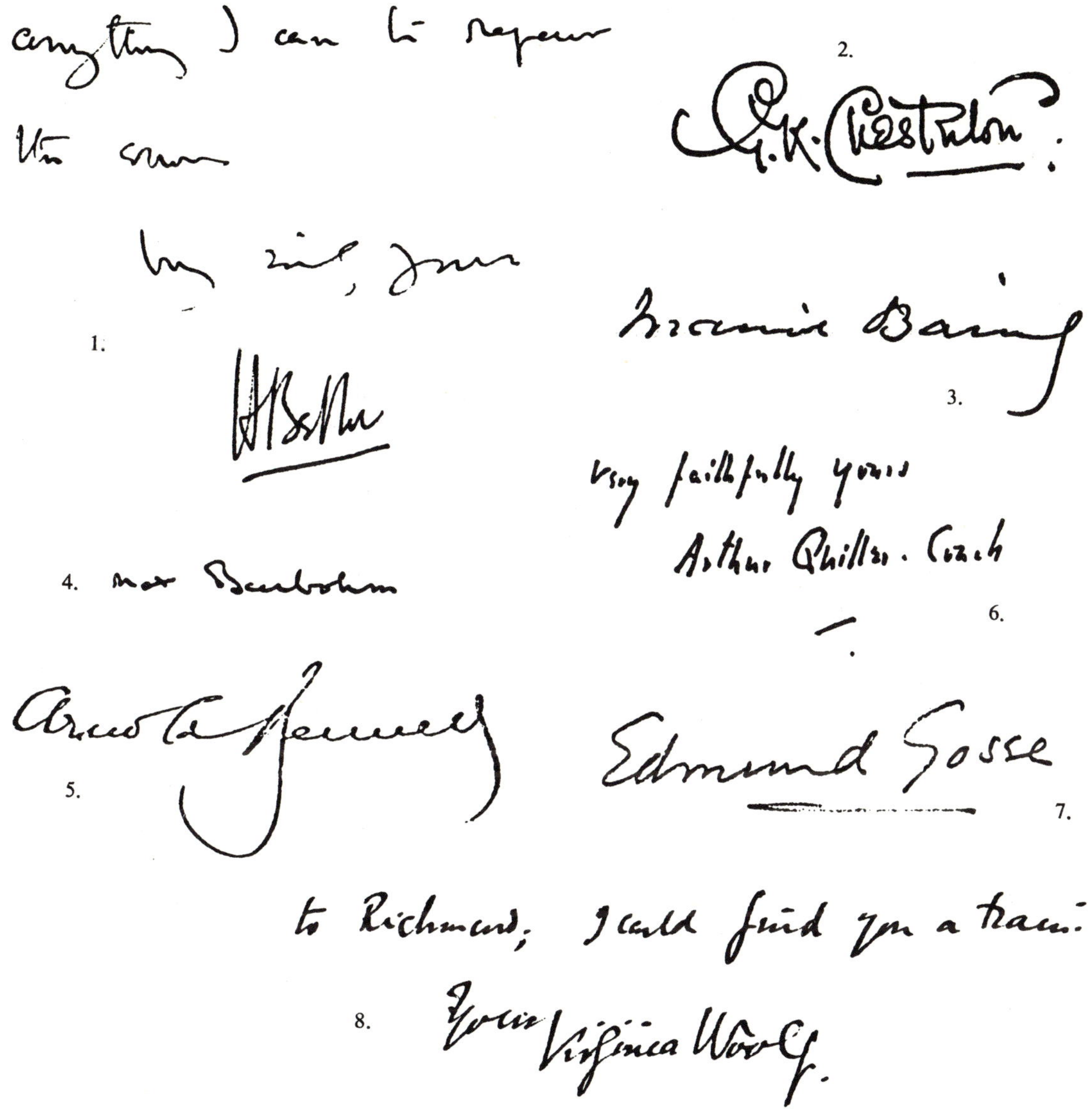

1. **(J.) Hilaire (P.) Belloc.** 1870–1953. Poet, historian and essayist. An interesting example for identification by collectors. Belloc's signature is upright and regular but his handwriting is smaller, sloped and less careful.
2. **Gilbert Keith Chesterton.** 1874–1936. Essayist, novelist and poet.
3. **Maurice Baring.** 1874–1946. Poet and novelist.
4. **Sir (H.) Max(imilian) Beerbohm.** 1872–1956. Essayist, novelist and caricaturist.
5. **E. Arnold Bennett.** 1867–1931. Novelist.
6. **Sir Arthur Quiller-Couch.** 1863–1944. Critic, poet and essayist; also a novelist, using the pseudonym 'Q'. Many of his letters are signed with this initial only.
7. **Sir Edmund W. Gosse.** 1849–1928. Critic.
8. **Virginia Woolf.** 1882–1941. Novelist.

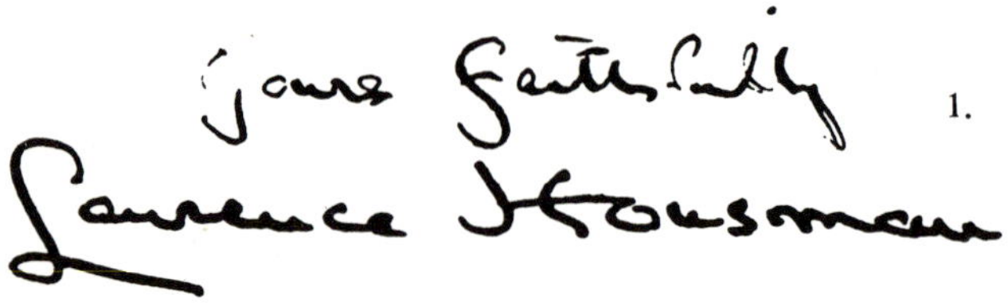

1.

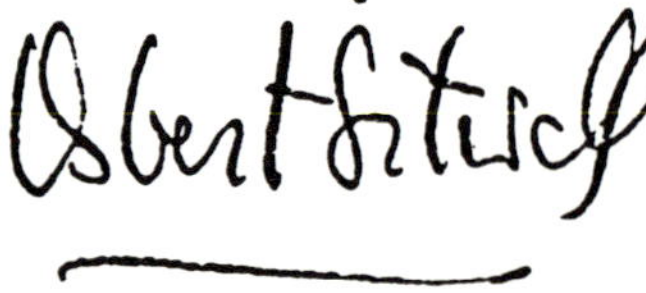

2.

3.

4.

5.

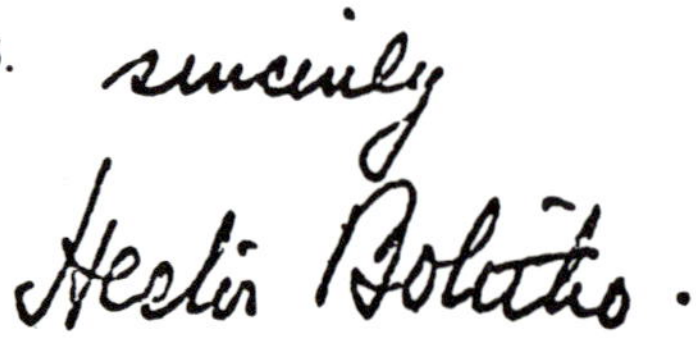

6.

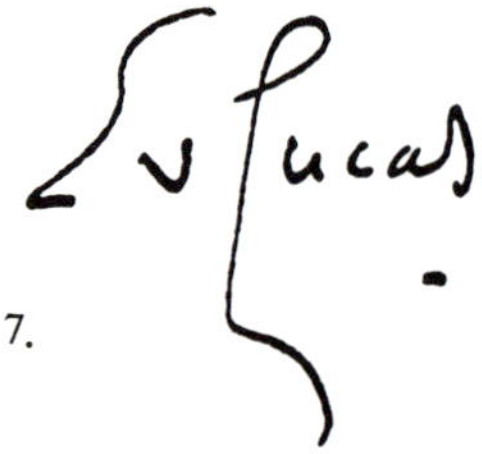

7.

8.

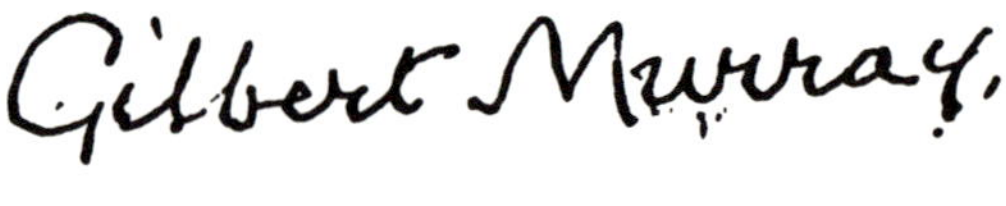

1. **Laurence Housman.** 1865–1959. Novelist and dramatist; brother of the poet A. E. Housman (see page 132).
2. **Sir Osbert Sitwell.** 1892–1969. Poet and novelist.
3. **Beverley Nichols.** 1899– . Novelist and journalist.
4. **Thomas Stearns Eliot.** 1888–1965. American-born but naturalized British poet, critic and dramatist. Won the Nobel Prize for Literature, 1948.
5. **Hector Bolitho.** 1898– . New Zealand biographer and travel writer.
6. **Axel Munthe.** 1857–1949. Swedish-born but naturalized British author of *The Story of San Michele*.
7. **Edward V. Lucas.** 1868–1938. Essayist, biographer and humorist.
8. **Gilbert A. Murray.** 1866–1957. Australian scholar; he was the leading classical historian and translator of Greek drama.

1.

2.

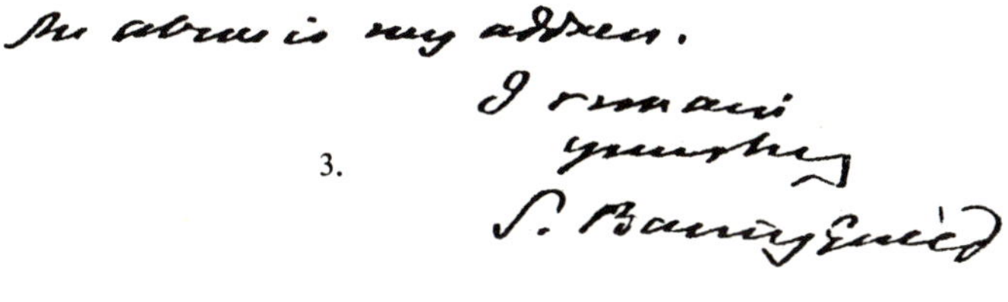
3.

4.

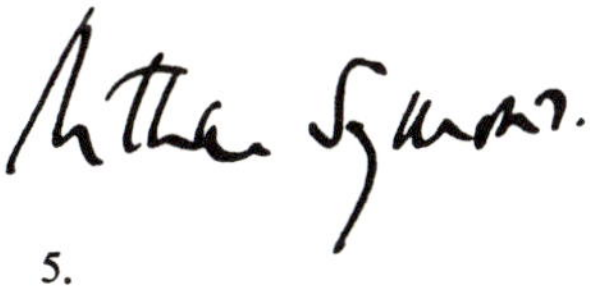
5.

6.

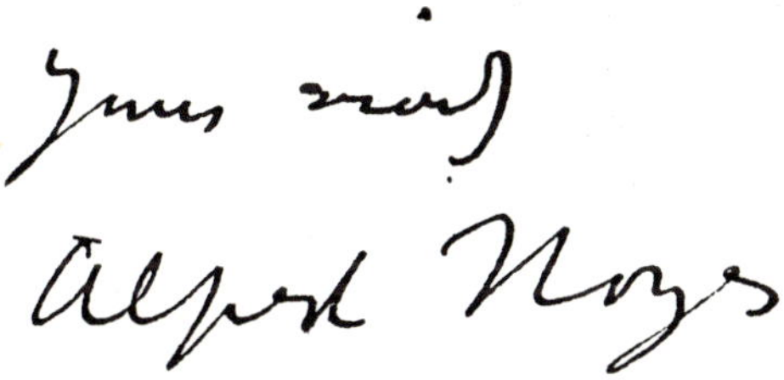
7.

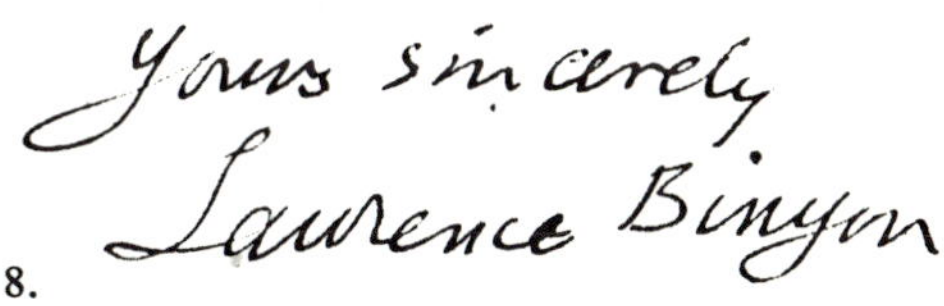
8.

1. **H. Austin Dobson.** 1840–1921. Also published monographs of Horace Walpole, Fielding, Goldsmith, etc.
2. **Alfred Austin.** 1835–1913. Succeeded Tennyson as Poet Laureate.
3. **Sabine Baring-Gould.** 1834–1924. More prolific as a novelist and miscellaneous writer, he is best known for the hymn *Onward, Christian Soldiers*.
4. **Sir Henry Newbolt.** 1862–1938.
5. **Arthur Symons.** 1865–1945. Also translated D'Annunzio and Baudelaire.
6. **Alice C. G. Meynell.** 1847–1922. Also an anthropologist and editor (with her husband, Wilfred Meynell).
7. **Alfred Noyes.** 1880–1958.
8. **Laurence Binyon.** 1869–1943. Also an art critic and dramatist, his poem 'For the Fallen', with its immortal lines, 'They shall grow not old, as we that are left grow old . . .', is his own memorial.

1. 

2.

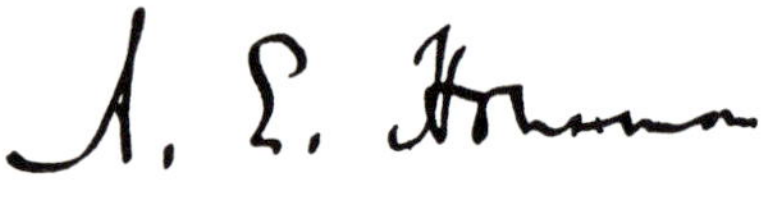
3.

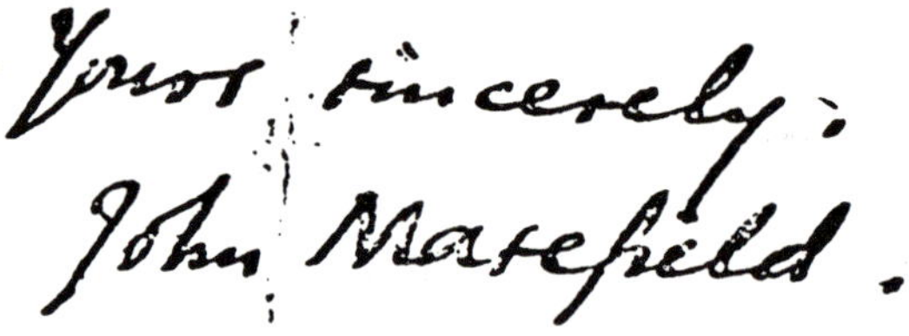
4.

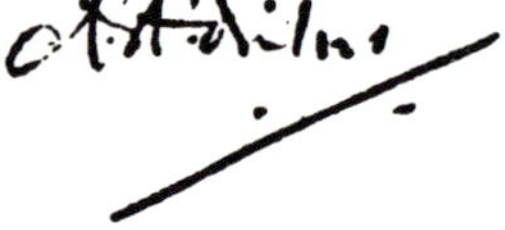
5.

6. 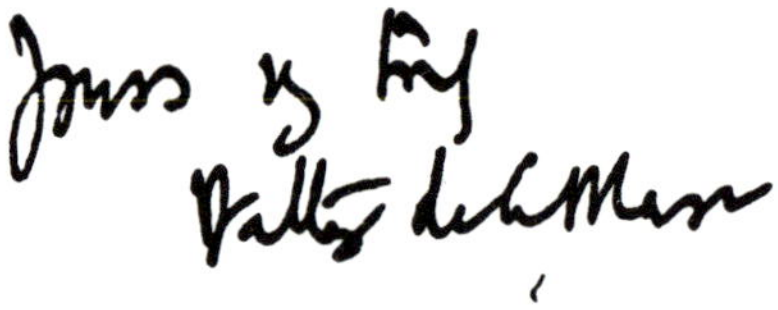

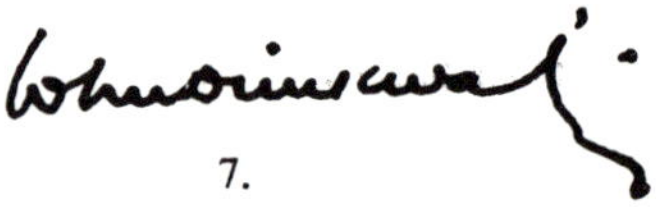
7.

8. 

1. **Rudyard Kipling.** 1865–1936. Equally famous as a short-story writer. Kipling letters from the latter part of his life are almost invariably typed; holograph examples are exceedingly rare.
2. **Robert Bridges.** 1844–1930. Poet Laureate. He frequently signed with his initials only.
3. **Alfred Edward Housman.** 1859–1936. His best known work is *A Shropshire Lad.*
4. **John Masefield.** 1878–1967. Poet Laureate. His handwriting is not always as heavy as in this example.
5. **Alan A. Milne.** 1882–1956. In addition to his poems for children he is remembered as a humorist and as the creator of 'Winnie the Pooh'.
6. **Walter de la Mare.** 1873–1956.
7. **John Drinkwater.** 1882–1937.
8. **Sir Rabindranath Tagore.** 1861–1941. Indian poet-philosopher. The first Asian to win the Nobel Prize for Literature (1913).

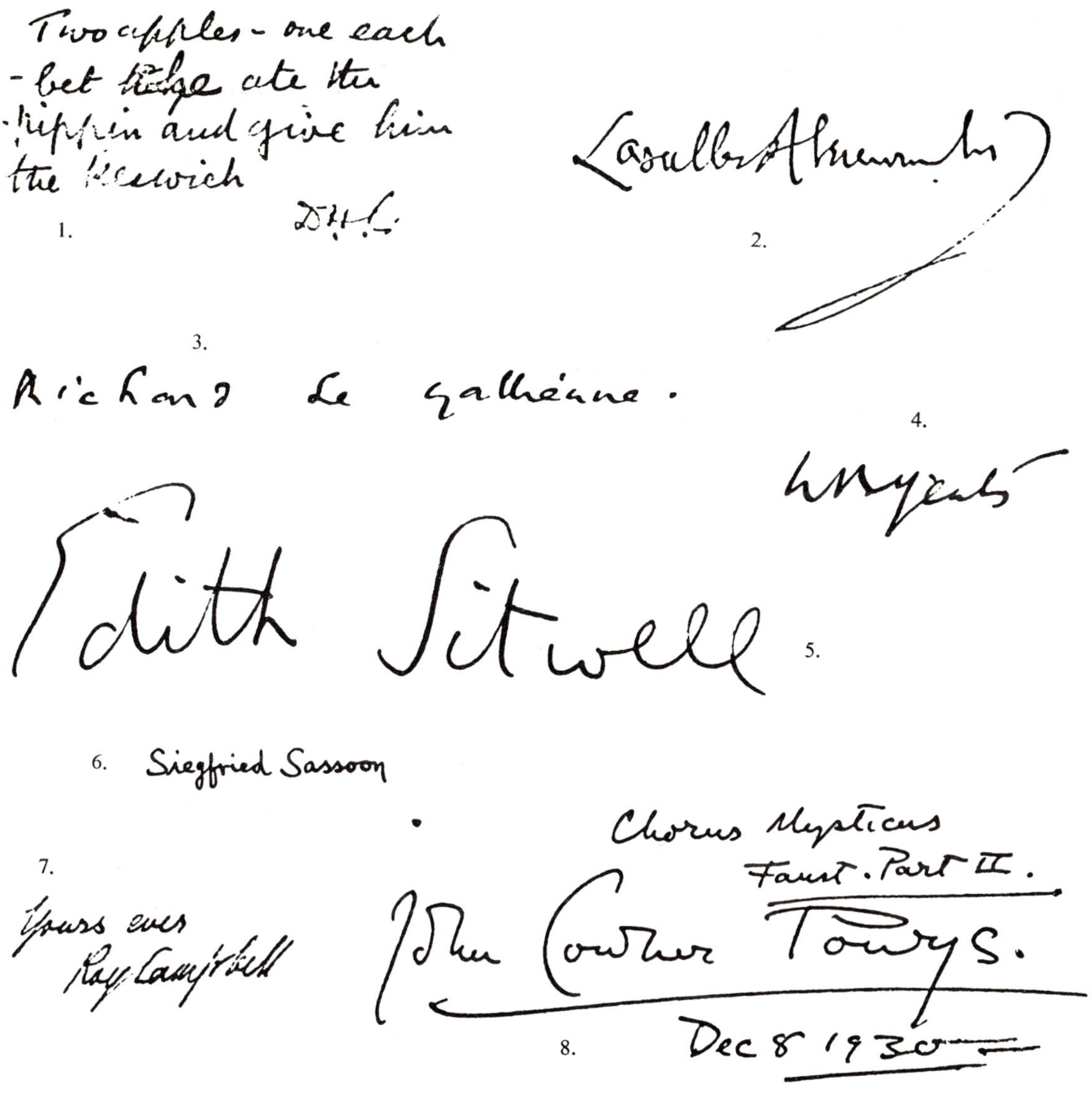

1. **David Herbert Lawrence.** 1885–1930. Equally famous as a novelist. His comparatively scarce autograph is now avidly sought-after.
2. **Lascelles Abercrombie.** 1881–1938.
3. **Richard Le Gallienne.** 1866–1947.
4. **William Butler Yeats.** 1865–1939. The autograph of this distinguished Irish poet-dramatist is much in demand.
5. **Dame Edith Sitwell.** 1887–1964.
6. **Siegfried L. Sassoon.** 1886–1967.
7. **Roy Campbell.** 1901–57. South-African poet.
8. **John Cowper Powys.** 1872–1963. Also known for his philosophical essays and as a novelist.

1.

2.

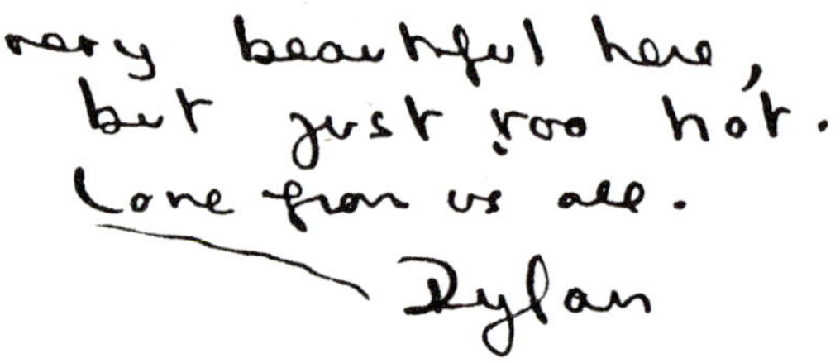

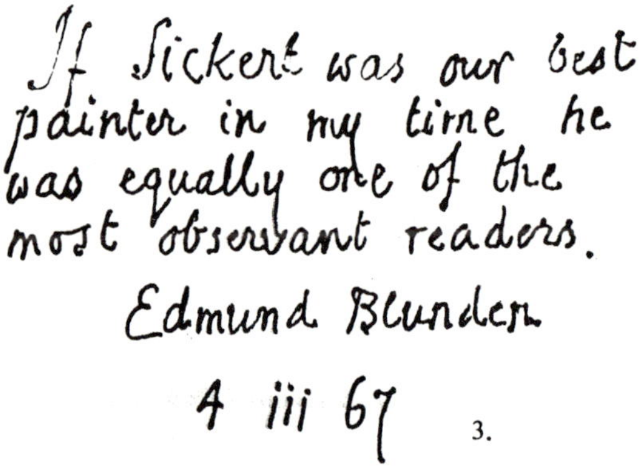

3.

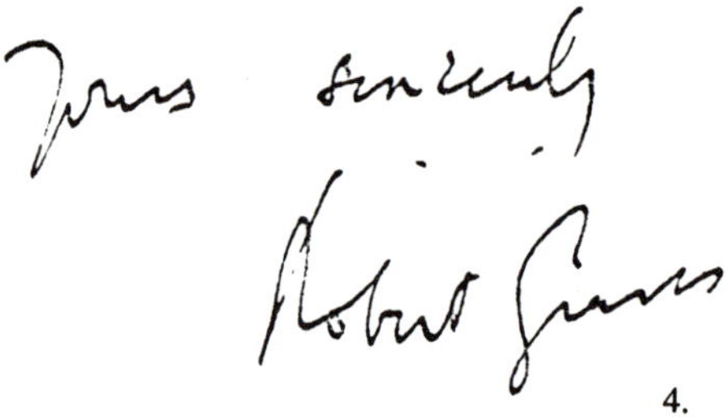

4.

6.

5.

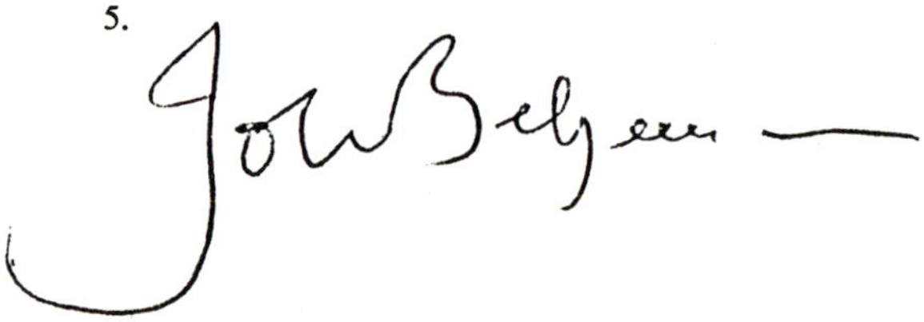

7.

8.

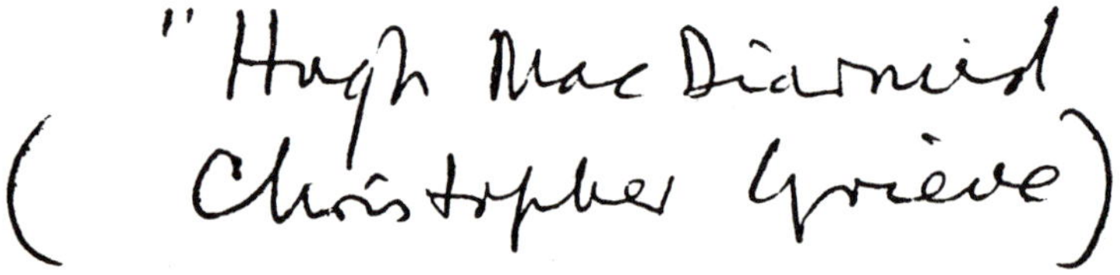

9.

1. **Louis MacNeice.** 1907–63.
2. **Dylan Thomas.** 1914–53. At present the rare autograph of this poet is one of the most sought-after in contemporary literature.
3. **Edmund Blunden.** 1896– . Written on the fly-leaf of Sickert's personal copy of Blunden's book on B. R. Haydon.
4. **Robert Graves.** 1895– .
5. **Sir John Betjeman.** 1906– .
6. **Sir Sacheverell Sitwell.** 1897– . Distinguished as both a poet and a critic. Younger brother of Sir Osbert and Dame Edith Sitwell (see pages 130, 133).
7. **Sir Alan P. Herbert.** 1890– . Humorous versifier, librettist and novelist.
8. **'Hugh MacDiarmid' (Christopher M. Grieve).** 1892– . One of the leaders of the Scottish literary renascence.
9. **Cecil Day-Lewis.** 1904– . The present Poet Laureate. He has also written many detective stories under the pseudonym 'Nicholas Blake'.

1.

2.

3.

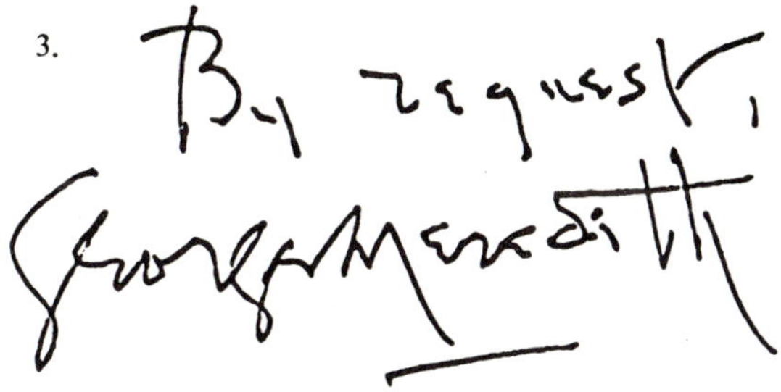

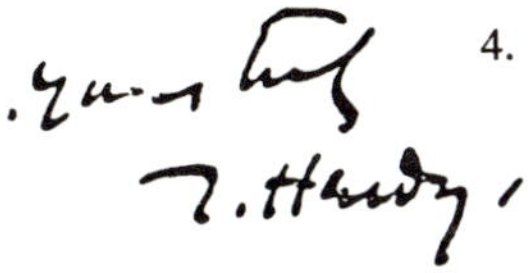

4.

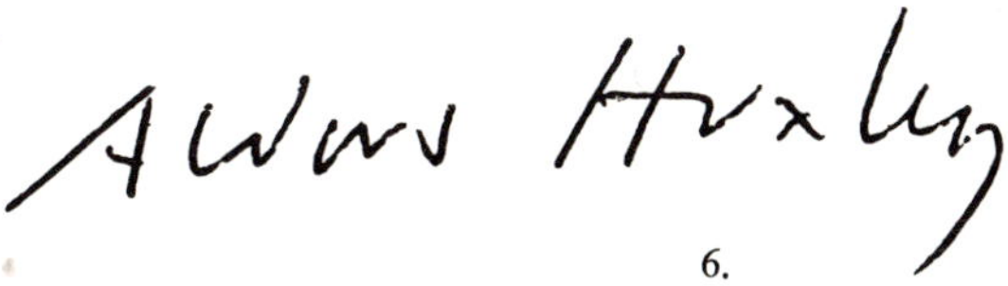

6.

5.

8.

7.

9.

1. **Sir (J.) Percy Fitzpatrick.** 1862–1931. South-African statesman, celebrated for his novel *Jock of the Bushveld.*
2. **Olive Schreiner.** 1855–1920. Author of *The Story of a South African Farm.*
3. **George Meredith.** 1828–1909.
4. **Thomas Hardy.** 1840–1928. Equally distinguished as a poet. Hardy autographs, once plentiful, are now so much in demand that they are becoming scarce.
5. **Herbert George Wells.** 1866–1946.
6. **Aldous (L.) Huxley.** 1894–1963.
7. **(Marguerite) Radclyffe Hall.** 1886–1943. Her novel *The Well of Loneliness* (1928), with its theme of lesbianism, was banned in Britain but not in the U.S.
8. **W. Somerset Maugham.** 1874–1965.
9. **Daphne du Maurier.** 1907–   . Lady Browning. Daughter of Sir Gerald du Maurier (see page 159).

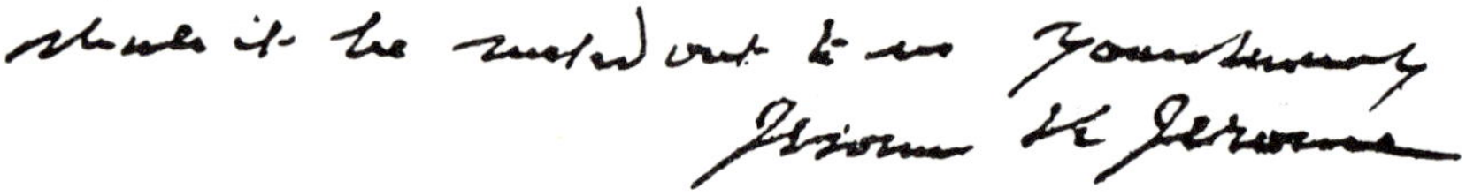

1.

2.

3.

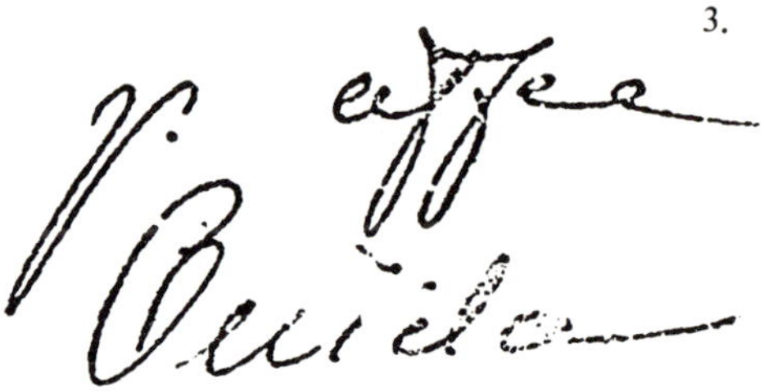

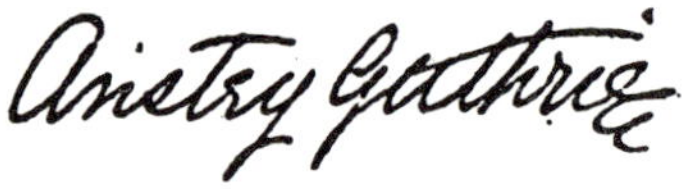

4.

5.

6.

7.

8.

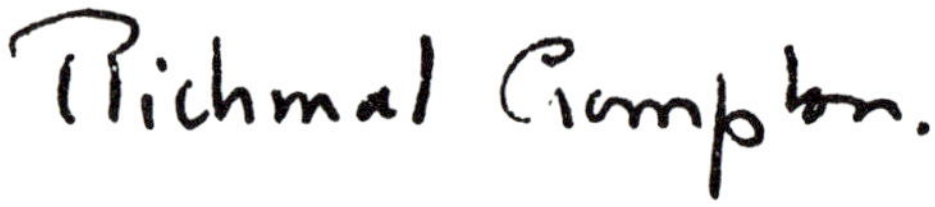

9.

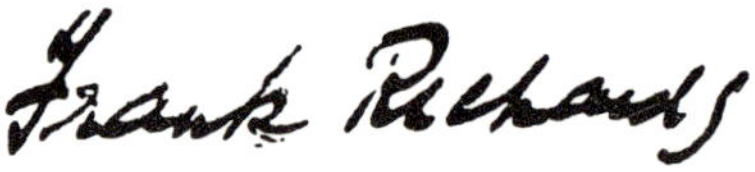

1. **Jerome K. Jerome.** 1859–1927. Humorist, author of *Three Men in a Boat*.
2. **'Marie Corelli' (Mary Mackay).** 1855–1924. Romantic novelist.
3. **'Ouida' (Louise de la Ramée).** 1839–1908. Author of *Under Two Flags*.
4. **T. Anstey Guthrie ('Francis Anstey').** 1856–1934. Humorist, best known for his novel *Vice Versa*.
5. **William John Locke.** 1863–1930. Author of *The Beloved Vagabond*. Also a dramatist.
6. **Pelham G. Wodehouse.** 1881– . Humorist.
7. **William Wymark Jacobs.** 1863–1943. Writer of the humorous and the macabre.
8. **'Richmal Crompton' (Richmal Crompton Lamburn).** 1890–1969. For many years a schoolmistress, she was the author of the 'William' books.
9. **Frank Richards.** 1875–1961. Author of the 'Billy Bunter' books for boys.

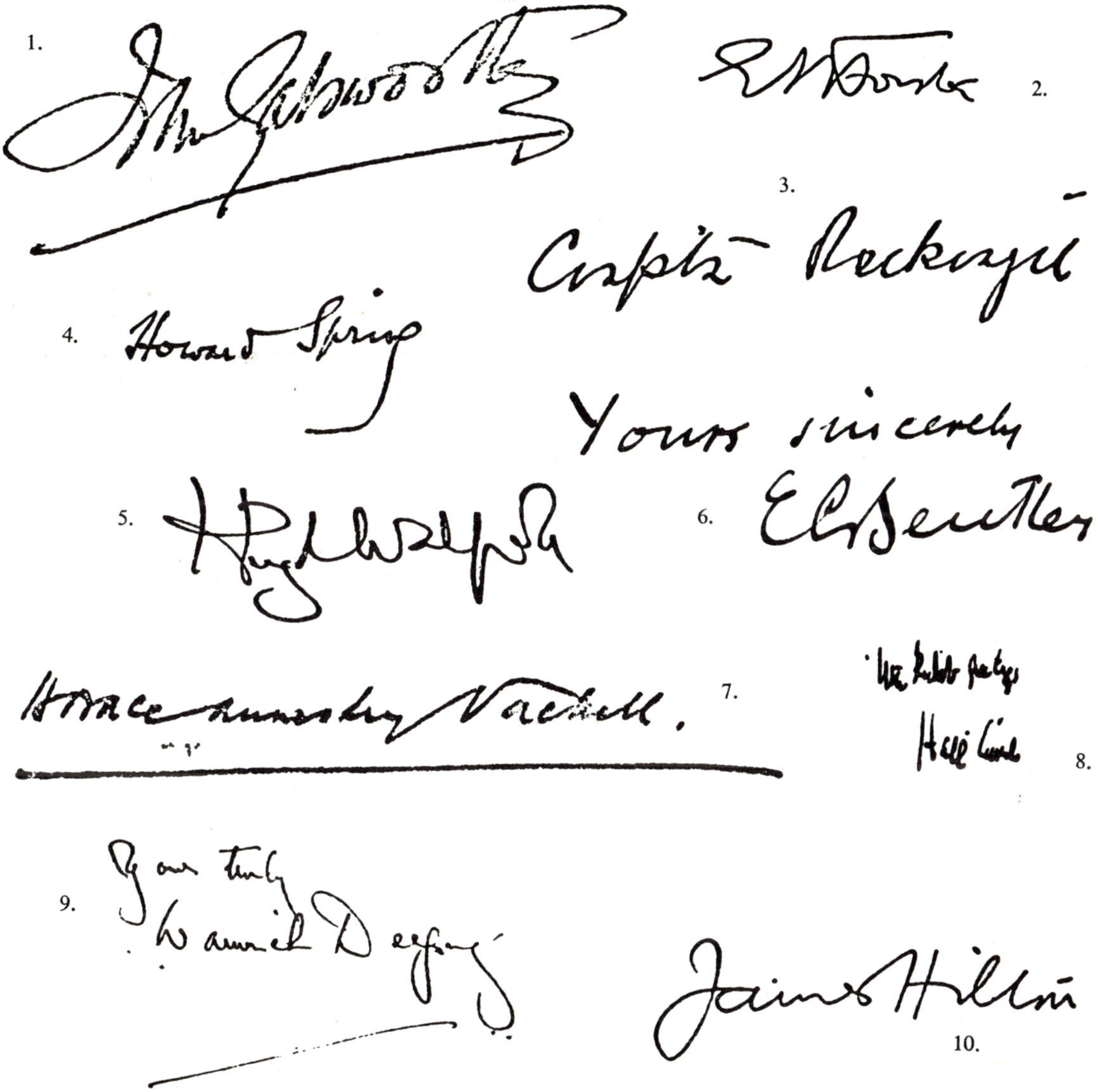

1. **John Galsworthy.** 1867–1933. Won the Nobel Prize for Literature, 1932.
2. **Edward Morgan Forster.** 1879–1970. His masterpiece was *A Passage to India*.
3. **Sir (E. M.) Compton Mackenzie.** 1883–
4. **Howard Spring.** 1889–1965.
5. **Sir Hugh (S.) Walpole.** 1884–1941.
6. **Edmund Clerihew Bentley.** 1875–1956. His novel *Trent's Last Case* (1913) began a new era in the style of detective-story writing. Also he originated and gave his name to the two-couplet nonsense verse, the 'clerihew'.
7. **Horace Annesley Vachell.** 1861–1955. Author of *The Hill*.
8. **Sir (T. H.) Hall Caine.** 1853–1931. His small writing is fairly easily identified; also he had a curious habit of leaving very considerable margins on both sides of his autograph letters.
9. **(G.) Warwick Deeping.** 1877–1950. Author of *Sorrell and Son*.
10. **James Hilton.** 1900–54. Author of *Goodbye, Mr Chips*.

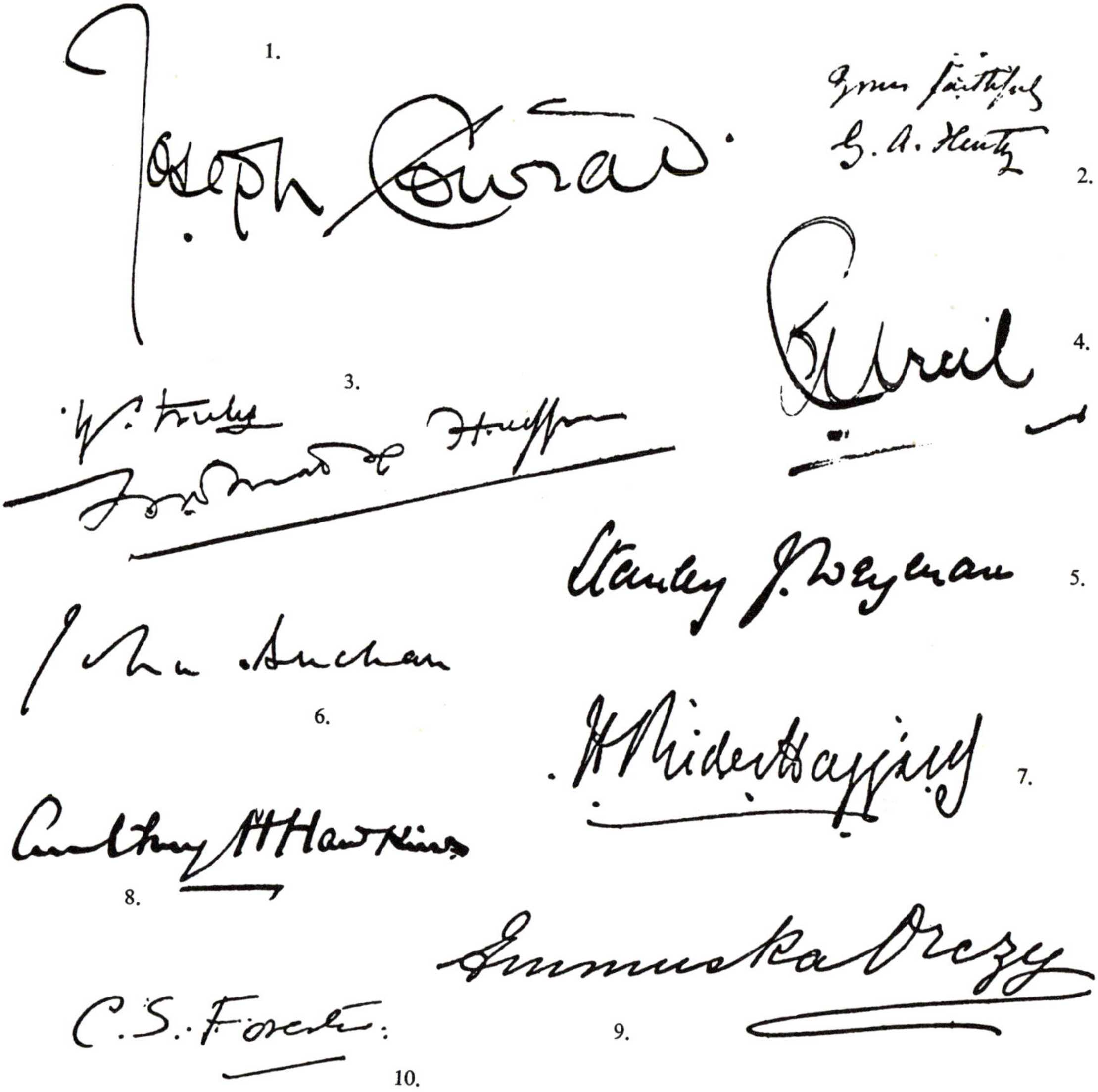

1. **Joseph Conrad.** 1857–1924. Polish-born, he was naturalized British in 1884. His autograph is greatly sought-after.
2. **George A. Henty.** 1832–1902. Prolific writer of historical adventure books for boys.
3. **Ford Madox Hueffer.** 1873–1939. In 1923 changed his surname to Ford. Collaborated with Conrad.
4. **Percival C. Wren.** 1885–1941. Creator of 'Beau Geste'.
5. **Stanley J. Weyman.** 1855–1928. Wrote *Under the Red Robe.*
6. **John Buchan (Lord Tweedsmuir).** 1875–1940. Governor-General of Canada, 1935. His signature is usually found as 'Tweedsmuir' after that date.
7. **Sir H. Rider Haggard.** 1856–1925. Author of *King Solomon's Mines.*
8. **'Anthony Hope' (Sir Anthony Hope Hawkins).** 1863–1933. Author of *The Prisoner of Zenda.*
9. **Baroness Emmuska Orczy.** 1865–1947. Author of *The Scarlet Pimpernel.*
10. **Cecil Scott Forester.** 1899–1966. Creator of 'Captain Hornblower'.

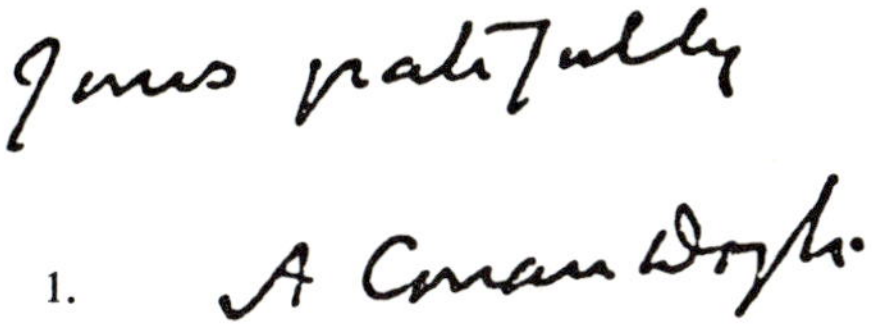
1.

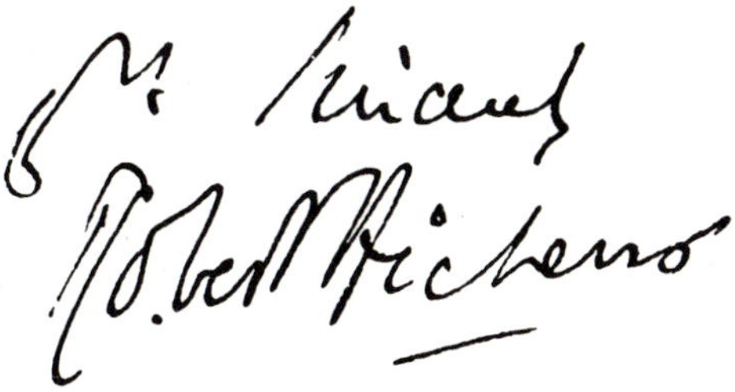
2.

3.
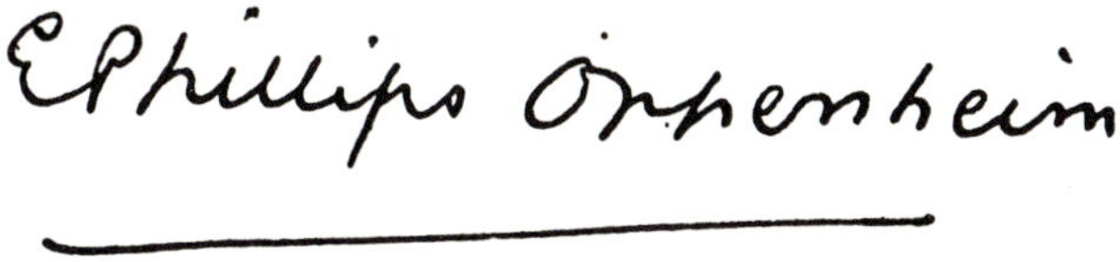

4.

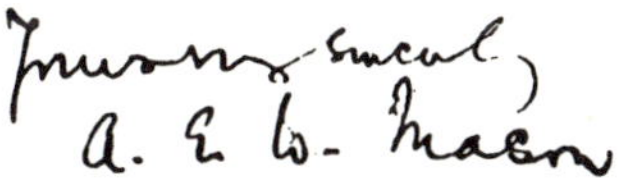
5.

6.

7.

8.

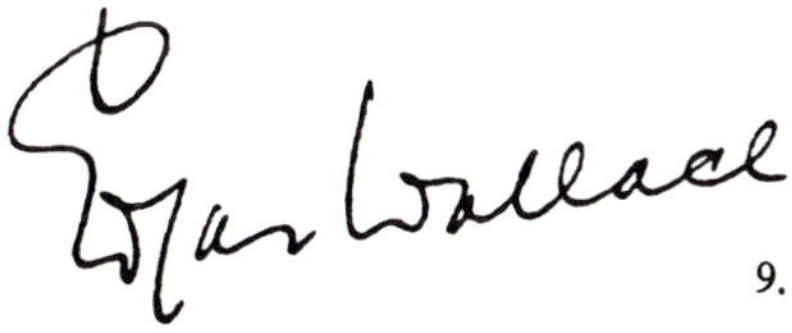
9.

1. **Sir Arthur Conan Doyle.** 1859–1930. Creator of 'Sherlock Holmes'. Collectors are warned that some of Conan Doyle's letters are written and/or signed on his behalf by an amanuensis whose handwriting is rather more regular than, but similar to, his own.
2. **Robert Hichens.** 1864–1950. Wrote *The Garden of Allah.*
3. **E. Phillips Oppenheim.** 1866–1946.
4. **'Sax Rohmer' (A. Sarsfield Ward).** 1886–1959. Creator of 'Dr Fu Manchu'.
5. **Alfred E. W. Mason.** 1865–1948. Author of historical and detective novels.
6. **George D. H. Cole.** 1889–1958. Author of detective stories (all written in collaboration with his wife) and distinguished economist.
7. **Agatha Christie.** 1891– . In private life Mrs M. E. Mallowan.
8. **Ian Fleming.** 1908–64. Creator of 'James Bond'.
9. **Edgar Wallace.** 1875–1932.

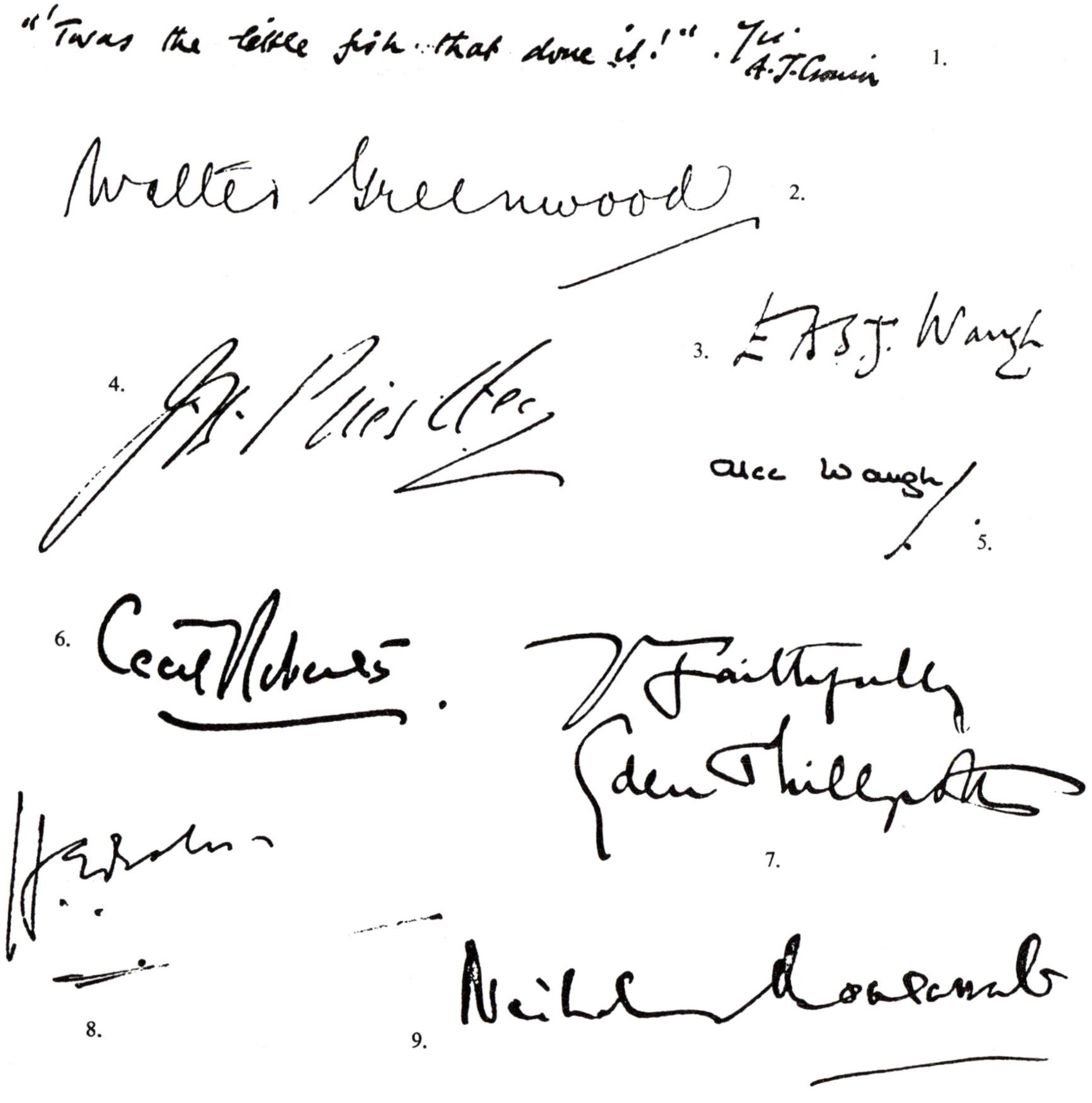

1. **Archibald Joseph Cronin.** 1896– . A former doctor. His novels include *The Citadel* and *Hatter's Castle*.
2. **Walter Greenwood.** 1903– . Also a dramatist, his best known novel is *Love on the Dole*.
3. **Evelyn (A. St J.) Waugh.** 1903–66. Author of *Decline and Fall, Men at Arms*, etc.
4. **John Boynton Priestley.** 1894– . Equally distinguished as a playwright and a critic.
5. **Alec (Alexander Raban) Waugh.** 1898– . Brother of Evelyn Waugh, 3 above, he first made his name with that classic of school life, *The Loom of Youth*.
6. **Cecil (E. M.) Roberts.** 1892– . Also a poet and playwright.
7. **Eden Phillpotts.** 1862–1960. A prolific author, he wrote over 250 books.
8. **Herbert Ernest Bates.** 1905– . Also a playwright, short-story writer and literary critic.
9. **Nicholas (J. T.) Monsarrat.** 1910– . Author of *The Cruel Sea*.

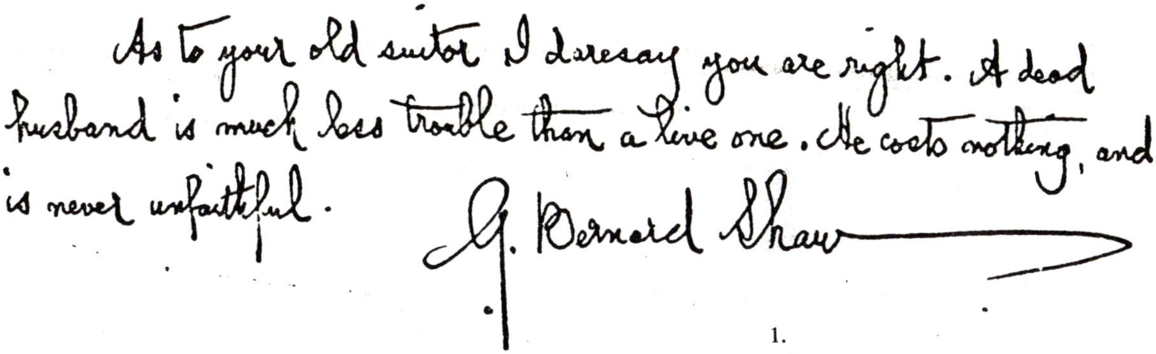

1.

2.

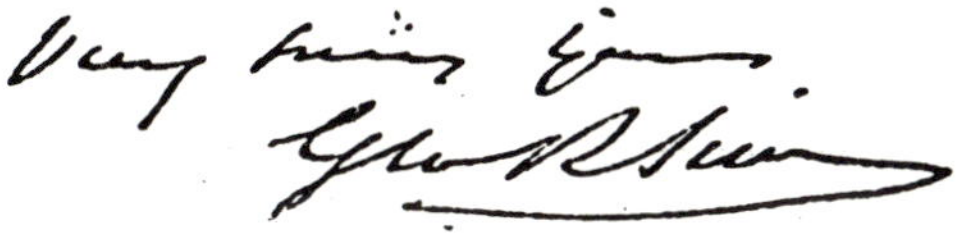

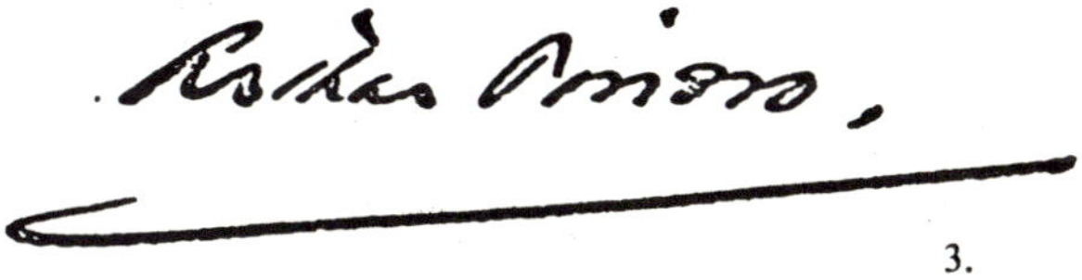

3.

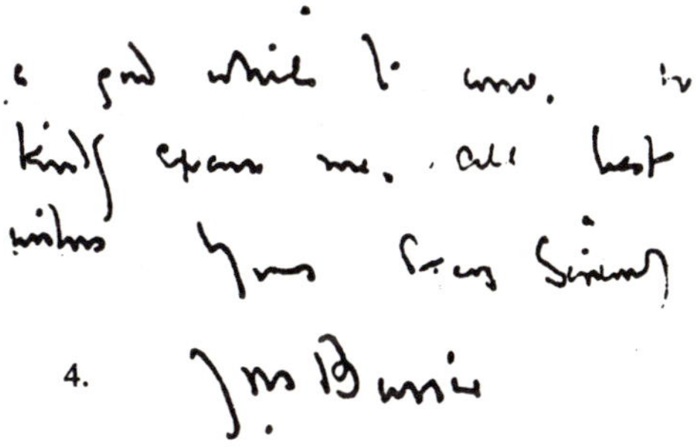

4.

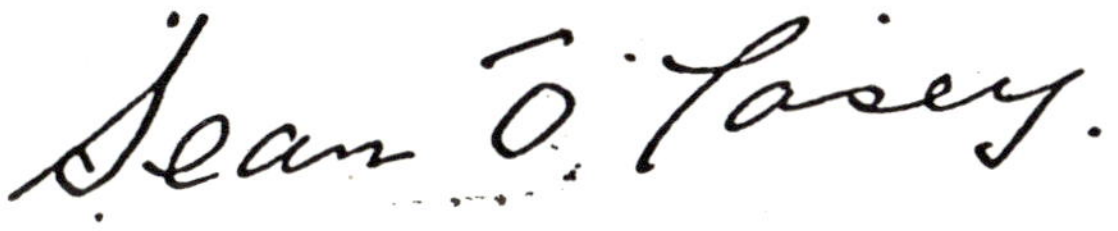

5.

6.

7.

1. **George Bernard Shaw.** 1856–1950. See page 22.
2. **George Robert Sims.** 1847–1922. Author of such melodramas as *The Lights of London*, he also wrote articles under the pseudonym 'Dragonet'. Sims was himself an autograph collector and wrote a small book on the subject (see Bibliography).
3. **Sir Arthur W. Pinero.** 1855–1934. Author of still popular Victorian and Edwardian farces.
4. **Sir James M. Barrie.** 1860–1937. Universally known for *Peter Pan*. Care must be taken by the collector in identifying Barrie autographs. He wrote in two different hands and some of his 'autograph' letters were written for him. The example above is typical of his best-known handwriting. His other holograph is larger and more readable.
5. **Sean O'Casey.** 1884–1964.
6. **Patrick Hamilton.** 1904–62. Author of *Rope*.
7. **Sir Noël Coward.** 1899–   . Distinguished also as an actor and composer.

ARTISTS: SEVENTEENTH- TO EARLY NINETEENTH-CENTURY PAINTERS

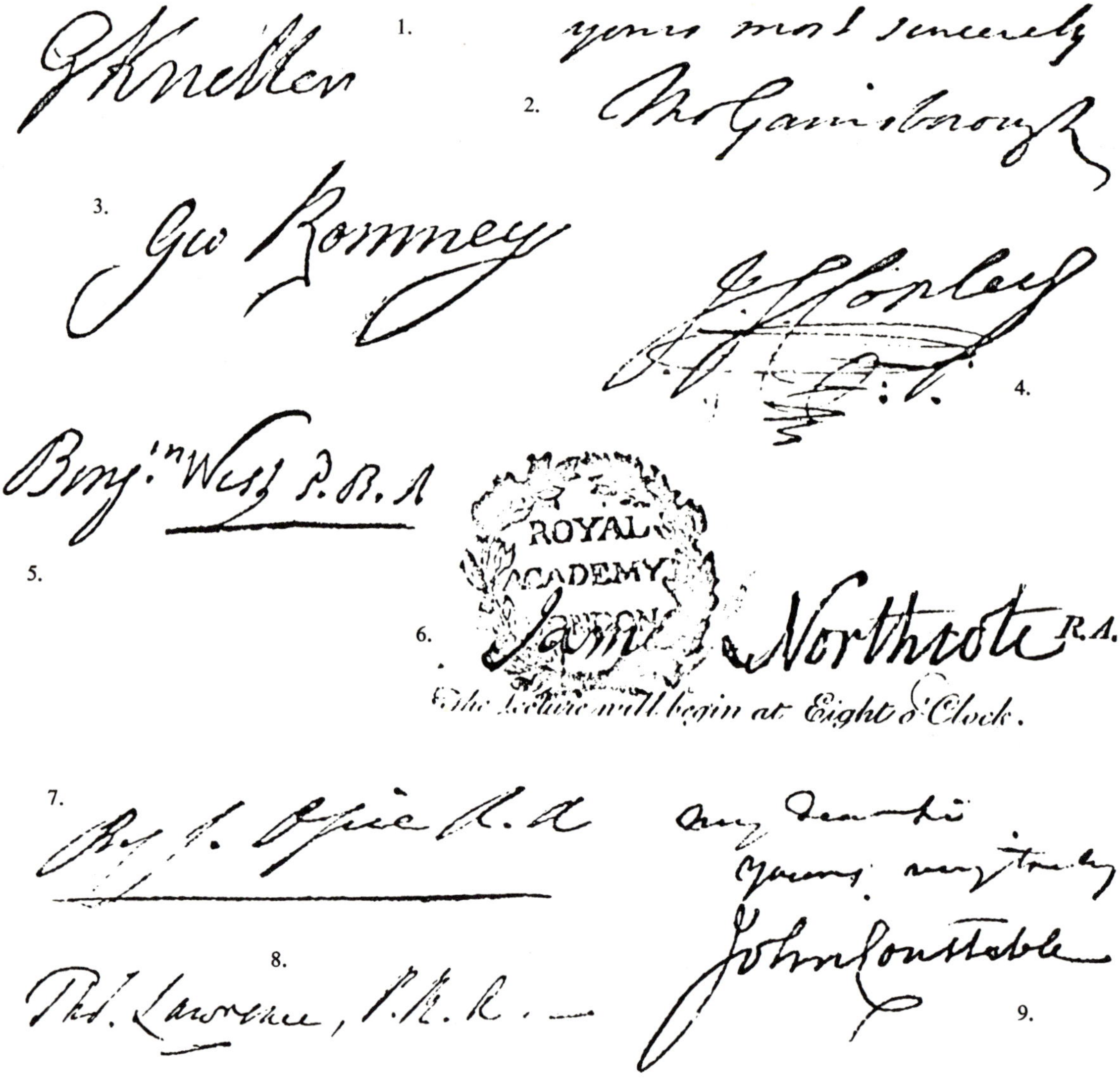

1. **Sir Godfrey Kneller.** 1646–1723. Court painter to the later Stuarts, Lely's successor.
2. **Thomas Gainsborough.** 1727–88. One of the great English masters. A valuable autograph.
3. **George Romney.** 1734–1802. Portrait painter. Painted over thirty portraits of Lady Hamilton.
4. **John Singleton Copley.** 1737–1815. Born in Boston, U.S.A., this celebrated historical and portrait painter lived for forty years in Britain and became a Royal Academician.
5. **Benjamin West.** 1738–1820. American-born, he lived in London for nearly sixty years and was President of the Royal Academy, as which he signs 'P.R.A.' above.
6. **James Northcote.** 1746–1831. Historical and portrait painter.
7. **John Opie.** 1761–1807. 'The Cornish Wonder'. Historical and portrait painter.
8. **Sir Thomas Lawrence.** 1769–1830. Portrait painter. Signed above as 'P.R.A.' (President, Royal Academy).
9. **John Constable.** 1776–1837. Landscape painter.

1.

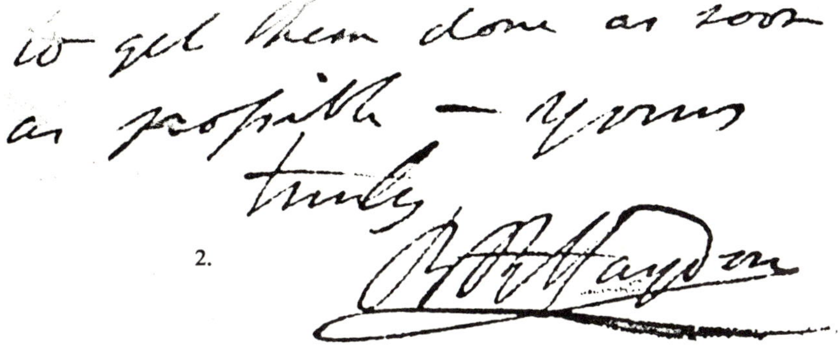

2.

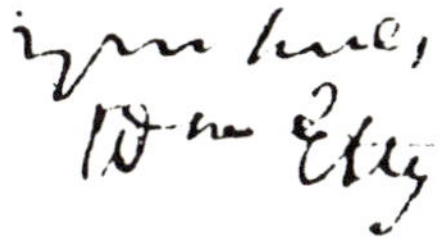

3.

4.

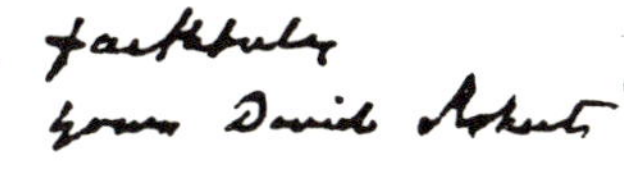

5.

6.

7.

8.

1. **Joseph M. W. Turner.** 1775–1851. One of the greatest masters of land- and sea-scapes, and of water-colour.
2. **Benjamin R. Haydon.** 1786–1846. Turbulent and ill-fated historical painter.
3. **William Etty.** 1787–1849. Known for his nudes, classical and historical subjects.
4. **David Roberts.** 1796–1864. Scots painter and traveller. This very small autograph is typical.
5. **Sir David Wilkie.** 1785–1841.
6. **Sir Charles L. Eastlake.** 1793–1865. Historical painter; President of the Royal Academy.
7. **William Mulready.** 1786–1863. The autograph of this Irish painter interests philatelists and postal history collectors because he designed the first (ornamental) penny-postage envelope: the Mulready envelope, 1840.
8. **Edward Lear.** 1812–88. An accomplished landscape painter, Lear is remembered for his illustrated travel books and his celebrated *Book of Nonsense*.

1.

2.

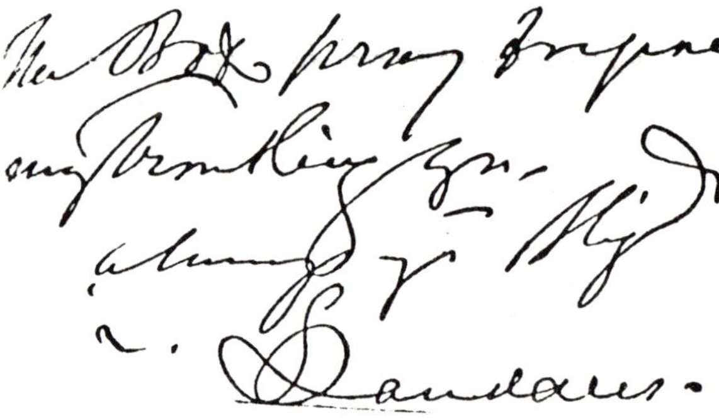

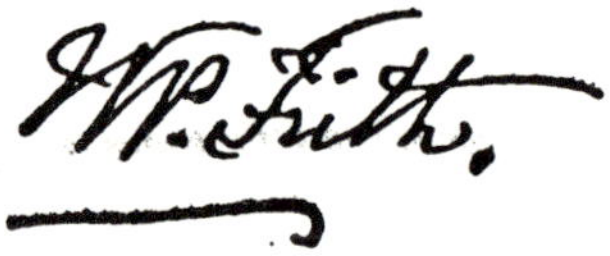

3.

4.

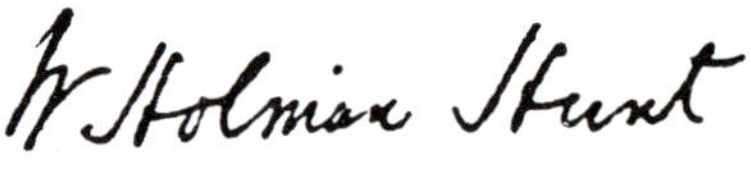

5.

6.

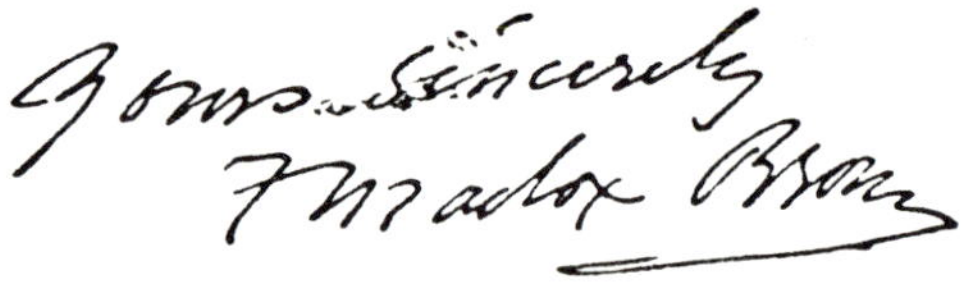

7.

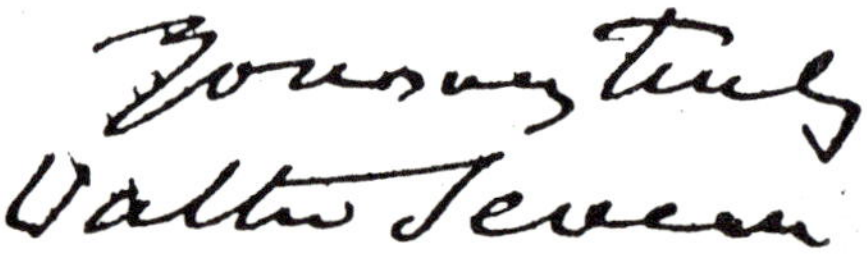

8.

9.

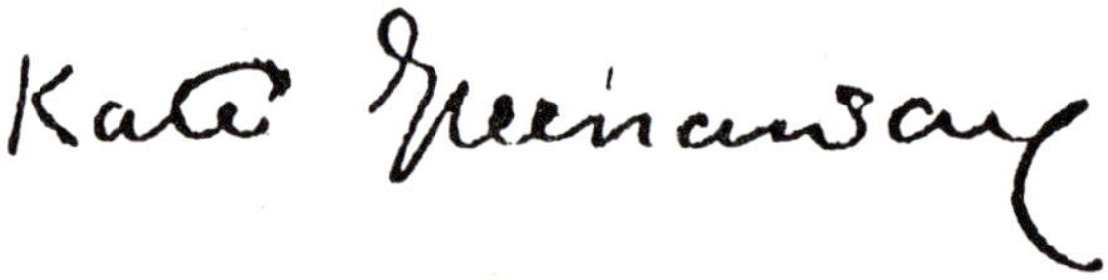

1. **Frederic, Lord Leighton.** 1830–96. President of the Royal Academy. Leighton's extrovert signature is never found as a peer because he died the day after he was made one.
2. **Sir Edwin H. Landseer.** 1802–73. This famous animal painter's signature is often more complicated than the example above and he frequently signed with an elaborate monogram only.
3. **William P. Frith.** 1819–1909.
4. **Sir Edward Burne-Jones.** 1833–98. This painter, who was much influenced by the Pre-Raphaelites, often wrote a less regular hand or signed with initials only.
5. **William Holman Hunt.** 1827–1910. Pre-Raphaelite, famed for his 'Light of the World'.
6. **Sir John E. Millais.** 1829–96. Pre-Raphaelite, often signed 'J. E. Millais'.
7. **Ford Madox Brown.** 1821–93. Pre-Raphaelite.
8. **Walter Severn.** 1830–1904. Water-colourist.
9. **Catherine (Kate) Greenaway.** 1846–1901. Painter, famed for writing and illustrating children's books.

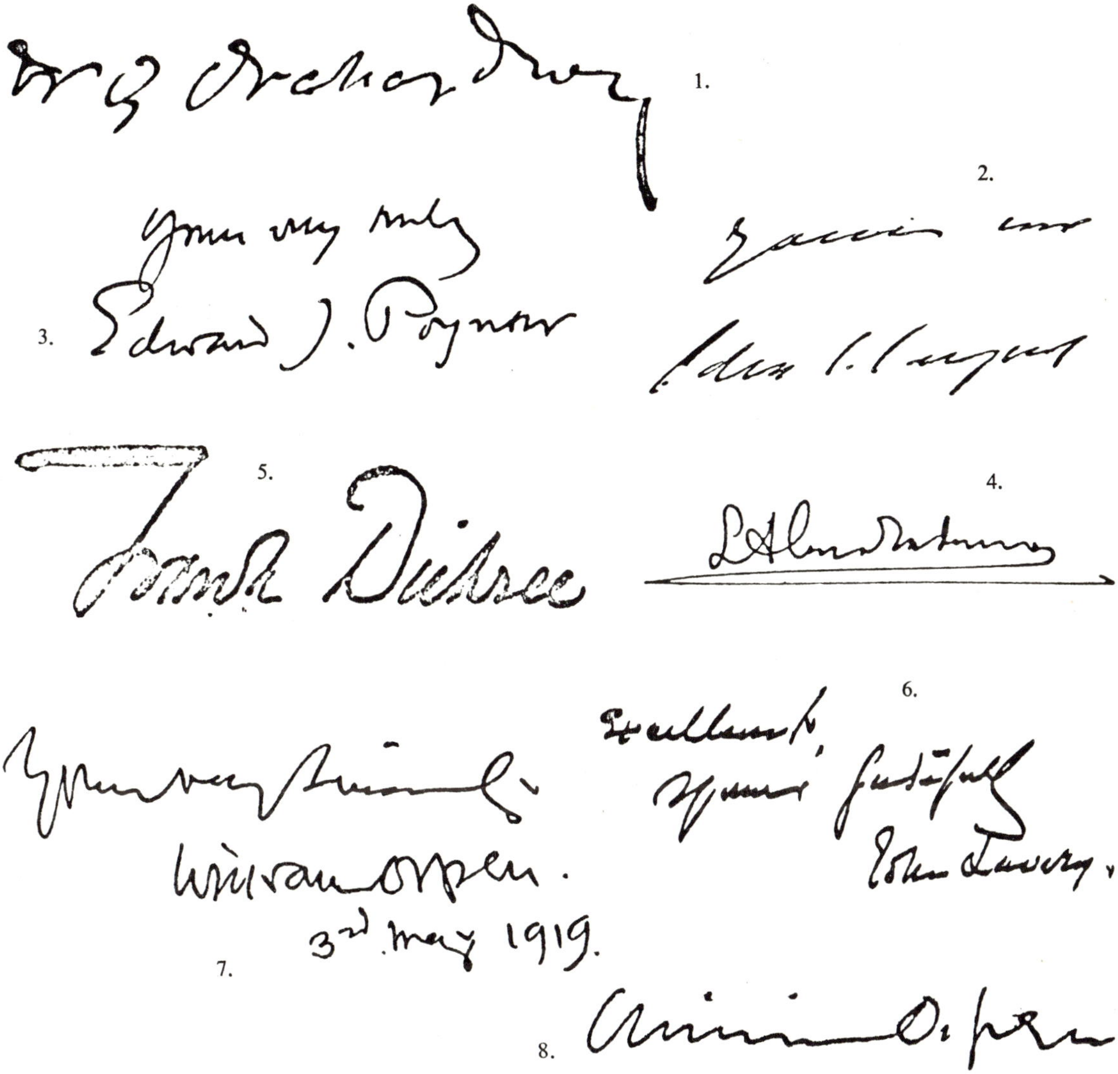

1. **Sir William Q. Orchardson.** 1832–1910. Painter of historical and social themes.
2. **John Singer Sargent.** 1856–1925. This renowned American painter lived and worked mostly in England, becoming a Royal Academician and the most fashionable portrait painter of his time. His autograph, particularly his signature, is not easily identified.
3. **Sir Edward J. Poynter.** 1836–1919. President of the Royal Academy, 1896.
4. **Sir Laurence Alma-Tadema.** 1836–1912. Classical painter.
5. **Sir Frank Dicksee.** 1853–1928. President of the Royal Academy, 1924.
6. **Sir John Lavery.** 1856–1941. Irish portrait painter.

7 and 8. **Sir William Orpen.** 1878–1931. Portrait, genre and war-scene painter. Here are perfect examples of how someone writing in a hurry, as in 8 above, can produce a totally different style to his normal one. Yet both examples were written in the same year, 1919. For discussion on this subject, see page 37.

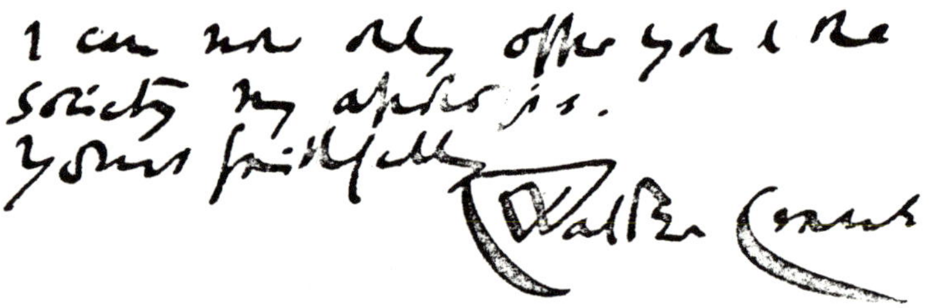

1.

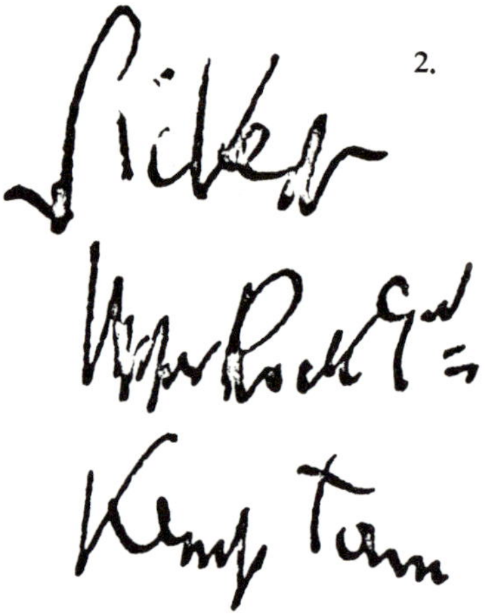

2.

3.

4.

5.

6.

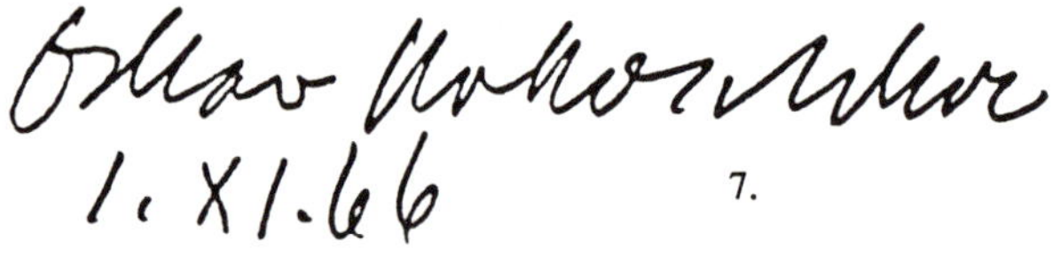

7.

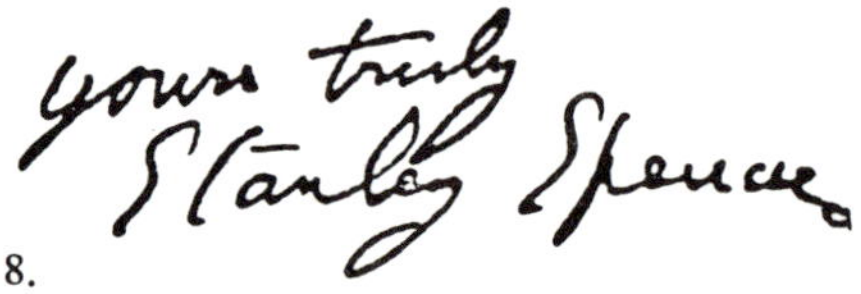

8.

1. **Walter Crane.** 1845–1915. Painter and illustrator, associated with William Morris in the romantic movement of decorative art.
2. **Walter R. Sickert.** 1860–1942. One of the most important of the British impressionists.
3. **Paul Nash.** 1889–1946. War artist, designer, engraver and near-Surrealist.
4. **Dame Laura Knight.** 1877–1970. The first woman Royal Academician, particularly known for her ballet and circus scenes.
5. **Augustus John.** 1878–1961. Painter-etcher.
6. **Sir Frank Brangwyn.** 1867–1956. Painter-etcher, famed for his murals.
7. **Oskar Kokoschka.** 1886– . Expressionist painter and dramatist. Austrian-born, he became a naturalized Briton in 1947.
8. **Sir Stanley Spencer.** 1891–1959. Known in particular for his two paintings of the *Resurrection*, in the Tate Gallery, London.

1. **George Cruikshank.** 1792–1878. Also a celebrated illustrator (of Dickens's *Oliver Twist*, etc.). Note the differing styles in handwriting and signature; see also page 32.
2. **Thomas Rowlandson.** 1756–1827. Famous for his caricatures of Napoleon, he also illustrated Sterne's *A Sentimental Journey*.
3. **John Leech.** 1817–64. A major *Punch* cartoonist and illustrator.
4. **Sir John Tenniel.** 1820–1914. Cartoonist of *Punch* and illustrator of *Alice in Wonderland.* Note the monogram with which he signed his work, after his signature above.
5. **George du Maurier.** 1834–96. Wrote and illustrated three novels, notably *Trilby*.
6. **Phil May.** 1864–1903. Cartoonist and poster artist.
7. **Sir Bernard Partridge.** 1861–1945. Political cartoonist of *Punch*.
8. **Bruce Bairnsfather.** 1888–1959. Famous for his World War I character 'Old Bill' (shown above as part of his autograph), he was also official war cartoonist with the U.S. Army during World War II.

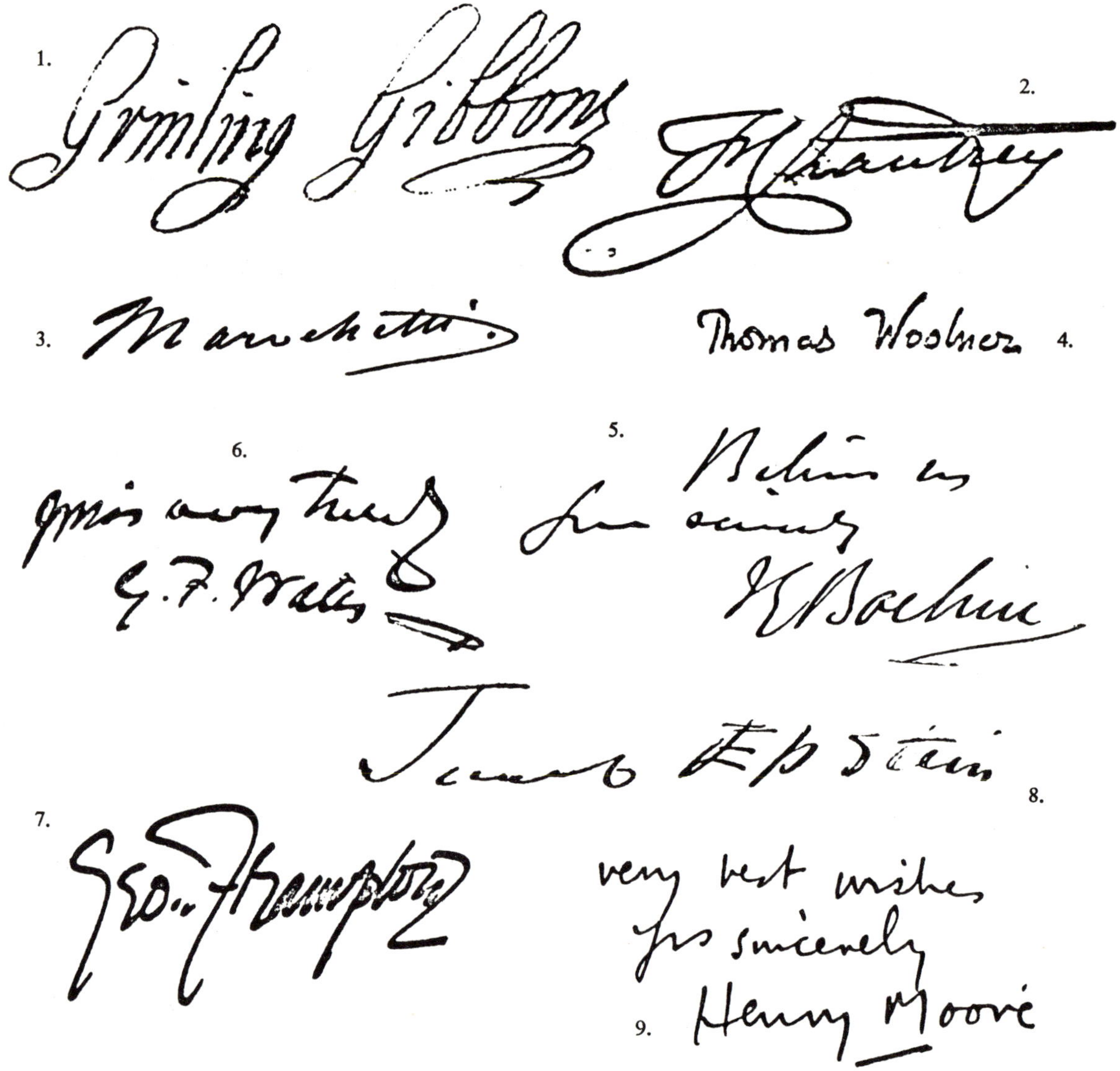

1. **Grinling Gibbons.** 1648–1720. Woodcarver and sculptor who worked with Wren. A very rare autograph.
2. **Sir Francis L. Chantrey.** 1781–1841. Left his fortune to the Royal Academy for the purchase of British works of art.
3. **Carlo, Baron Marochetti.** 1805–67. Produced the statue of Richard Cœur-de-Lion outside the Houses of Parliament.
4. **Thomas Woolner.** 1825–92. Pre-Raphaelite.
5. **Sir Joseph E. Boehm.** 1834–90. Produced the statue of Carlyle on the Chelsea Embankment.
6. **George Frederick Watts.** 1817–1904. Both painter and sculptor, he was briefly married to Ellen Terry.
7. **Sir George J. Frampton.** 1860–1928. Sculptor of the Edith Cavell Memorial and of Peter Pan in Kensington Gardens.
8. **Sir Jacob Epstein.** 1880–1959. One of the greatest and most controversial sculptors of his time.
9. **Henry S. Moore.** 1898–   . Perhaps the most original and powerful of living sculptors.

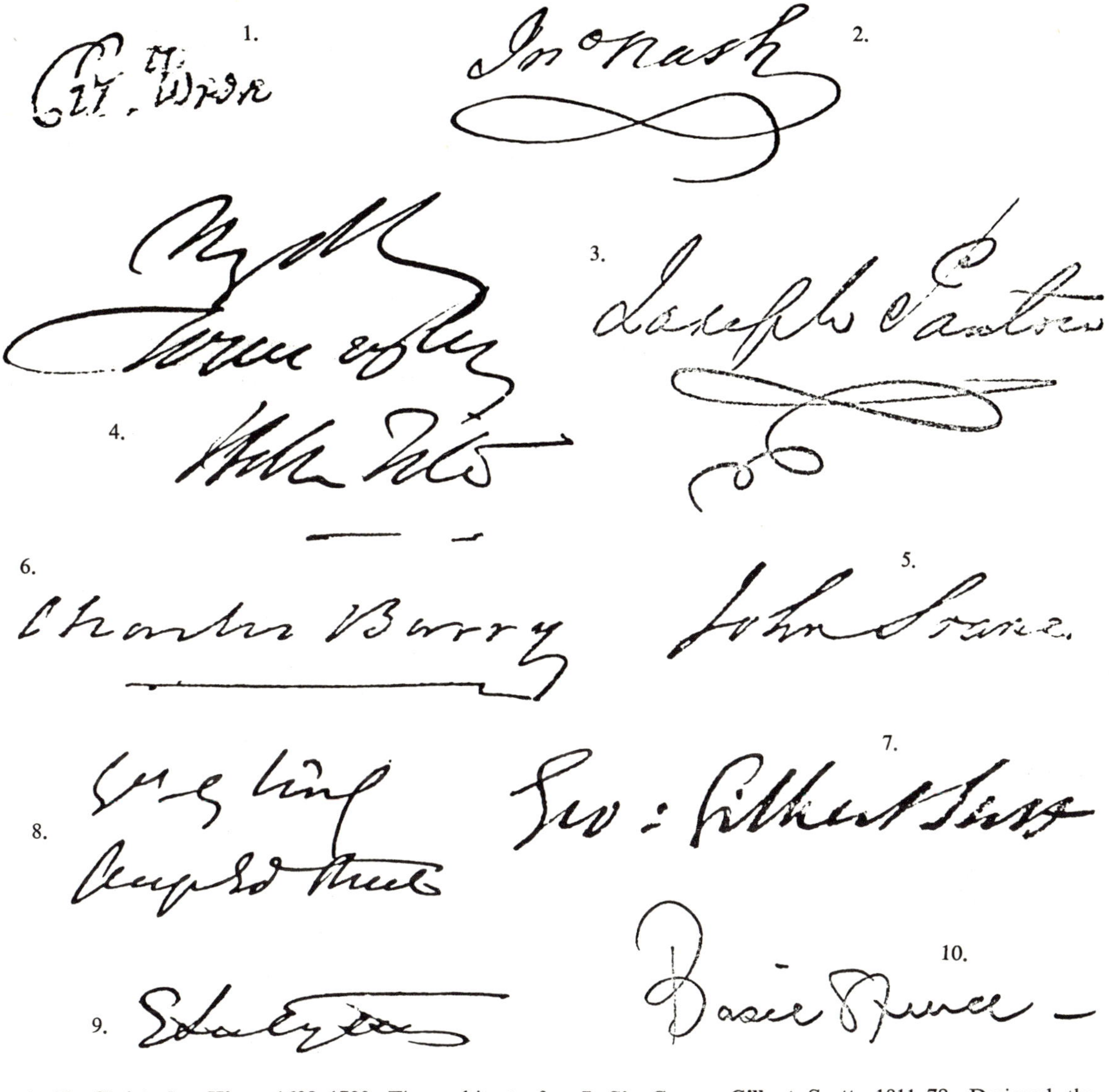

1. **Sir Christopher Wren.** 1632–1723. The architect of St Paul's Cathedral. A scarce autograph.
2. **John Nash.** 1752–1835. Regency architect (of Regent's Park, etc.).
3. **Sir Joseph Paxton.** 1801–65. Architect (of the Crystal Palace) and both a landscape and a working gardener (Chatsworth).
4. **Sir William Tite.** 1798–1873. Built many railway stations and rebuilt the Royal Exchange.
5. **Sir John Soane.** 1753–1837. Designed the Bank of England; his London house is now the Soane Museum.
6. **Sir Charles Barry.** 1795–1860. Architect of the Houses of Parliament.
7. **Sir George Gilbert Scott.** 1811–78. Designed the Albert Memorial, St Pancras Station, etc.
8. **George E. Street.** 1824–81. Architect of the London Law Courts.
9. **Sir Edwin L. Lutyens.** 1869–1944. Perhaps the greatest architect since Wren; designed the Roman Catholic Cathedral, Liverpool, and the Cenotaph, Whitehall.
10. **Sir Basil U. Spence.** 1907– . The leading contemporary British architect. Designed Coventry Cathedral.

1.

2.

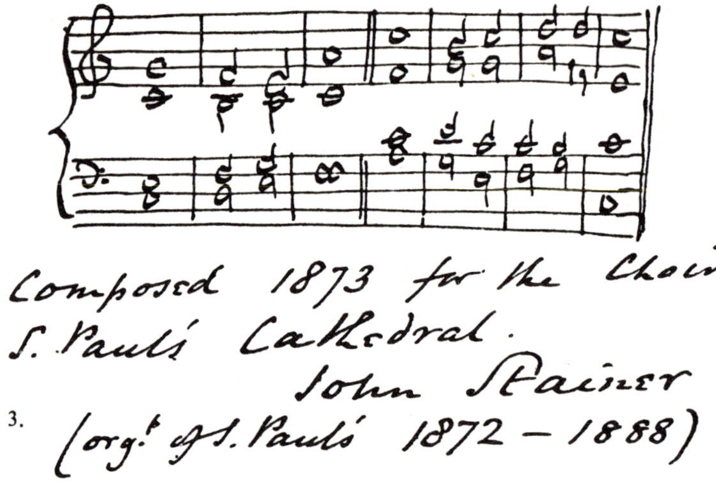

3.

4.

5.

6.

7.

8.

9.

1. **Sir George T. Smart.** 1776–1867. Composer and impresario. Musical director at Covent Garden.
2. **William Crotch.** 1775–1847. The first Principal of the Royal Academy of Music.
3. **Sir John Stainer.** 1840–1901. Composed cantatas and church music. A distinguished organist. An example of his holograph music.
4. **Michael W. Balfe.** 1808–70. Composed the operetta *The Bohemian Girl.*
5. **Sir Henry R. Bishop.** 1786–1855. The first musician to be knighted. Composed operas and songs such as *Home, Sweet Home.*
6. **Sir Julius Benedict.** 1804–85. Also a pianist and conductor, he accompanied Jenny Lind in America (1850).
7. **Sir Alexander C. Mackenzie.** 1847–1935. Principal of the Royal Academy of Music. An example of his holograph music.
8. **Sir Joseph Barnby.** 1838–96. Composer of hymns and other sacred music.
9. **Sir George J. Elvey.** 1816–93. Composer of anthems and organist of St George's Chapel, Windsor.

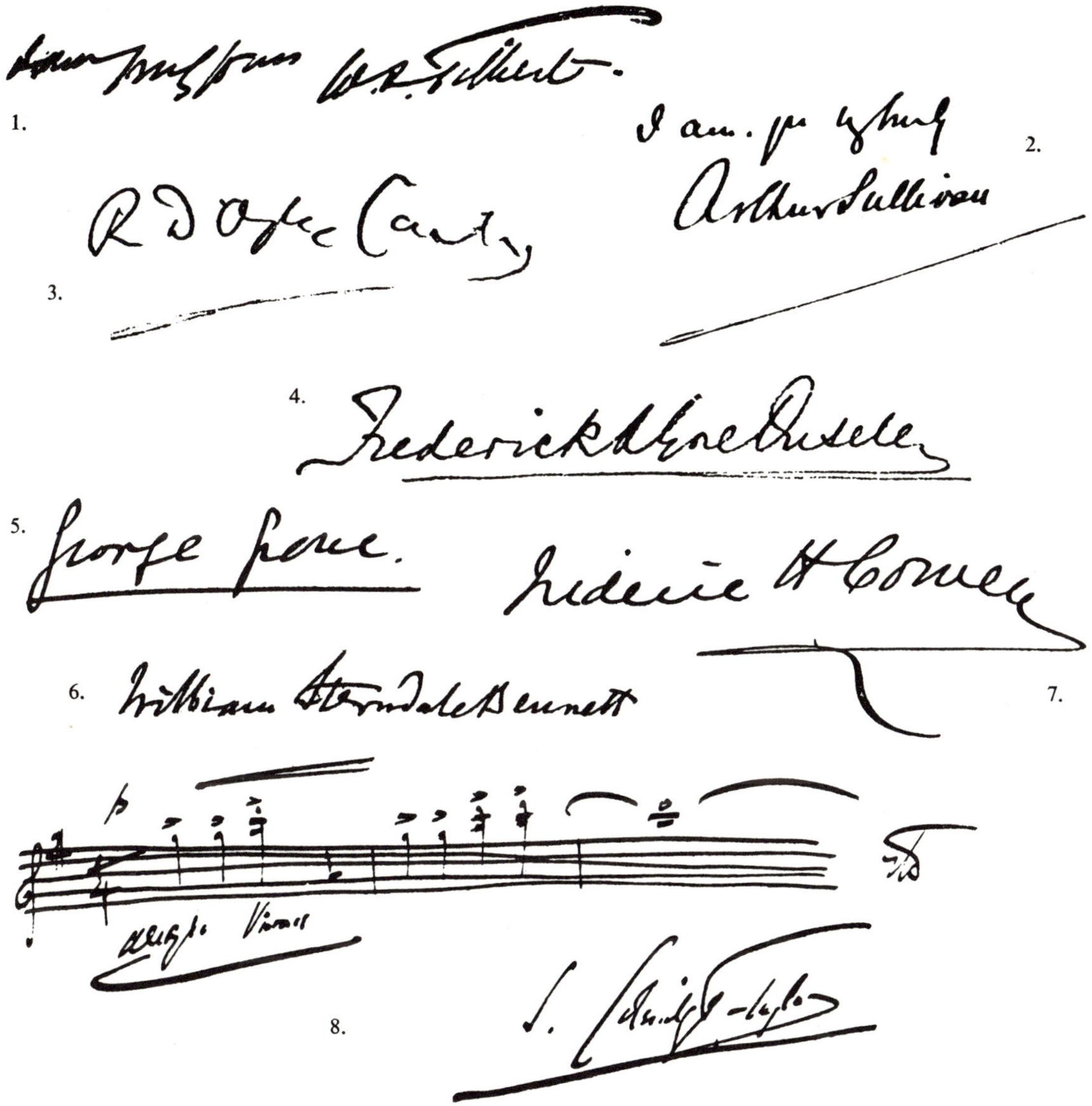

1. **Sir William S. Gilbert.** 1836–1911. Librettist of the famed 'Gilbert and Sullivan' ('Savoy') light operas.
2. **Sir Arthur Sullivan.** 1842–1900. Composer (with Gilbert as librettist) of the 'Gilbert and Sullivan' light operas.
3. **Richard D'Oyly Carte.** 1844–1901. Impresario; produced, at the Savoy Theatre (which he built), the 'Gilbert and Sullivan' light operas.
4. **Sir Frederick A. Gore Ouseley.** 1825–89. Also a notable theorist and organist.
5. **Sir George Grove.** 1820–1900. A musicologist, edited the *Dictionary of Music and Musicians.* He was also a civil engineer and director of the Crystal Palace Company.
6. **Sir William Sterndale Bennett.** 1816–75. Principal of the Royal College of Music.
7. **Sir Frederic H. Cowen.** 1852–1935. Prolific composer of songs (some 300), symphonies and cantatas.
8. **Samuel Coleridge-Taylor.** 1875–1912. Composer of *Hiawatha.* An example of his holograph music.

1. **Haydn Wood.** 1882–1959. A prolific composer, he was also a violinist. Above is an example of his holograph music—from his best-known ballad *Roses of Picardy.*
2. **Sir Charles V. Stanford.** 1852–1924. Professor of Music at Cambridge, he composed much church music and a number of operas.
3. **John Ireland.** 1879–1962. A particularly original composer, he studied under Stanford, 2 above.
4. **Percy Grainger.** 1882–1961. Australian-born, he became an American citizen in 1917. Particularly known for his folk music.
5. **Albert W. Ketèlbey.** 1875–1959. Autograph extract from his most famous work *In a Monastery Garden.*

1.

2.

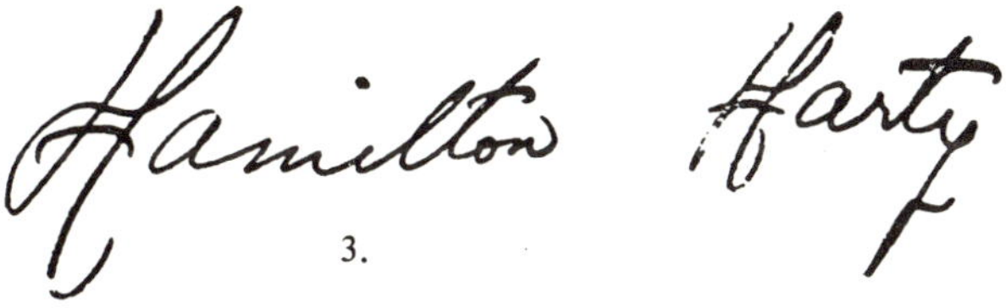

3.

4.

5.

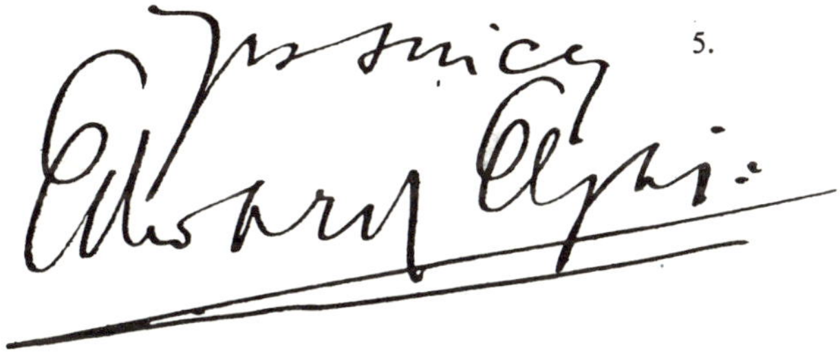

6.

7.

8.

1. **Gustav T. Holst.** 1874–1934. One of our major composers, he was of Swedish ancestry.
2. **Sir Edward German.** 1862–1936. A holograph excerpt from his *Richard III* suite.
3. **Sir H. Hamilton Harty.** 1879–1941.
4. **Sir C. Hubert H. Parry.** 1848–1918. Director of the Royal College of Music. A distinguished musical historian.
5. **Sir Edward W. Elgar.** 1857–1934. One of the most influential British composers of all time. Master of the King's Musick.
6. **Sir F. Paolo Tosti.** 1846–1916. Italian-born, he became a naturalized British subject. Particularly known for his songs, of which *Good-bye* is the best known.
7. **Sir Arthur Somervell.** 1863–1937.
8. **Roger Quilter.** 1877–1953. His works include operas, a children's overture and songs.

1. **Frederick Delius.** 1862–1934. A scarce autograph. He was blind from 1924 and many 'Delius' letters were, in fact, written by his wife.
2. **Sir William T. Walton.** 1902–   . One of our greatest contemporary composers.
3. **Eric Coates.** 1886–1957. Composer of the *London Suite*, etc.
4. **Ralph Vaughan Williams.** 1872–1958. One of the major composers of his time.
5. **E. Benjamin Britten.** 1913–   . Also distinguished as a conductor. Founder of the Aldeburgh Festival.
6. **Sir Arthur Bliss.** 1891–   . Master of the Queen's Musick.
7. **Richard Addinsell.** 1904–   . Composer of the *Warsaw Concerto*.
8. **Constant Lambert.** 1905–51. A holograph music example. Lambert's early death made his autograph uncommon.

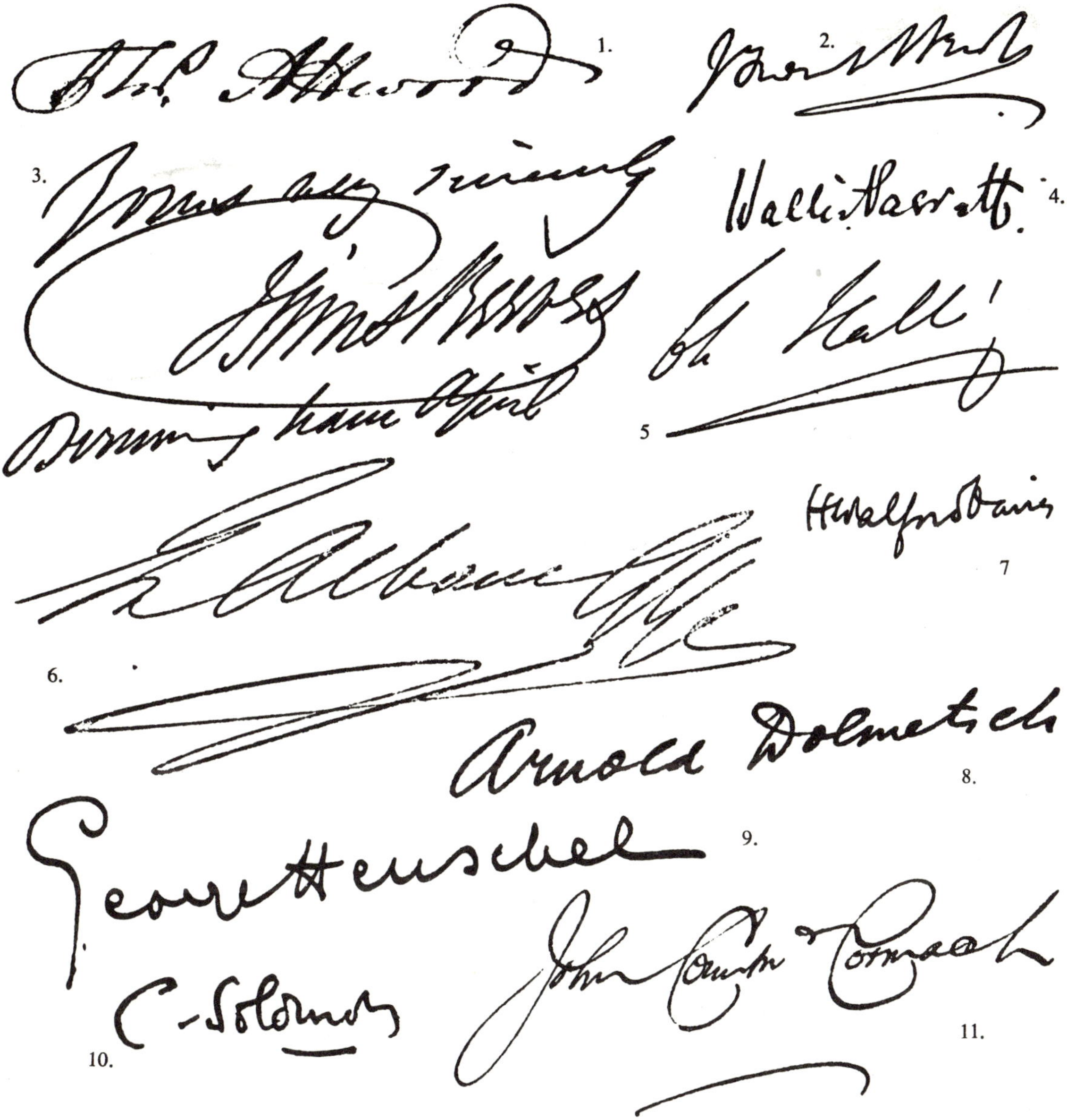

1. **Thomas Attwood.** 1765–1838. Organist (of St Paul's) and composer.
2. **Sir J. Frederick Bridge.** 1844–1924. Organist and composer.
3. **John Sims Reeves.** 1818–1900. Operatic tenor.
4. **Sir Walter Parratt.** 1841–1924. Organist and composer. Master of the Queen's Musick to Queen Victoria.
5. **Sir Charles Hallé.** 1819–95. Conductor and pianist. Founded the Hallé Orchestra, 1858.
6. **Dame Emma Albani.** 1852–1930. Famous Canadian operatic soprano. She has added her married name 'Gye' to her signature above.
7. **Sir H. Walford Davies.** 1869–1941. Conductor, organist and composer. Master of the King's Musick.
8. **E. Arnold Dolmetsch.** 1858–1940. Naturalized British musician of Swiss origin. Collected, played and made copies of early musical instruments.
9. **Sir George Henschel.** 1850–1934. German-born, naturalized British composer, conductor, singer and pianist.
10. **'Solomon' (Solomon Cutner).** 1902–   . Pianist.
11. **Count John McCormack.** 1884–1945. Irish tenor, later an American citizen.

1. **Sir Charles Santley.** 1834–1922. A distinguished baritone, he was also a skilled painter.
2. **Jenny Lind (Goldschmidt).** 1820–87. 'The Swedish Nightingale'; naturalized British, 1859.
3. **Dame Nellie Melba.** 1861–1931. Australian soprano.
4. **Sir Henry J. Wood.** 1869–1944. Conductor. Founder of the 'Proms' (Promenade Concerts).
5. **Sir Thomas Beecham.** 1879–1961. Conductor and impresario.
6. **Sir Adrian Boult.** 1889– . Conductor of the London Philharmonic Orchestra.
7. **Benno Moiseiwitsch.** 1890–1963. Russian-born, this famous pianist took British nationality in 1937.
8. **Sir H. Malcolm W. Sargent.** 1895–1967. Followed in the steps of Sir Henry Wood, 4 above, as Conductor-in-Chief of the Promenade Concerts.
9. **Sir John Barbirolli.** 1899–1970. Conductor of the Hallé Orchestra.
10. **Louis Kentner.** 1905– . Polish-born pianist of international repute. Naturalized British, 1946.

PERSONALITIES OF THE THEATRE: SEVENTEENTH- TO NINETEENTH-CENTURY

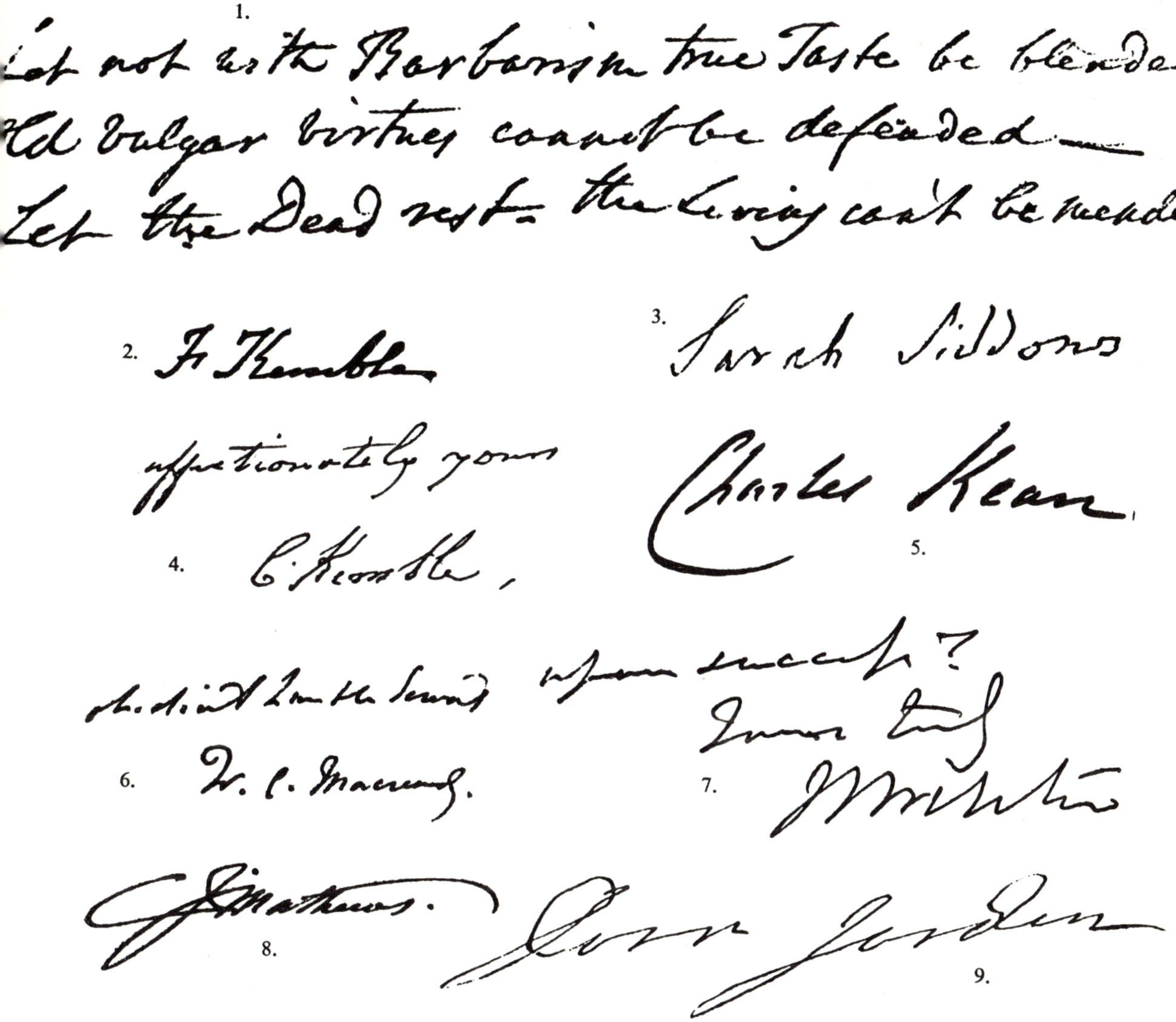

1. **David Garrick.** 1717–79. Autograph lines from a poem. Garrick holographs are now both scarce and highly sought-after.
2. **Frances ('Fanny') Kemble.** 1809–93. Her signature is also found in her married name, 'Butler'.
3. **Sarah Siddons.** 1755–1831. Mrs Siddons's signature as 'S. Siddons' is slightly more common than as 'Sarah Siddons'.
4. **Charles Kemble.** 1775–1854. The shaky (though still characteristic) signature of an old, ill man. He died three months after writing this.
5. **Charles Kean.** 1811(?)–68.
6. **W. C. Macready.** 1793–1873.
7. **Benjamin N. Webster.** 1797–1882.
8. **Charles James Mathews.** 1803–78. Sometimes confused with his father Charles; he always included his second initial in his signature, however.
9. **Dorothea Jordan.** 1762–1816. Irish actress; mistress of William IV. She often signed, as above, with her Christian name abbreviated to 'Dora'.

1.

2.

3.

4.

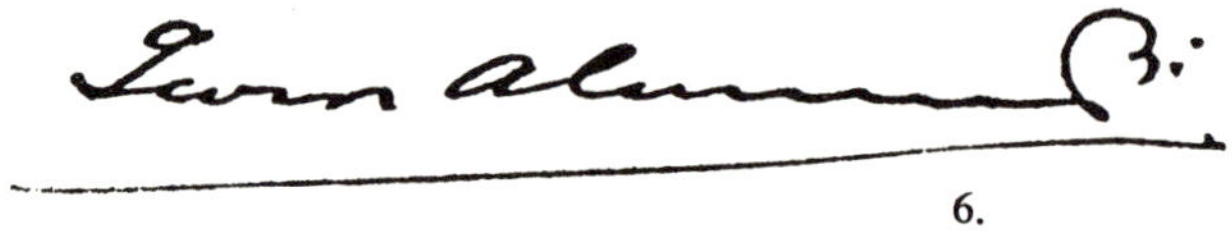

6.

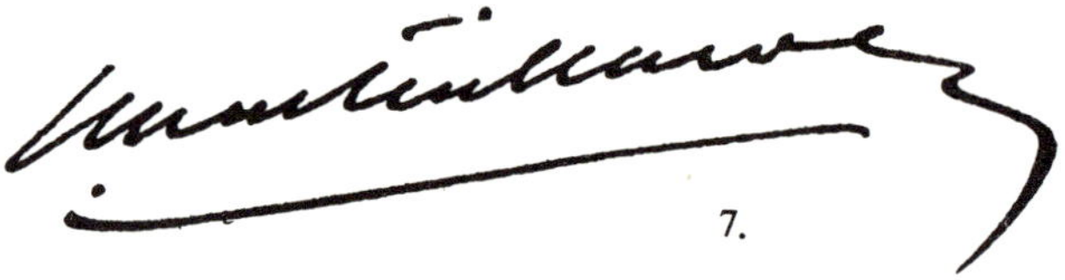

5.

7.

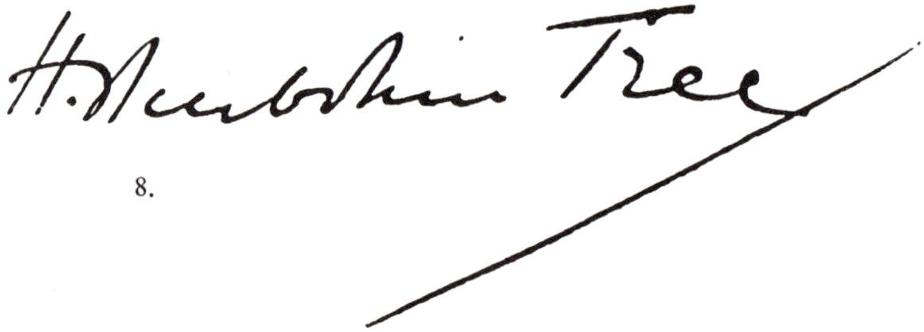

8.

1. **Sir Squire Bancroft.** 1841–1926.
2. **Wilson Barrett.** 1846–1904.
3. **Dame Ellen Terry.** 1848–1928.
4. **Sir Johnston Forbes-Robertson.** 1853–1937.
5. **Sir Henry Irving.** 1838–1905. The first actor to be knighted. Irving's writing is difficult to read and he used two different styles, one being less flowing, slightly larger and more upright than the example above.
6. **Sir George Alexander.** 1858–1918.
7. **Sir John Martin-Harvey.** 1863–1944.
8. **Sir Herbert Beerbohm Tree.** 1853–1917. The half-brother of the essayist and caricaturist Sir Max Beerbohm (see page 129).

PERSONALITIES OF THE THEATRE: A TWENTIETH-CENTURY MISCELLANY

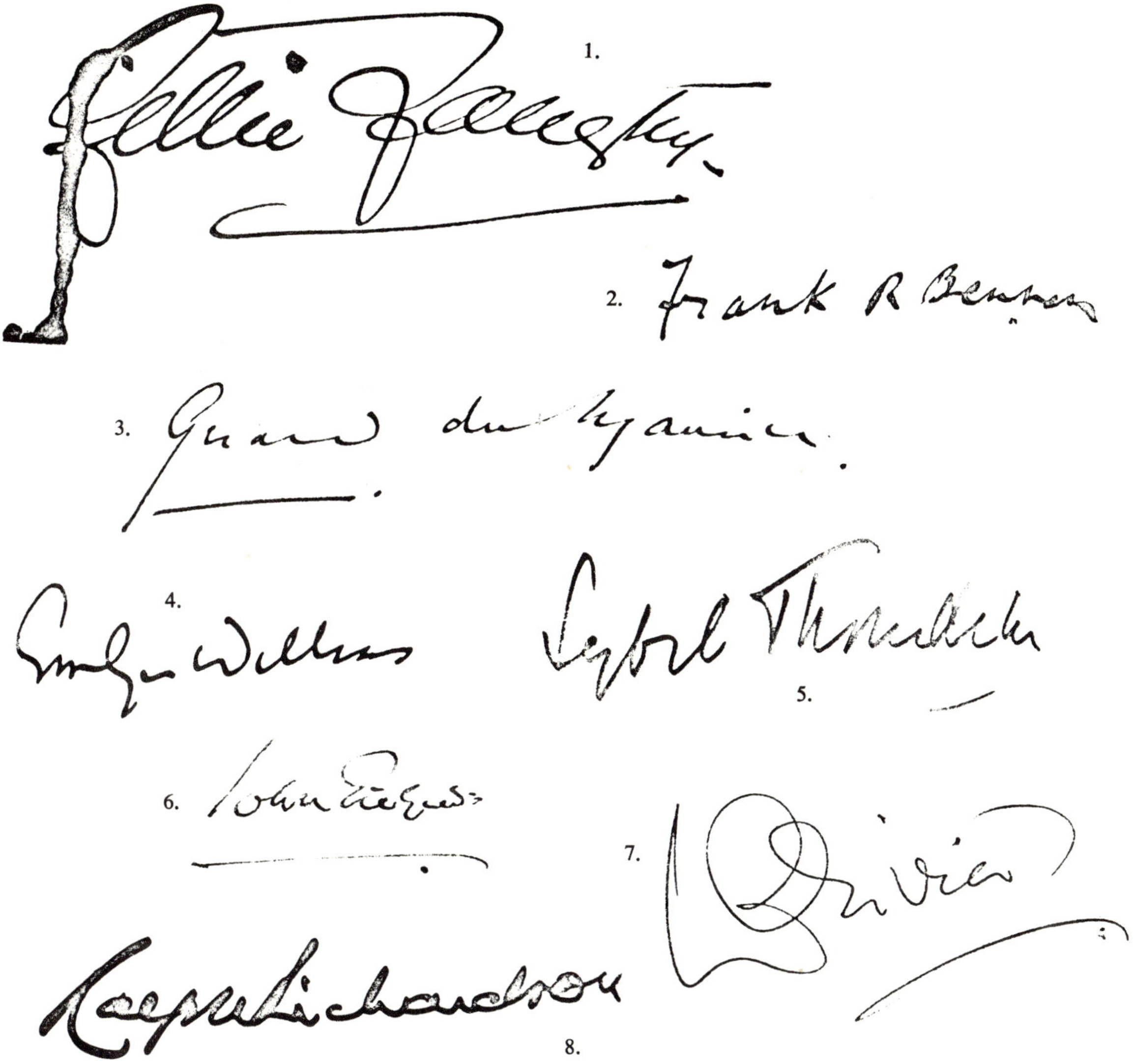

1. **Lillie Langtry.** 1852–1929. 'The Jersey Lily'. Her maiden name was Emily Le Breton, Langtry being her first married name. Later she became Lady de Bathe.
2. **Sir Frank Benson.** 1858–1939. Actor-manager, best remembered for the Shakespearian company which he founded.
3. **Sir Gerald du Maurier.** 1873–1934. The actor-manager son of the artist George du Maurier and father of the novelist Daphne (see pages 147, 135).
4. **Emlyn Williams.** 1905– . Actor and playwright.
5. **Dame Sybil Thorndike.** 1882– . Lady Casson, the widow of the actor-manager Sir Lewis Casson.
6. **Sir John Gielgud.** 1904– .
7. **Laurence, Lord Olivier.** 1907– . The first theatrical peer.
8. **Sir Ralph Richardson.** 1902– .

PERSONALITIES OF THE THEATRE: COMEDIANS AND MUSIC-HALL ARTISTES

1.

2.

3.

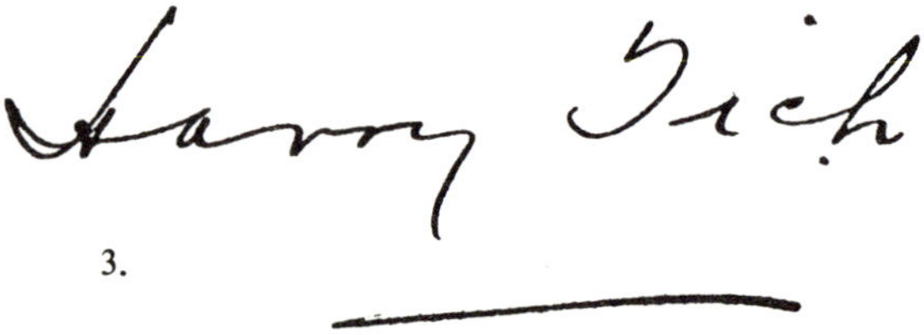

4.

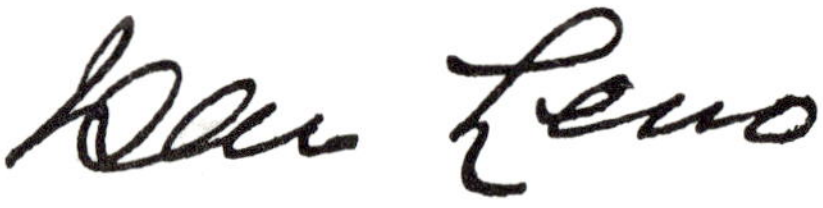

5.

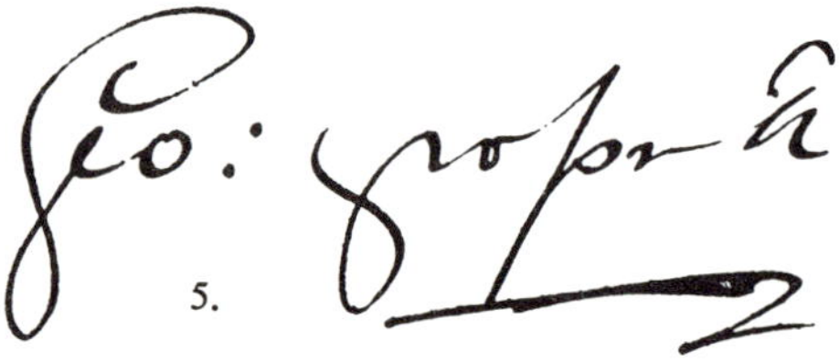

6.

7.

8.

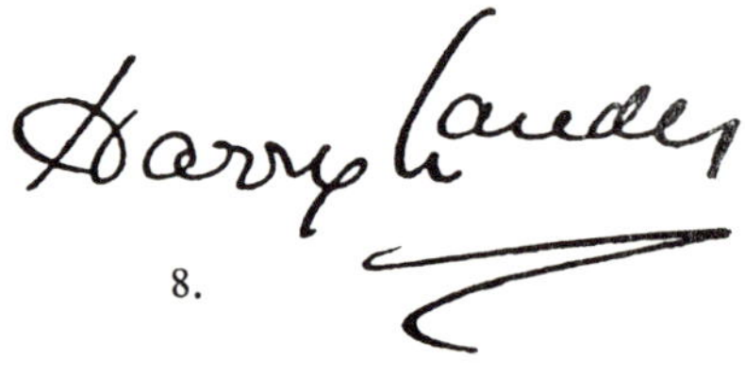

1. **John B. Buckstone.** 1802–79. Comedian and dramatist.
2. **Sir George Robey.** 1869–1954. Typical self-caricature. The original is in blue and red ink.
3. **'Little Tich' (Harry Relph).** 1868–1928. Signed above as 'Harry Tich' but his signature is often found in his real name.
4. **'Dan Leno' (George Galvin).** 1861–1904. Signature sometimes found in his real name.
5. **George Grossmith (senior).** 1847–1912. Easily confused with his son, George, junior, but the latter's signature is more regular and slants strongly to the right.
6. **Vesta Tilley.** 1864–1952. Signed in her married surname. The famous male impersonator was Lady de Frece.
7. **Charles Chaplin.** 1889–
8. **Sir Harry Lauder.** 1870–1950. Lauder, like Robey, often drew self-caricatures. The original of the above comes from one of these.

EMPIRE AND COMMONWEALTH PERSONALITIES: LEADING FIGURES OF INDIA AND THE EAST (1) UNDER THE EMPIRE

1.

2.

3.

4.

6.

5.

8.

7.

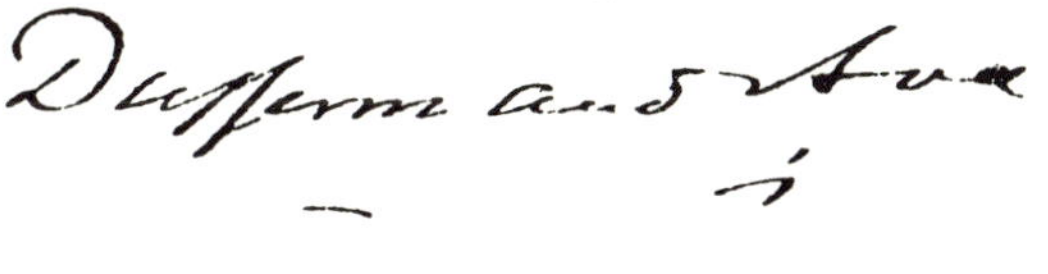

1. **Warren Hastings.** 1732–1818. Governor-General of India, acquitted of charges of corruption after a trial lasting seven years.
2. **Sir James Brooke.** 1803–68. The 'White Rajah' of Sarawak.
3. **Richard (C.), Marquis Wellesley.** 1760–1842. Governor-General of India, 1797–1805. Brother of Wellington.
4. **J. A. Broun-Ramsay, Marquis of Dalhousie.** 1812–60. The 'greatest of Indian pro-consuls' Governor-General, 1847–56.
5. **John (L. M.), Lord Lawrence.** 1811–79. Governor-General of India, 1863–9.
6. **James Bruce, 8th Earl of Elgin.** 1811–63. Governor-General of India, 1861–3, and of Canada, 1847–54. Often confused with his father, of 'Elgin Marbles' fame. Signs here both his earldoms, 'Elgin and Kinkardine'.
7. **Thomas G. Baring, Earl Northbrook.** 1826–1904. Governor-General of India, 1872–6.
8. **Frederick T. H. T. Blackwood, Marquis of Dufferin and Ava.** 1826–1902. Viceroy of India, 1884. Governor-General of Canada, 1872–8.

EMPIRE AND COMMONWEALTH PERSONALITIES: LEADING FIGURES OF INDIA AND THE EAST (2) TWENTIETH-CENTURY

1.

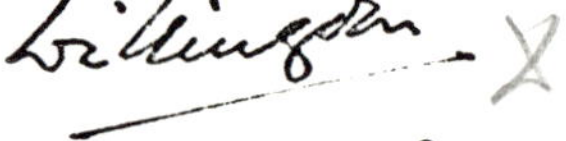

2.

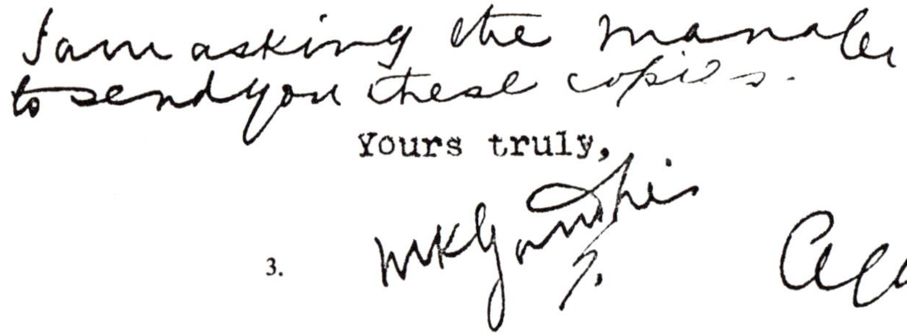

3.

4.

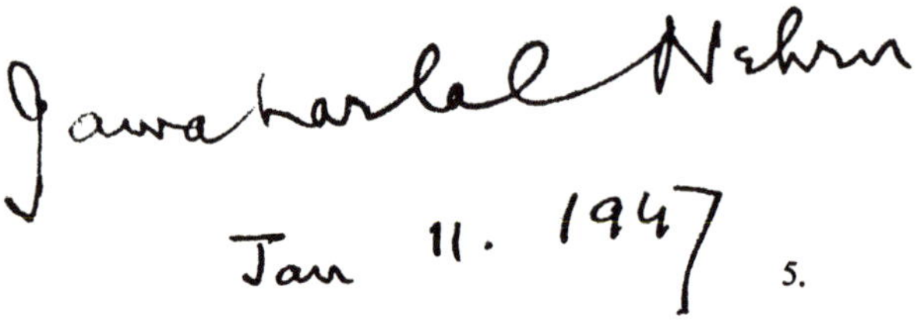

5.

6.

7.

8.

1. **Charles, Lord Hardinge of Penhurst.** 1858–1944. Viceroy of India, 1910–16.
2. **F. Freeman-Thomas, Marquis of Willingdon.** 1866–1941. Viceroy of India, 1931–6. Governor-General of Canada, 1926–30.
3. **Mohandas K. Gandhi.** 1869–1948. The 'Mahatma'. The autograph of this great Indian leader and patriot is much in demand.
4. **Aga Khan III.** 1877–1957. Sultan Sir Mohammed Shah, hereditary head of the Ismaeli Muslims. President of the League of Nations, 1937.
5. **Jawaharlal Nehru.** 1889–1964. The first Prime Minister of India (1947).
6. **Field-Marshal Mohammad Ayub Khan.** President (1958–69) of Pakistan.
7. **Sir Sarvepalli Radhakrishnan.** 1888– . A great Indian scholar and philosopher, he was President of his country, 1962–7.
8. **Sir Oliver Goonetilleke.** 1892– . Governor-General of Ceylon, 1954–62.

EMPIRE AND COMMONWEALTH PERSONALITIES: LEADING FIGURES OF AFRICA UNDER THE EMPIRE

1.

2.

3.

4.

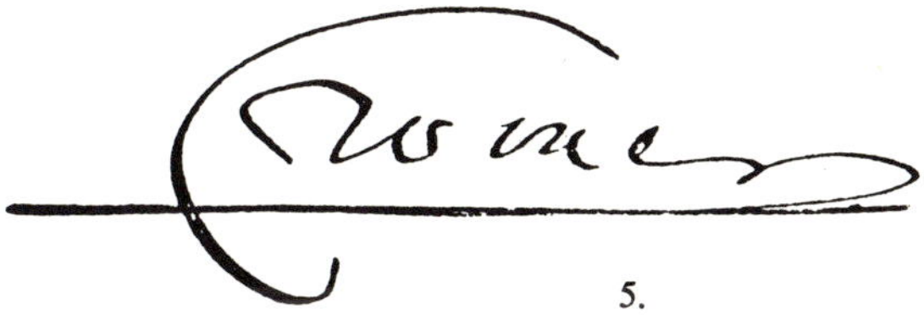

5.

6.

7.

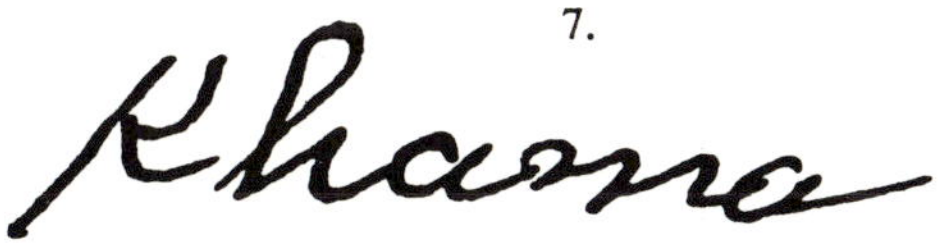

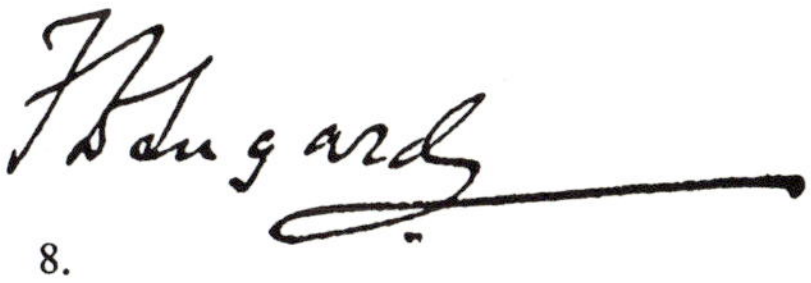

8.

1. **King Cetywayo.** 1836(?)–84. The great Zulu chieftain. An extremely rare signature.
2. **King Lewanika.** 1843–1916. Enlightened Barotse chieftain, nicknamed 'Kobosi'.
3. **Cecil John Rhodes.** 1853–1902. Empire builder, Prime Minister of the Cape, 'founder' of Rhodesia and diamond magnate. Instituted the Rhodes Scholarships.
4. **Sir Leander Starr Jameson.** 1853–1917. Led the rash 'Jameson Raid' on Boer territory; later Prime Minister of the Cape.
5. **Evelyn Baring, Earl of Cromer.** 1841–1917. Administrator in Egypt.
6. **Alfred, Viscount Milner.** 1854–1925. High Commissioner for South Africa, 1897–1905. Later Minister for War.
7. **Khama.** 1835–1923. As Chief of the Bamangwato, the main tribe of Bechuanaland, one of the most powerful and enlightened African rulers of his time.
8. **Frederick (J. D.), Lord Lugard.** 1858–1945. The 'founder' of Nigeria.

EMPIRE AND COMMONWEALTH PERSONALITIES: LEADING FIGURES OF AUSTRALIA AND THE PACIFIC

1.

2.

3.

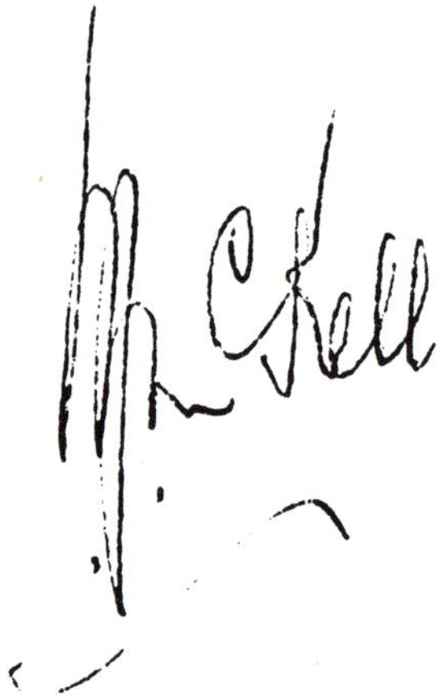

4.

5.

6.

7.

1. **William M. Hughes.** 1864–1952. Prime Minister, 1915–23.
2. **Joseph A. Lyons.** 1879–1939. Prime Minister of Tasmania, 1923–9, and of Australia, 1932–9.
3. **Stanley Melbourne, Viscount Bruce.** 1883–1967. Prime Minister, 1923–9.
4. **Sir William J. McKell.** 1891–   . Governor-General, 1947–53.
5. **Joseph B. Chifley.** 1885–1951. Prime Minister, 1945–1949.
6. **Sir Robert G. Menzies.** 1894–   . Twice Prime Minister, 1939–41 and 1949–66, he was appointed Lord Warden of the Cinque Ports in succession to Sir Winston Churchill: the first Australian to hold this ancient office, instituted by William the Conqueror and occupied by many of the most illustrious men in British history.
7. **Queen Salote Tupou III.** 1900–65. Educated in New Zealand, she was the ruler of Tonga for over forty years.

EMPIRE AND COMMONWEALTH PERSONALITIES: LEADING FIGURES OF CANADA

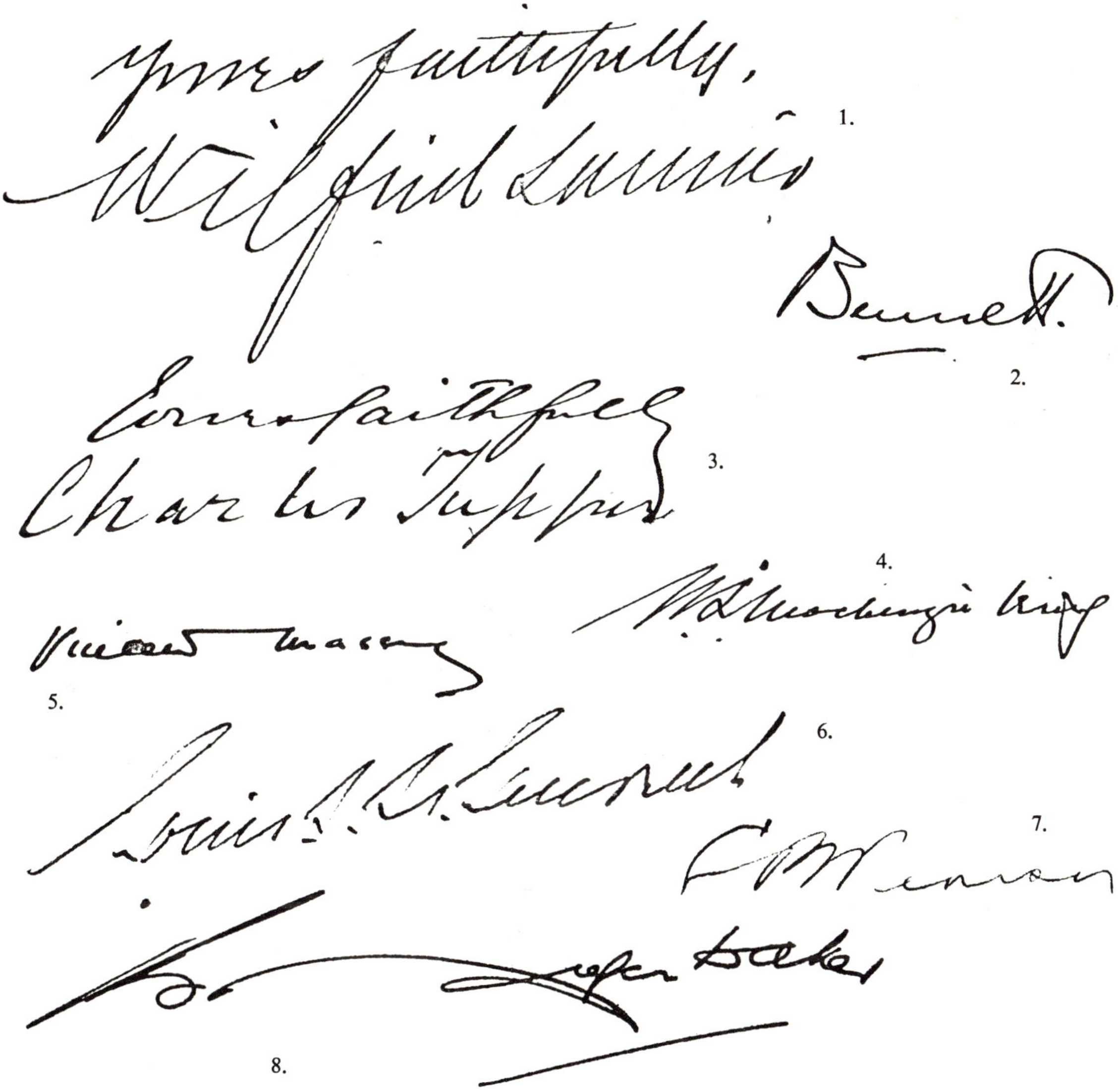

1. **Sir Wilfrid Laurier.** 1841–1919. The first French-Canadian and also the first Roman Catholic to be Prime Minister of Canada (1896).
2. **Richard (B.), Viscount Bennett.** 1870–1947. Prime Minister, 1930–5. Responsible for the Ottawa (Empire trade preference) Agreements.
3. **Sir Charles Tupper.** 1821–1915. Prime Minister of Nova Scotia, 1864–7, and of Canada, 1896.
4. **William L. Mackenzie King.** 1874–1950. A Liberal, he was three times Prime Minister, including throughout World War II. He held office for a total of over 21 years.
5. **Vincent Massey.** 1887– . Governor-General, 1952–9.
6. **Louis S. St Laurent.** 1882– . Prime Minister, 1948–57.
7. **Lester B. Pearson.** 1897– . Liberal leader. Prime Minister, 1963.
8. **John G. Diefenbaker.** 1895– . Conservative leader. Prime Minister, 1957–63.

EMPIRE AND COMMONWEALTH PERSONALITIES: LEADING FIGURES OF NEW ZEALAND

1.

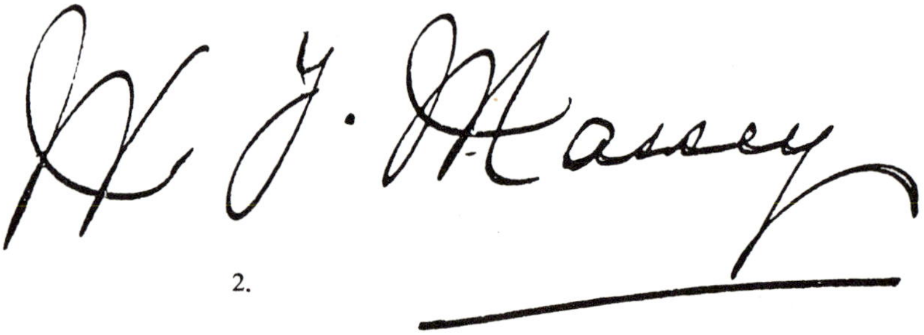

2.

3.

4.

5.

6.

7.

8.

1. **Sir George Grey.** 1812–98. Twice Governor of New Zealand, he entered politics there after his second Governorship, becoming Prime Minister, 1877–9. He had also been Governor of South Australia and of the Cape Colony.
2. **William Ferguson Massey.** 1856–1925. Prime Minister, 1912–25.
3. **Michael J. Savage.** 1872–1940. Prime Minister, 1935–40.
4. **Sir Joseph G. Ward.** 1856–1930. Twice Prime Minister, 1906–12 and 1928–30.
5. **Sir Walter Nash.** 1882– . Prime Minister, 1957–1960.
6. **Peter Fraser.** 1884–1950. Prime Minister, 1940–9.
7. **Keith J. Holyoake.** 1904– . Prime Minister, 1957 and again in 1960.
8. **Bernard (C.), Lord Freyberg, V.C.** 1889–1963. As a Lieutenant-General he commanded the 2nd New Zealand Expeditionary Force throughout World War II and was Governor-General, 1946–52.

EMPIRE AND COMMONWEALTH PERSONALITIES: LEADING FIGURES OF SOUTH AFRICA AND RHODESIA

1.

2.

3.

4.

5.

6.

7.

8.

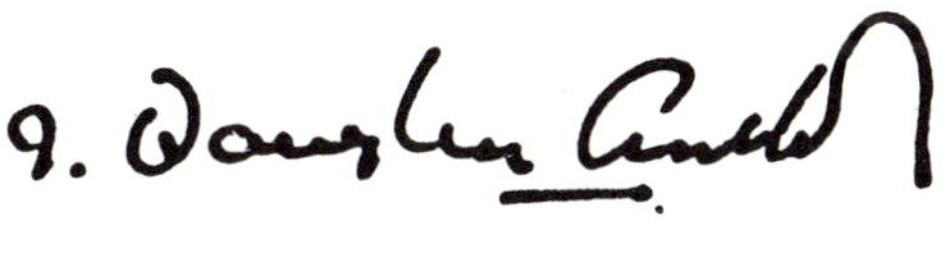

1. **General Louis Botha.** 1862–1919. After being Commander-in-Chief of the Boer forces during the South African War, he became Prime Minister of the Transvaal and then the first Prime Minister of the Union of South Africa (1910–19).
2. **Field-Marshal Jan C. Smuts.** 1870–1950. South Africa's most distinguished soldier and 'elder statesman'. Prime Minister, 1919–24 and 1939–48.
3. **General James B. M. Hertzog.** 1866–1942. Prime Minister of South Africa, 1924–39.
4. **Godfrey M. Huggins, Viscount Malvern.** 1883– . Prime Minister of Southern Rhodesia, 1933–53, and of the Federation of Rhodesia and Nyasaland, 1953–6.
5. **Sir Roy Welensky.** 1907– . Prime Minister of the Federation of Rhodesia and Nyasaland, 1956–63.
6. **R. S. Garfield Todd.** 1908– . Prime Minister of Southern Rhodesia, 1953–8.
7. **Sir Humphrey Gibbs.** 1902– . Governor of Rhodesia, 1959–69.
8. **Ian Douglas Smith.** 1919– . Prime Minister of Rhodesia, 1964– .

EMPIRE AND COMMONWEALTH PERSONALITIES: LEADING FIGURES OF POST-WAR INDEPENDENT COUNTRIES

1.

2.

3.

4.

5.

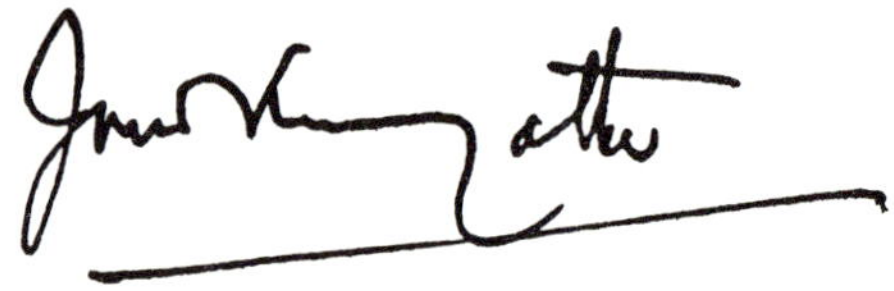

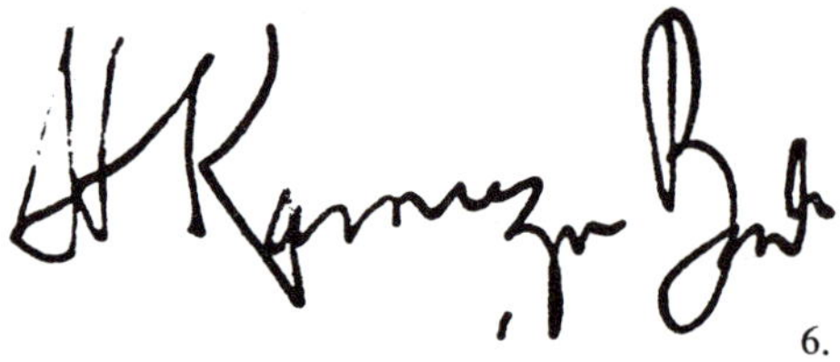

6.

7.

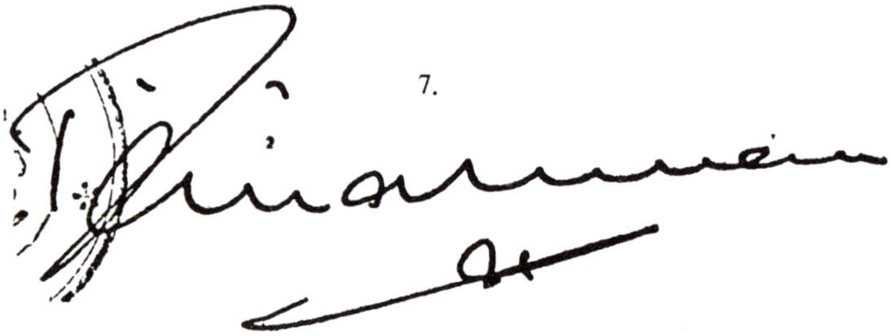

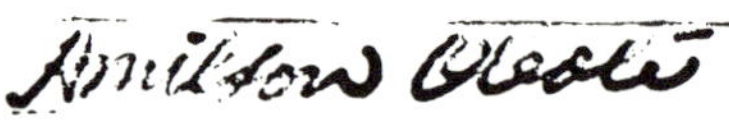

8.

9.

10.

1. **Kwame Nkrumah.** 1909– . First Prime Minister, 1957, and first President, 1960–6, of Ghana (formerly the Gold Coast.
2. **Julius K. Nyerere,** 1922– . First President of Tanzania, 1964, and of Tanganyika, 1962–4.
3. **Archbishop Makarios III.** 1913– . First President of Cyprus, 1960.
4. **D. Kenneth Kaunda.** 1924– . First President of Zambia (formerly Northern Rhodesia), 1964.
5. **Jomo Kenyatta.** 1889(?)– . First President of Kenya, 1964.
6. **Hastings K. Banda.** 1905– . First President of Malawi (formerly Nyasaland), 1966.
7. **Tunku Abdul Rahman Putra.** 1903– . Having been Malaya's first Prime Minister, he became the first Premier of the State of Malaysia, 1963.
8. **A. Milton Obote.** 1924– . First President of Uganda, 1966.
9. **King Sobhuza II.** 1899– . Ingwenyama (King) of Swaziland. He is the world's longest ruling monarch: since December 1899.
10. **Sir Seretse Khama.** 1921– . First President of Botswana (formerly Bechuanaland Protectorate), 1966.

1.

2.

3.

4.

5.

6.

7.

8.

9.

10.

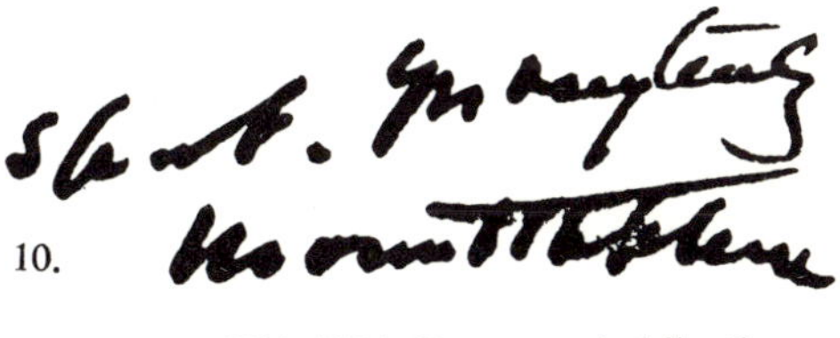

1. **Sir Thomas Gresham.** 1519–79. The most illustrious merchant financier of his era. 'King's Merchant' for Edward VI in Antwerp; Elizabeth I's Ambassador in Brussels; founder of the Royal Exchange and Gresham College. A rare Tudor autograph.
2. **Sir Francis Child.** 1642–1713. Banker. Lord Mayor of London.
3. **Sir John Cutler.** 1608(?)–93. London merchant and philanthropist.
4. **Thomas Coutts.** 1735–1822. Founded Coutts Bank.
5. **John Laird.** 1805–74. Shipbuilder.
6. **Baron Lionel N. de Rothschild.** 1808–79. Head of Rothschild's Bank; the first Jewish Member of Parliament.
7. **Michael T. Bass.** 1799–1884. Brewer and philanthropist.
8. **John Lubbock, Lord Avebury.** 1834–1913. Banker, economist, politician and entomologist. Instituted Bank Holidays.
9. **Donald A. Smith, Lord Strathcona.** 1820–1914. Canadian financier and politician; co-founder of the Canadian Pacific Railway.
10. **George Stephen, Lord Mount Stephen.** 1829–1921. Canadian manufacturer and philanthropist; co-founder of the Canadian Pacific Railway.

MAGNATES OF COMMERCE AND INDUSTRY (2)

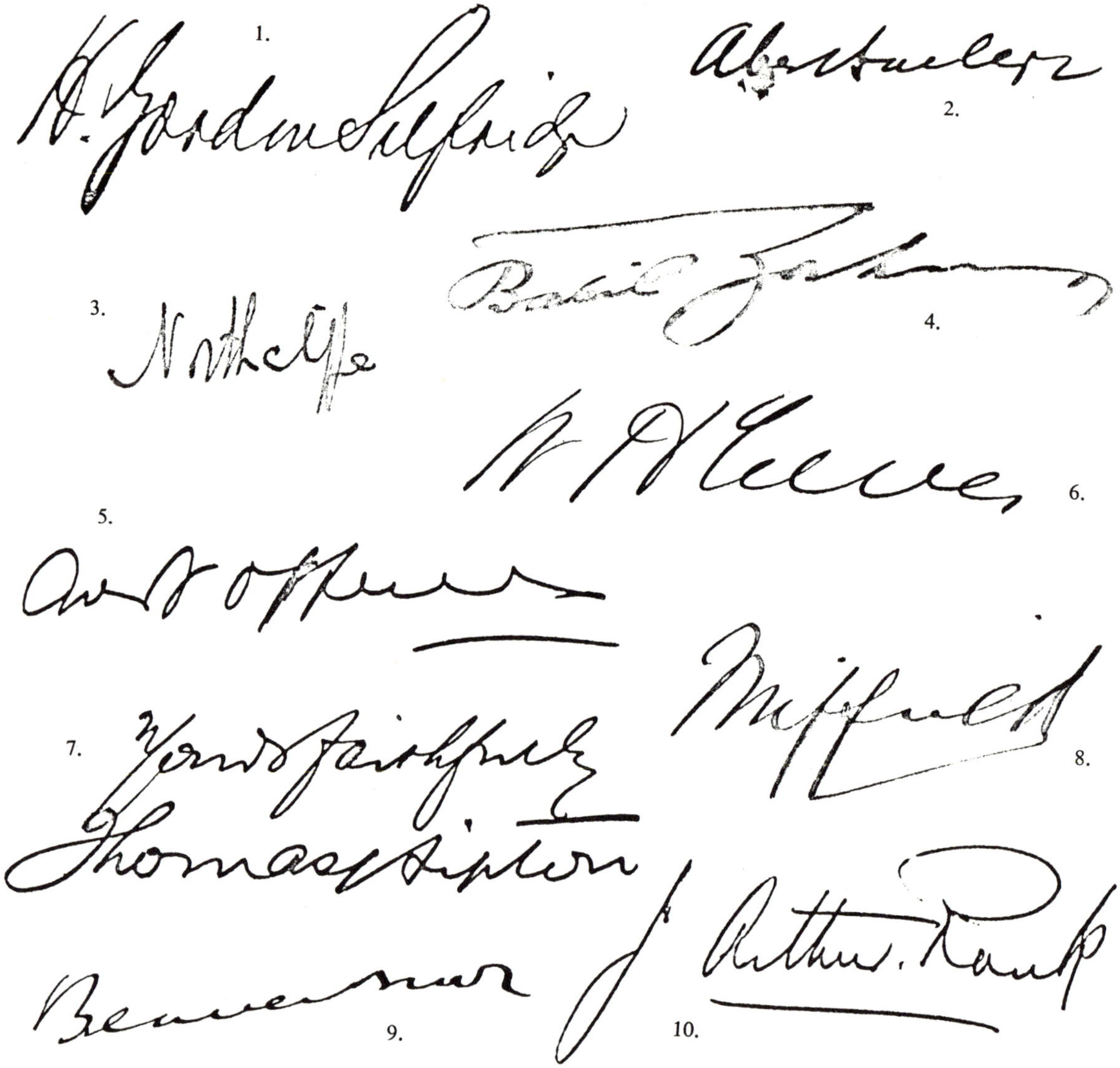

1. **H. Gordon Selfridge.** 1858–1947. American-born founder of the Oxford Street departmental store. Naturalized British, 1937.
2. **Sir Abe Bailey.** 1864–1940. South-African gold-mining millionaire, financier and race-horse owner.
3. **Alfred C. W. Harmsworth, Viscount Northcliffe.** 1865–1922. Newspaper proprietor, of *The Times*, the *Daily Mail* and the *Daily Mirror* (which he founded).
4. **Sir Basil Zaharoff.** 1850–1936. Armaments magnate and financier.
5. **Sir Ernest Oppenheimer.** 1880–1957. South-African diamond magnate.
6. **William H. Lever, Viscount Leverhulme.** 1851–1925. Soap manufacturer and philanthropist.
7. **Sir Thomas J. Lipton.** 1850–1931. Grocer and yachtsman.
8. **William R. Morris, Viscount Nuffield.** 1877–1963. Motor manufacturer and philanthropist; established the Nuffield Foundation.
9. **William M. Aitken, Lord Beaverbrook.** 1879–1964. Canadian-born newspaper proprietor and statesman; owned the *Daily Express*, the *Sunday Express* and the *Evening Standard*.
10. **J. Arthur, Lord Rank.** 1888– . Film magnate; President of the Rank Organization.

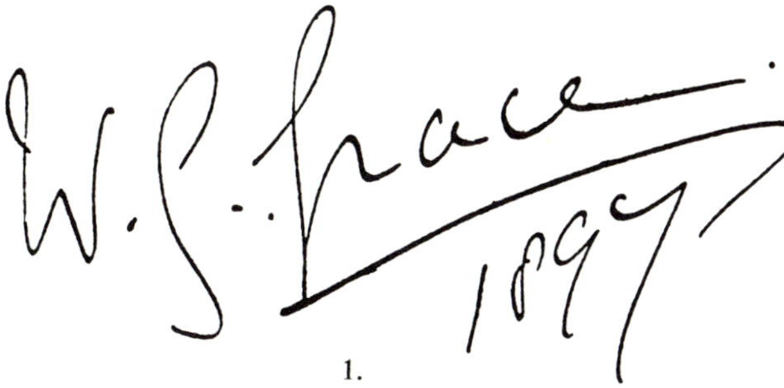

1.

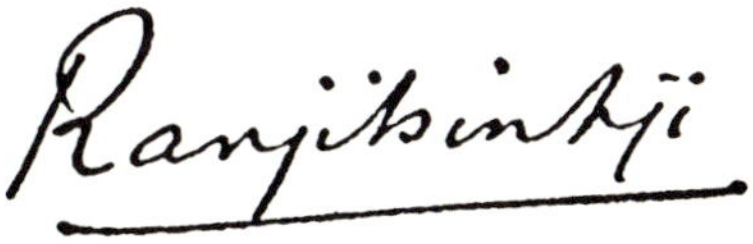

2.

3.

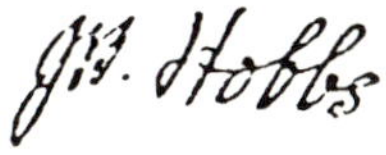

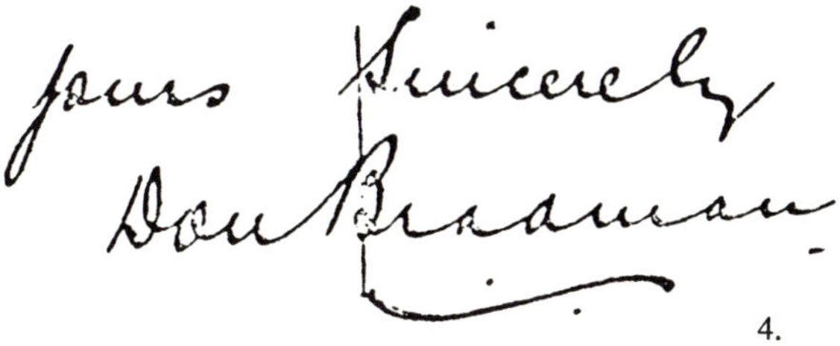

4.

5.

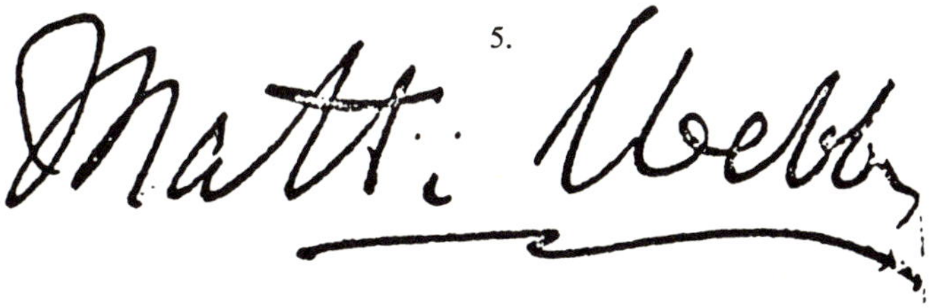

6.

7.

8.

1. **William G. Grace.** 1848–1915. 'W.G.'. One of the most famous names in cricketing history.
2. **Prince Ranjitsinghi.** 1872–1933. Maharajah of Nawanagar. One of the greatest Indian cricketers.
3. **Sir John B. Hobbs.** 1882–1963. 'Jack Hobbs', the England and Surrey cricketer and one of the outstanding batsmen of his day.
4. **Sir Donald G. Bradman.** 1908– . Australian cricket captain, he set up many batting records.
5. **Captain Matthew Webb.** 1848–83. Swimmer; the first to swim the English Channel (1875). Drowned trying to swim the Niagara rapids.
6. **Sir Malcolm Campbell.** 1885–1949. Racing motorist; held world land and sea speed records.
7. **James ('Jimmy') Wilde.** 1892–1969. Boxer: world fly-weight champion.
8. **Donald Campbell.** 1921–1967. Several times holder of the world water speed record. Son of Sir Malcolm, 6 above.

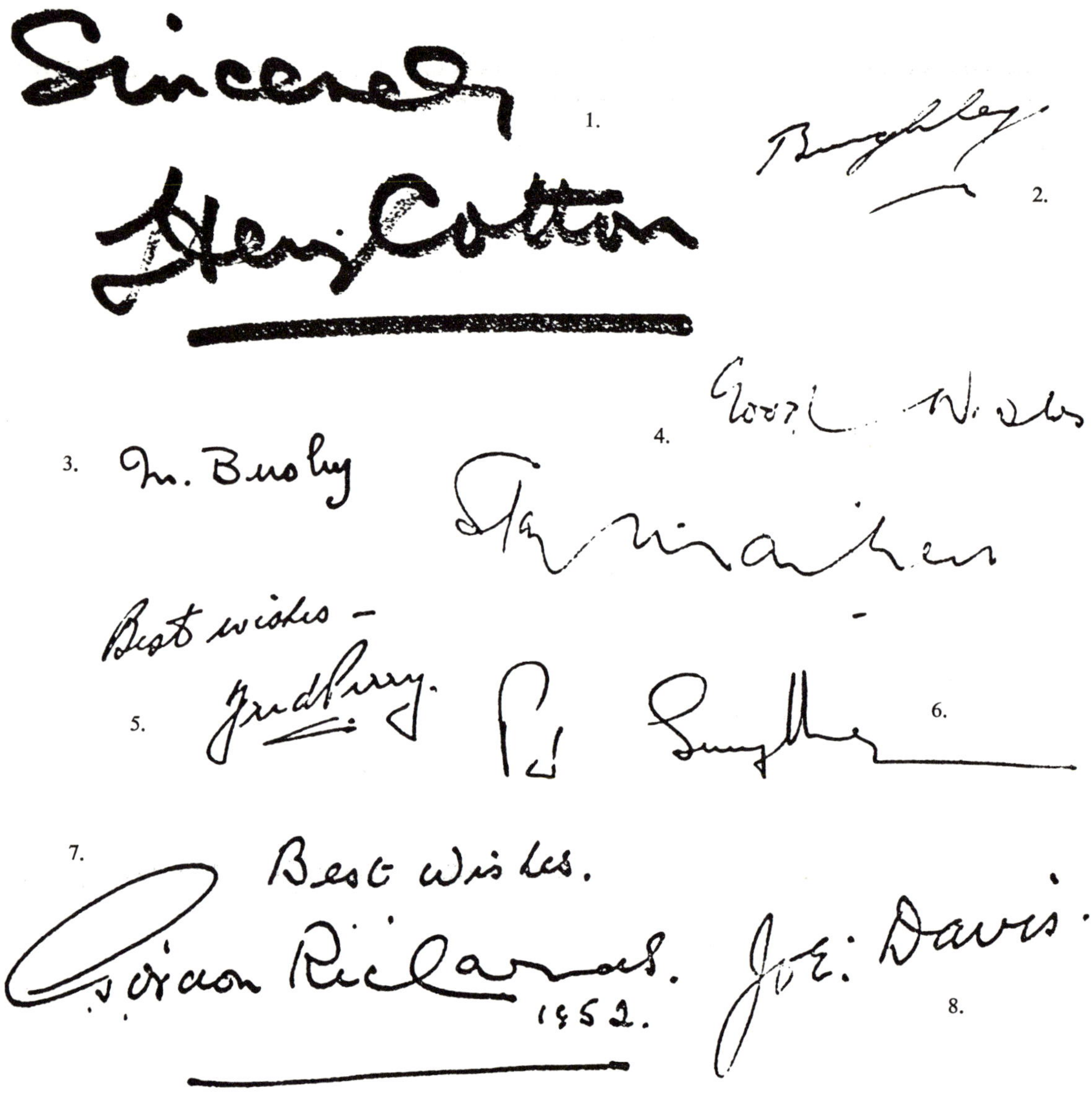

1. **T. Henry Cotton.** 1907– . Golfer; winner of countless golf tournaments, including (three times) the British Open.
2. **David G. B. Cecil, Lord Burghley, Marquis of Exeter.** 1905– . Athlete (hurdler). Chairman of the British Olympic Association.
3. **Sir Matthew Busby.** 1909– . Footballer. Manager of Manchester United.
4. **Sir Stanley Matthews.** 1915– . The first professional footballer to be knighted, he played for England in fifty-five international matches.
5. **Frederick J. Perry.** 1909– . Britain's most successful tennis player. Won the Wimbledon singles championship for three successive years, 1934–6.
6. **Pat Smythe (Patricia R. Koechlin)** 1928– . Olympic horsewoman. Winner of a host of international show-jumping events and author of several books on this subject.
7. **Sir Gordon Richards.** 1904– . Many times champion jockey, he established the world record (over 4,500) for winning rides.
8. **Joe Davis.** 1901– . Snooker and billiards champion.

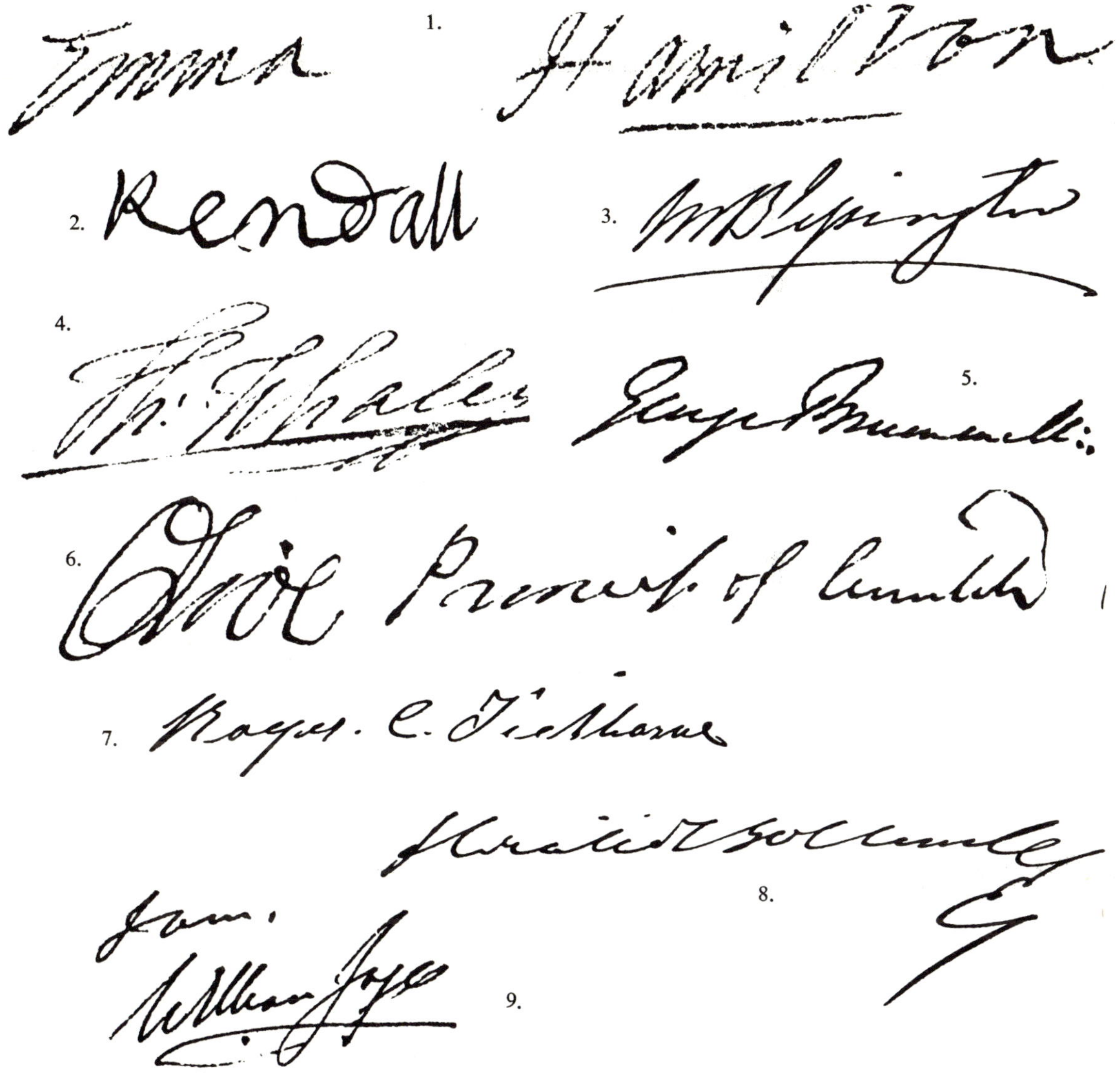

1. **Emma, Lady Hamilton.** 1761(?)–1815. Nelson's mistress. This example is larger than usual. The original is written in a music book.
2. **Ehrengard von der Schulenburg, Duchess of Kendall.** 1667–1743. Mistress of George I.
3. **Marguerite, Countess of Blessington.** 1789–1849. Authoress. Mistress of Count D'Orsay.
4. **Thomas Whaley.** 1766–1800. 'Buck' ('Jerusalem') Whaley. Irish eccentric. Walked to Jerusalem for a bet.
5. **George B. Brummell.** 1778–1840. 'Beau Brummell'. Celebrated dandy.
6. **Olivia Serres.** 1772–1834. Imposter. Claimed to be the daughter of the Duke of Cumberland. Styled herself 'Princess of Cumberland', as in example above.
7. **Arthur Orton.** 1834–98. Imposter. 'The Tichborne Claimant'. An Australian butcher, he claimed to be a long-lost baronet, Sir Roger Tichborne (see signature above).
8. **Horatio W. Bottomley.** 1860–1933. Fraudulent financier and journalist.
9. **William Joyce.** 1906–46. Traitor. 'Lord Haw-Haw'. Broadcast anti-British propaganda from Germany throughout World War II.

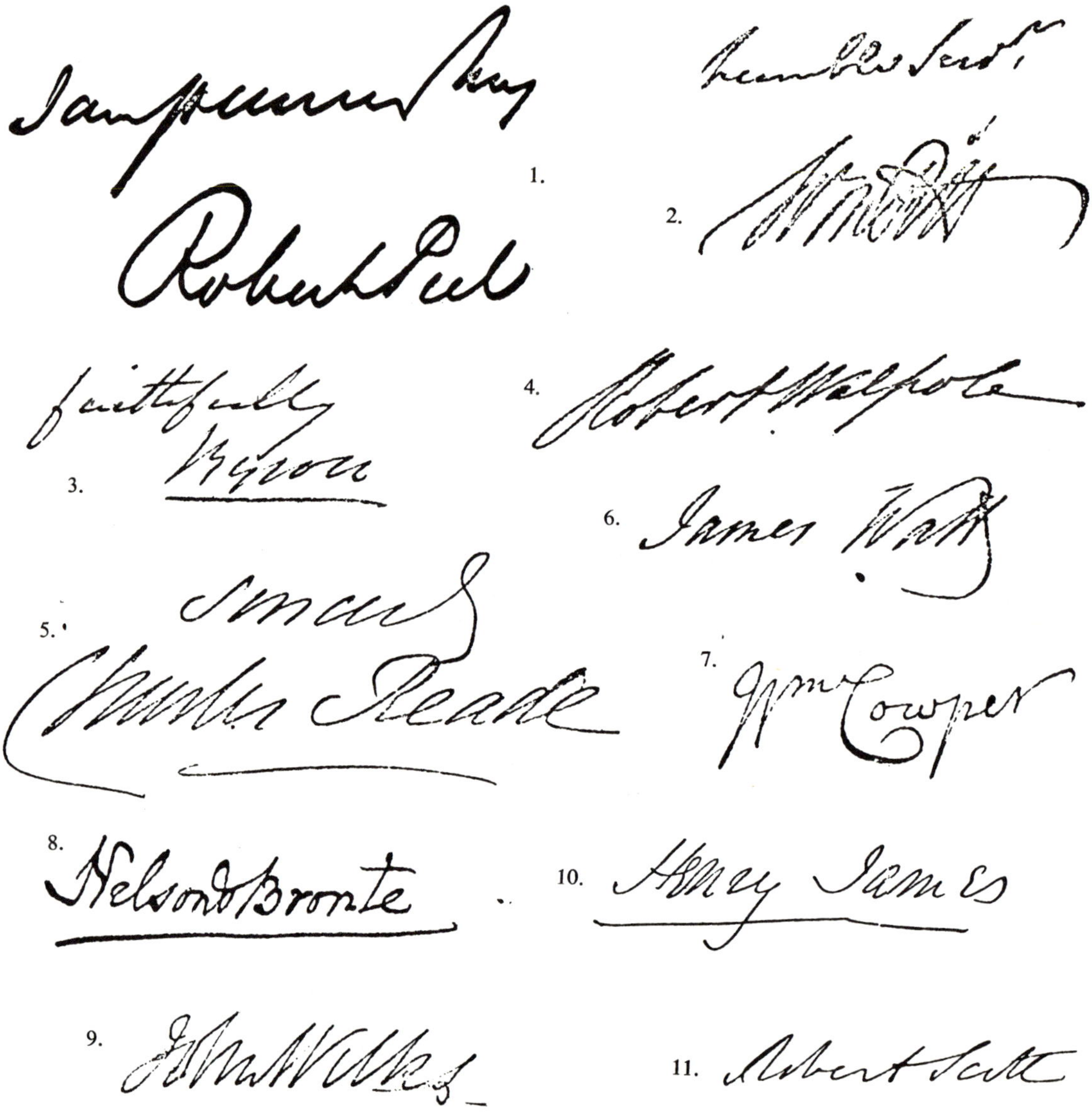

1. **Sir Robert Peel.** Not the Prime Minister (see page 61) but his son.
2. **William Pitt.** Neither of the famous Pitts (see page 60) but a minor contemporary, William Morton Pitt.
3. **Lord Byron.** Not the poet (see page 118) but his successor.
4. **Robert Walpole.** Not the Prime Minister (see page 59) but the classical scholar.
5. **Charles Reade, jnr.** The novelist's (see page 125) son, a minor author.
6. **James Watt, jnr.** Son of the great pioneer of steam engines (see page 113), himself an engineer.
7. **William Cowper.** Clerk of the Parliaments. Cousin of the poet (see page 116).
8. **Lord Nelson.** Not the great admiral (see page 90) but his brother and successor, the first Earl.
9. **John Wilks.** A minor politician, contemporaneous to John Wilkes (see page 72); no 'e' in surname, however.
10. **Henry James.** Not the novelist (see page 124) but the statesman, later Lord James.
11. **Robert Scott.** Lexicographer. Not Robert Falcon Scott of the Antarctic (see page 101).

Bibliography

Books in the English language dealing in whole or in part with British autographs.

WORKS ON AUTOGRAPH COLLECTING

H. T. Scott, *Autograph Collecting*, L. Upcott Gill, 1894. Over 200 facsimiles; two-thirds British.

'J.H.', *The Diversions of an Autograph Hunter*, Elliot Stock, 1894. Two pages of facsimiles; nine British examples.

G. B. Hill, *Talks about Autographs*, T. F. Unwin, 1896.

Adrian H. Joline, *Meditations of an Autograph Collector*, Harper, 1902. Mainly American.

George R. Sims, *Among my Autographs*, Chatto and Windus, 1904. A fair number of facsimiles (most are reduced in size), the majority being British.

A. M. Broadley, *Chats on Autographs*, T. Fisher Unwin, 1910. 135 facsimiles; all nationalities, over half British.

Adrian H. Joline, *Rambles in Autograph Land*, Putnam, New York, 1913. Some 70 facsimiles; half British, the rest mainly American.

Thomas F. Madigan, *Word Shadows of the Great*, Frederick A. Stokes, New York, 1930. Some 50 facsimile illustrations; largely American but a few British.

Lady Charnwood, *An Autograph Collection and the Making of it*, Ernest Benn, 1930.

Lady Charnwood, *Call Back Yesterday*, Eyre and Spottiswoode, 1937.

P. J. Croft, *Autographs*, Winifred A. Myers, 1959. Pamphlet reprinted from the *Concise Encyclopaedia of Antiques*.

Charles Hamilton, *Collecting Autographs and Manuscripts*, University of Oklahoma, 1961. 800 facsimiles; largely American but a number of British.

Winifred A. Myers, *How to Collect Autograph Letters and Manuscripts*, Myers, 1961. Pamphlet of talk given at the Antiquarian Booksellers Association; no facsimiles.

A. N. L. Munby, *The Cult of the Autograph Letter in England*, Athlone Press, 1962. No facsimiles.

Mary A. Benjamin, *Autographs: a Key to Collectors*, Walter R. Benjamin, New York, 1963.

BOOKS OF FACSIMILES (WITH REFERENCE NOTES)

Sir John Fenn, *Original Letters from the Archives of the Paston Family*, 5 vols, G. G. J. and J. Robinson, 1787.

John Thane, *British Autography*, J. Thane, 1789. Three volumes of facsimiles, with portraits, of British historical personages, mostly sixteenth- and seventeenth-century.

John Gough Nichols, *Autographs of Royal, Noble, Learned and Remarkable Personages*, J. B. Nichols and Sons, 1829. Facsimiles of English historical personages from the reign of Richard II to that of Charles II.

Joseph Netherclift, *Autographs of the Kings and Queens and Eminent Men of Great Britain*, 1835.

The Autograph Portfolio, Richard Glynn, 1837.

Joseph Netherclift, *Autograph Letters, Characteristic Extracts and Signatures*, 1838.

Joseph Netherclift and Son, *Collection of One Hundred Autograph Letters Written by Royal and Distinguished Persons*, 1849.

Charles John Smith, *Historical and Literary Curiosities*, Henry G. Bohn, 1852. A fair number of facsimiles; mostly British.

Frederick G. Netherclift and R. Sims, *The Autograph Miscellany*, 1855.

F. G. Netherclift and R. Sims, *Handbook to Autographs*, John Russell Smith, 1862. Numerous facsimiles; over half British.

The Autographic Mirror, Cassell, Petter and Galpin, 1864–6. Four volumes of facsimile sketches, letters, etc.; about half British, many French.

F. G. Netherclift and R. Sims, *The Autograph Souvenir*, 1865. About 80 facsimiles; half British.

Lawrence B. Phillips, *The Autographic Album*, Robert Hardwicke, 1866. 470 facsimiles; about three-fifths British.

A. W. Thibaudeau, *The Catalogue of the Morrison Collection*, 1883–92. Only 200 copies of this vast work were published. It contains a good number of facsimiles, but many are not British.

W. T. Stead, *Portraits and Autographs*, The Review of Reviews, 1891. Over 150 facsimiles and portraits; about two-thirds British.

Handwriting of the Kings and Queens of England, Religious Tract Society, 1893. Facsimiles from the Black Prince to Queen Victoria and her family.

Sir G. F. Warner, *Facsimiles of Royal, Historical, Literary and other Autographs in the Department of Manuscripts, British Museum*, 1899. 150 facsimile plates; mostly British.

Charles Geigy, *Handbook of Facsimiles of Famous Personages*, Basle, 1925. Many facsimiles; a reasonable proportion of British.

W. W. Greg, *English Literary Autographs, 1550–1650*, 3 vols, Oxford, 1925–32.

D. Flower and A. N. L. Munby, *English Poetical Autographs*, Cassell, 1938. 46 facsimile manuscripts.

Henry Morley, *English Literature in the Reign of Victoria*, Tauchnitz Edition (collection of British and American authors), Leipzig, 1841. 173 facsimiles, both British and American.

H. T. Scott and S. J. Davey, *A Guide to the Collector of Historical Documents, Literary Manuscripts and Autograph Letters*, S. J. Davey, 1891. A bibliography of facsimile publications.

Facsimile of Autographs of Subscribers to the Country Seats of Great Britain and Ireland, A. Clarke, 1895 (?). Fourteen pages of facsimiles of members of the aristocracy; the rest devoted to the landed gentry.

Rosa Baughan, *Character Indicated by Handwriting*, L. Upcott Gill, 1895 (?). A fair number of facsimiles of famous people; mainly British.

H.R.H. The Duchess of Albany, *The Duchess of Albany's Autograph Album*, Truscott, 1906. Limited edition of 250. 135 facsimiles; mainly British, including a number of little-known personalities.

J. A. Farrer, *Literary Forgeries*, Longmans, 1907.

Hall Caine (introducer), *King Albert's Book*, Daily Telegraph, 1914. Many facsimiles of leading figures of that time, including British.

Lonsdale Deighton, *The British Legion Album*, Cassell, 1924 (?). Many facsimiles of post World War I British and Allied personalities.

Field-Marshal Viscount Montgomery, *Ten Chapters*, Hutchinson, 1945. Lengthy facsimiles of Winston Churchill and several shorter notes and signatures of other Allied leaders in World War II.

INDEX

Bold figures refer to pages with facsimile examples

Wellington

Gladstone . Disraeli . Lloyd George

Soret Parnell

Massena

Fonigo

Ney

Nap III

Nap.

Josephine

St. Vincent

Ian Hamilton

Gorki's letters

Wm Congreve

Old Italian or German Document 13th cent

Irish

Mary Queen of Scots